HELLBOY AND THE BUREAU FOR PARANORMAL RESEARCH AND DEFENSE

1952

Created by MIKE MIGNOLA

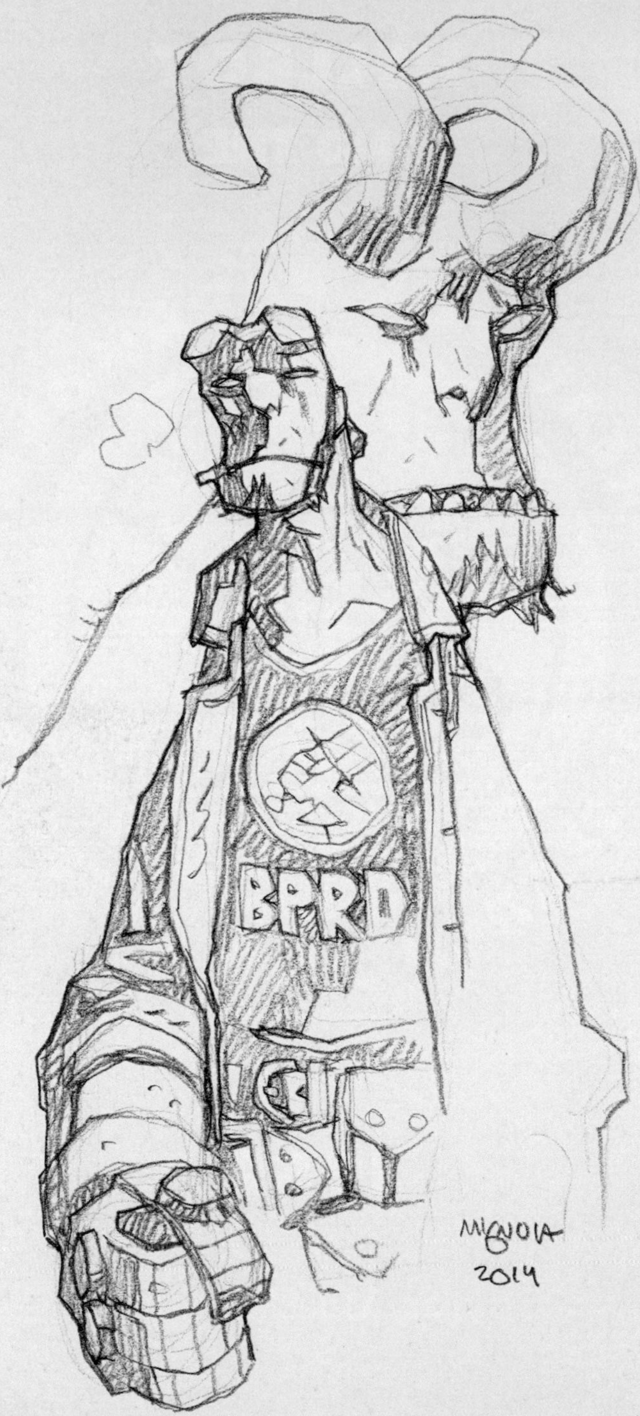
BPRD
MIGNOLA
2014

MIKE MIGNOLA'S

HELLBOY™
AND THE B.P.R.D. 1952

Story by
MIKE MIGNOLA & JOHN ARCUDI

Art by
ALEX MALEEV

Colors by
DAVE STEWART

Letters by
CLEM ROBINS

Cover art by
MIKE MIGNOLA & DAVE STEWART

Series covers by
ALEX MALEEV

Special thanks to Richard Starkings and Kevin Nowlan.

Neil Hankerson ✠ *Executive Vice President*
Tom Weddle ✠ *Chief Financial Officer*
Randy Stradley ✠ *Vice President of Publishing*
Michael Martens ✠ *Vice President of Book Trade Sales*
Scott Allie ✠ *Editor in Chief*
Matt Parkinson ✠ *Vice President of Marketing*
David Scroggy ✠ *Vice President of Product Development*
Dale LaFountain ✠ *Vice President of Information Technology*
Darlene Vogel ✠ *Senior Director of Print, Design, and Production*
Ken Lizzi ✠ *General Counsel*
Davey Estrada ✠ *Editorial Director*
Chris Warner ✠ *Senior Books Editor*
Cary Grazzini ✠ *Director of Print and Development*
Lia Ribacchi ✠ *Art Director*
Cara Niece ✠ *Director of Scheduling*
Mark Bernardi ✠ *Director of Digital Publishing*

Published by
Dark Horse Books
A division of Dark Horse Comics, Inc.
10956 SE Main Street
Milwaukie, OR 97222

DarkHorse.com
International Licensing: 503-905-2377

First edition: August 2015
ISBN 978-1-61655-660-0

Hellboy and the B.P.R.D.: 1952
Hellboy and the B.P.R.D.™ © 2014, 2015 Mike Mignola. Hellboy and all other prominently featured characters are trademarks of Mike Mignola. Dark Horse Books® and the Dark Horse logo are registered trademarks of Dark Horse Comics, Inc. All rights reserved. No portion of this publication may be reproduced or transmitted, in any form or by any means, without the express written permission of Dark Horse Comics, Inc. Names, characters, places, and incidents featured in this publication either are the product of the author's imagination or are used fictitiously. Any resemblance to actual persons (living or dead), events, institutions, or locales, without satiric intent, is coincidental.

This book collects *Hellboy and the B.P.R.D.: 1952* #1–#5.

1 3 5 7 9 10 8 6 4 2

Printed in China

Chapter One

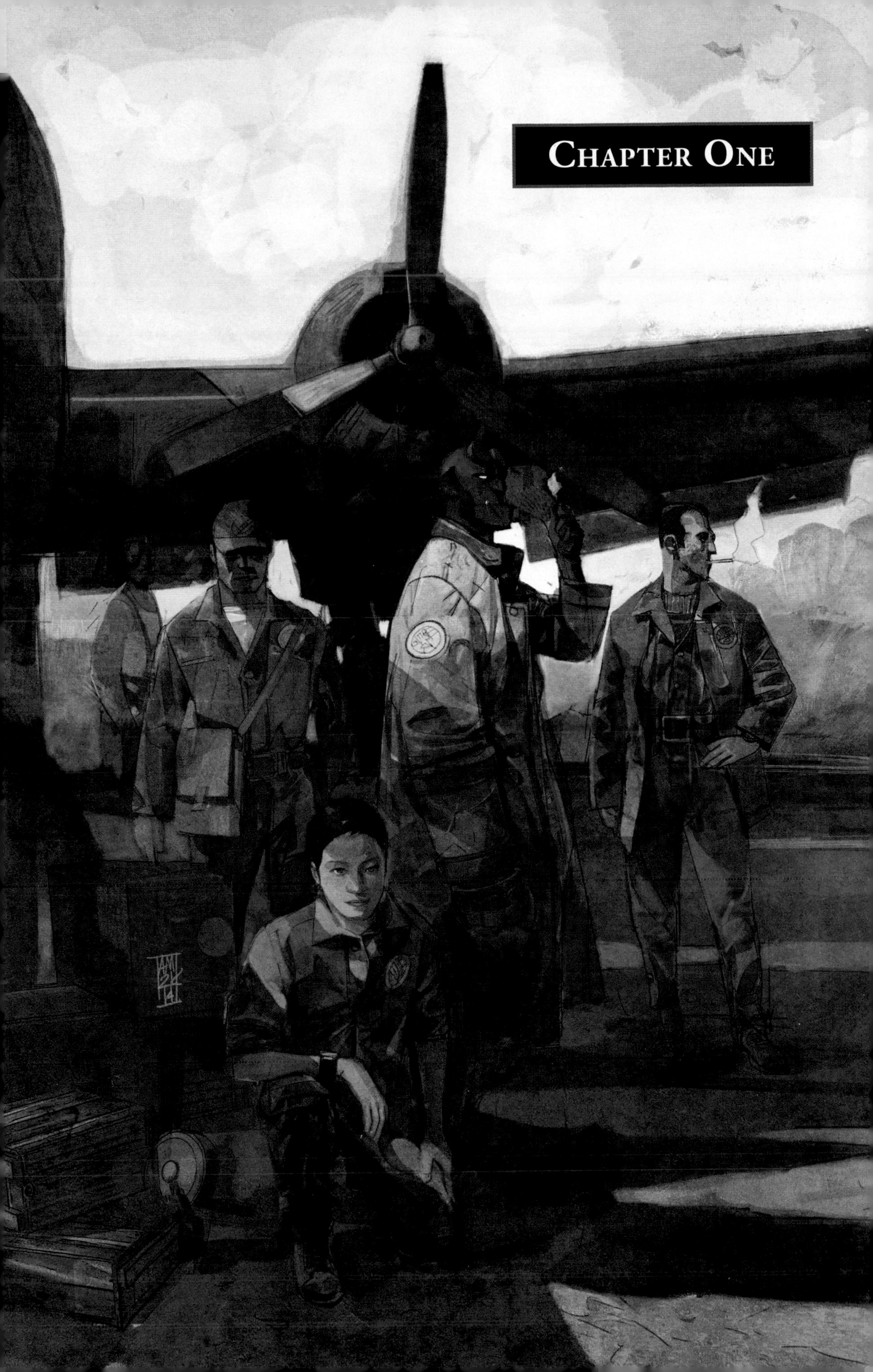

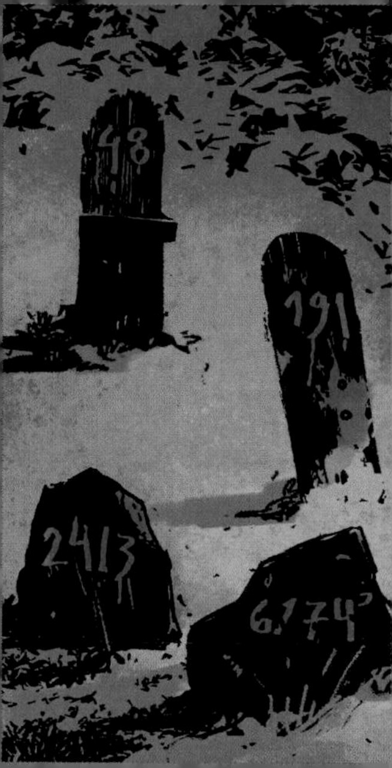
48
191
2413
6174

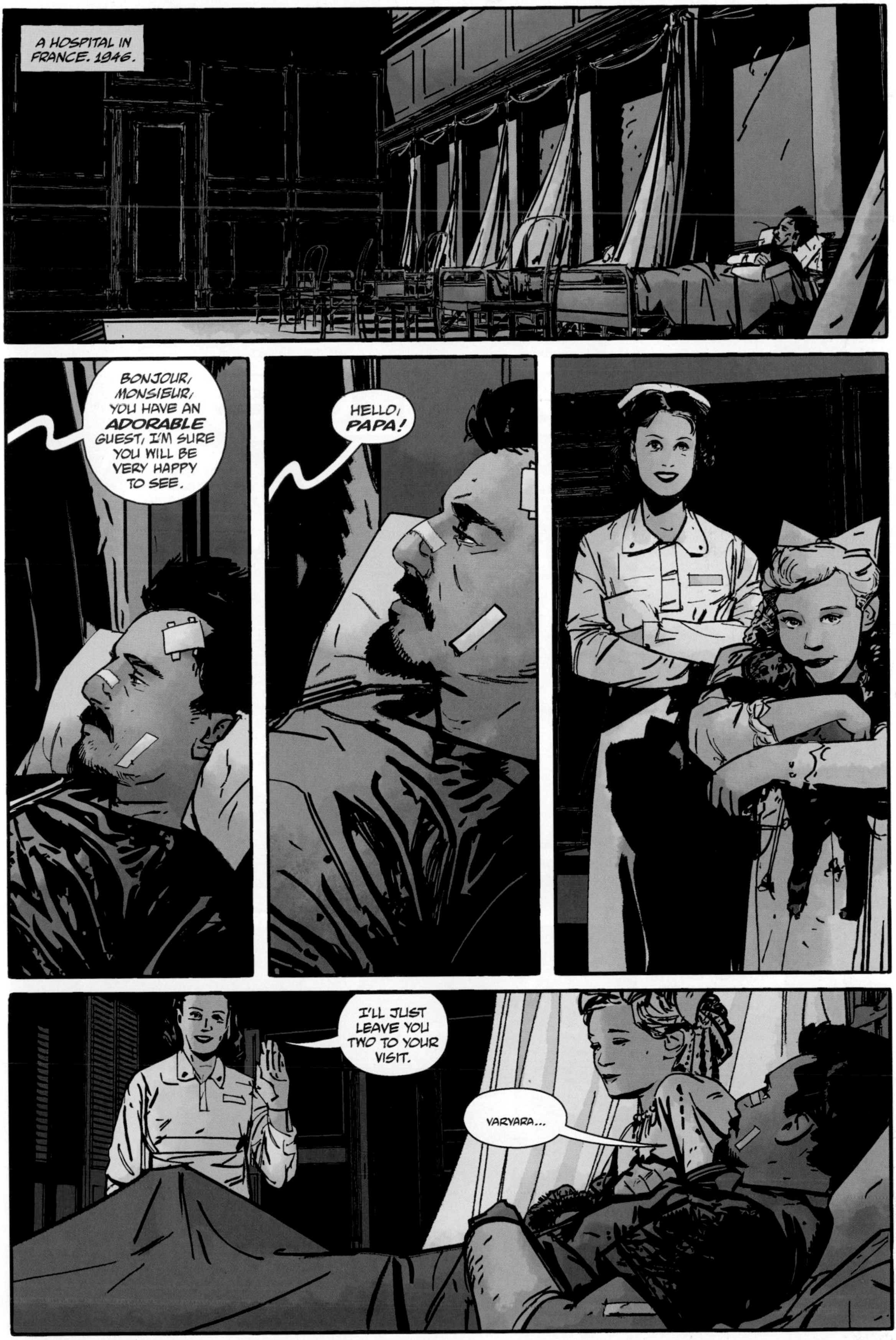
A HOSPITAL IN FRANCE. 1946.
BONJOUR, MONSIEUR, YOU HAVE AN ADORABLE GUEST, I'M SURE YOU WILL BE VERY HAPPY TO SEE.
HELLO, PAPA!
I'LL JUST LEAVE YOU TWO TO YOUR VISIT.
VARVARA...

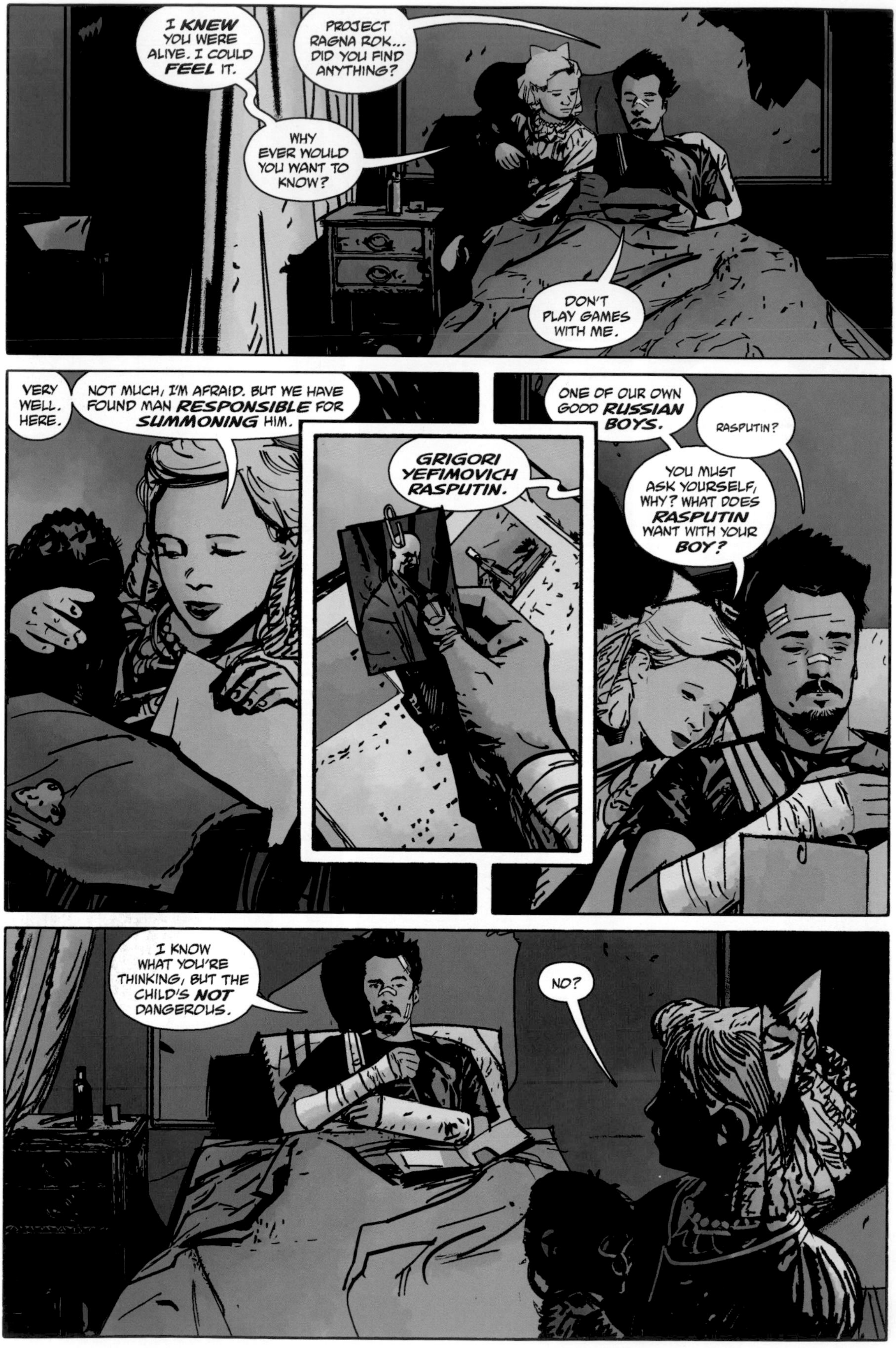
I KNEW YOU WERE ALIVE. I COULD FEEL IT.
PROJECT RAGNA ROK... DID YOU FIND ANYTHING?
WHY EVER WOULD YOU WANT TO KNOW?
DON'T PLAY GAMES WITH ME.
VERY WELL. HERE.
NOT MUCH, I'M AFRAID. BUT WE HAVE FOUND MAN RESPONSIBLE FOR SUMMONING HIM.
GRIGORI YEFIMOVICH RASPUTIN.
ONE OF OUR OWN GOOD RUSSIAN BOYS.
RASPUTIN?
YOU MUST ASK YOURSELF, WHY? WHAT DOES RASPUTIN WANT WITH YOUR BOY?
I KNOW WHAT YOU'RE THINKING, BUT THE CHILD'S NOT DANGEROUS.
NO?

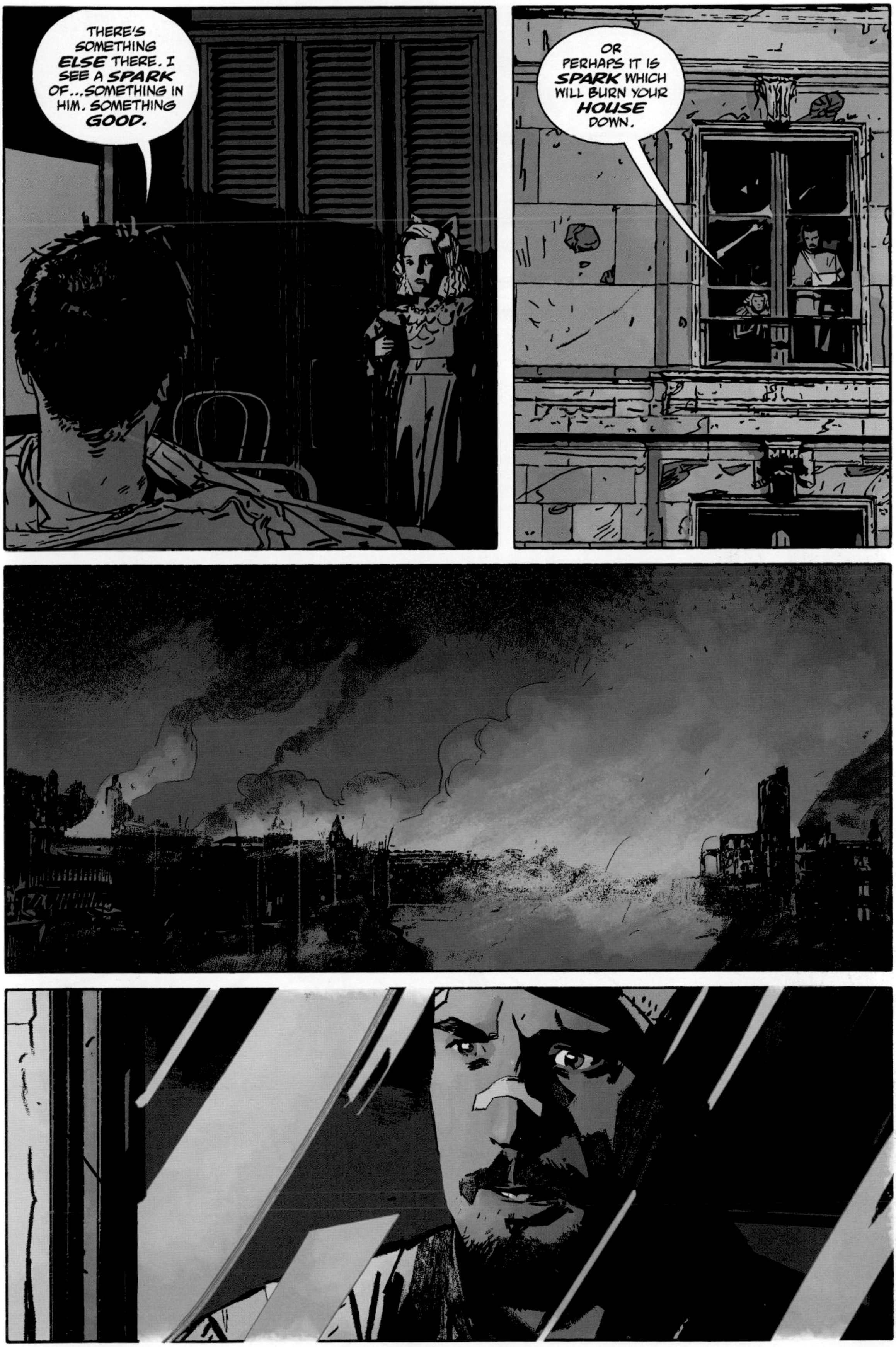
THERE'S SOMETHING ELSE THERE. I SEE A SPARK OF...SOMETHING IN HIM. SOMETHING GOOD.
OR PERHAPS IT IS SPARK WHICH WILL BURN YOUR HOUSE DOWN.

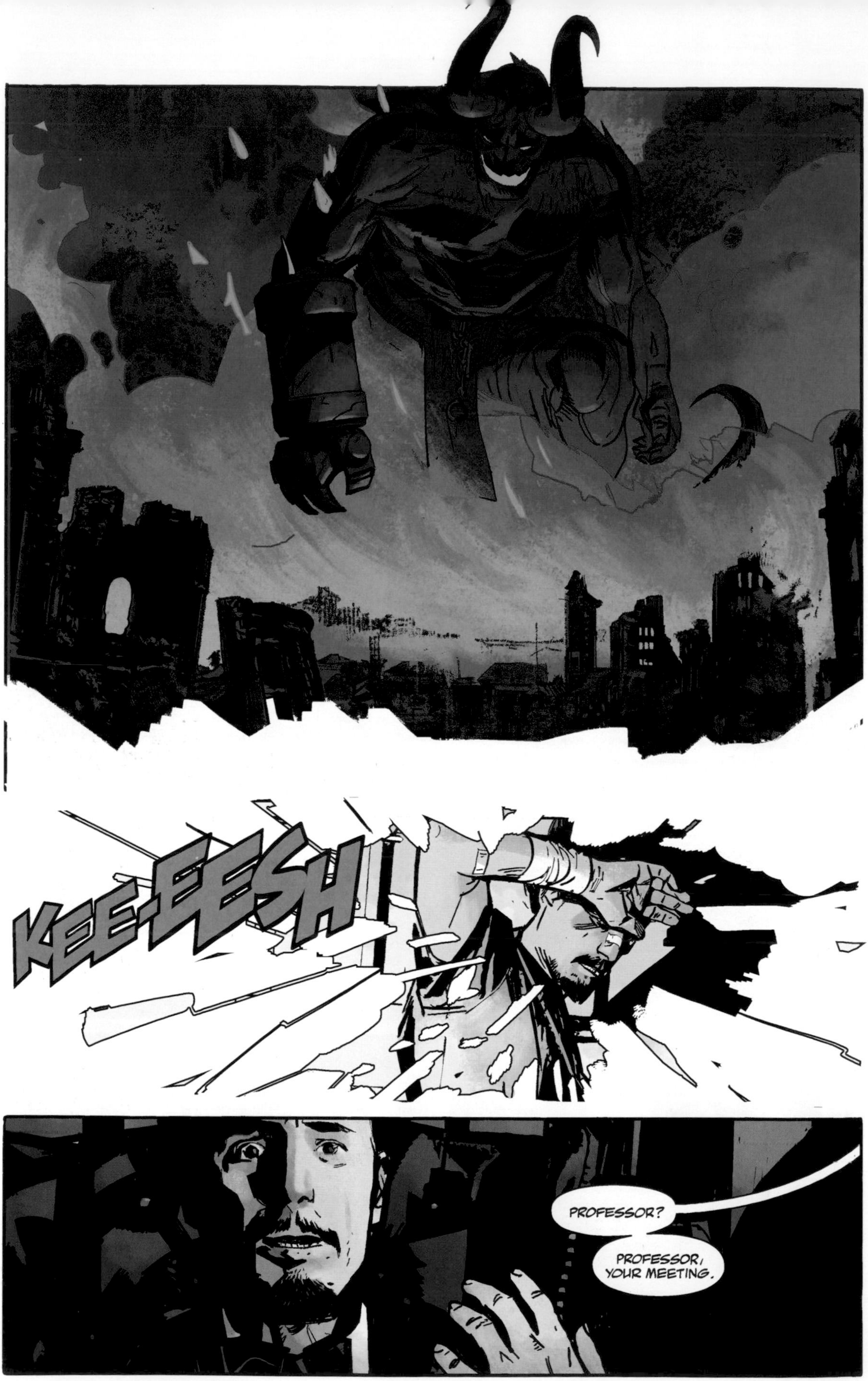
KEE-EESH
PROFESSOR?
PROFESSOR, YOUR MEETING.

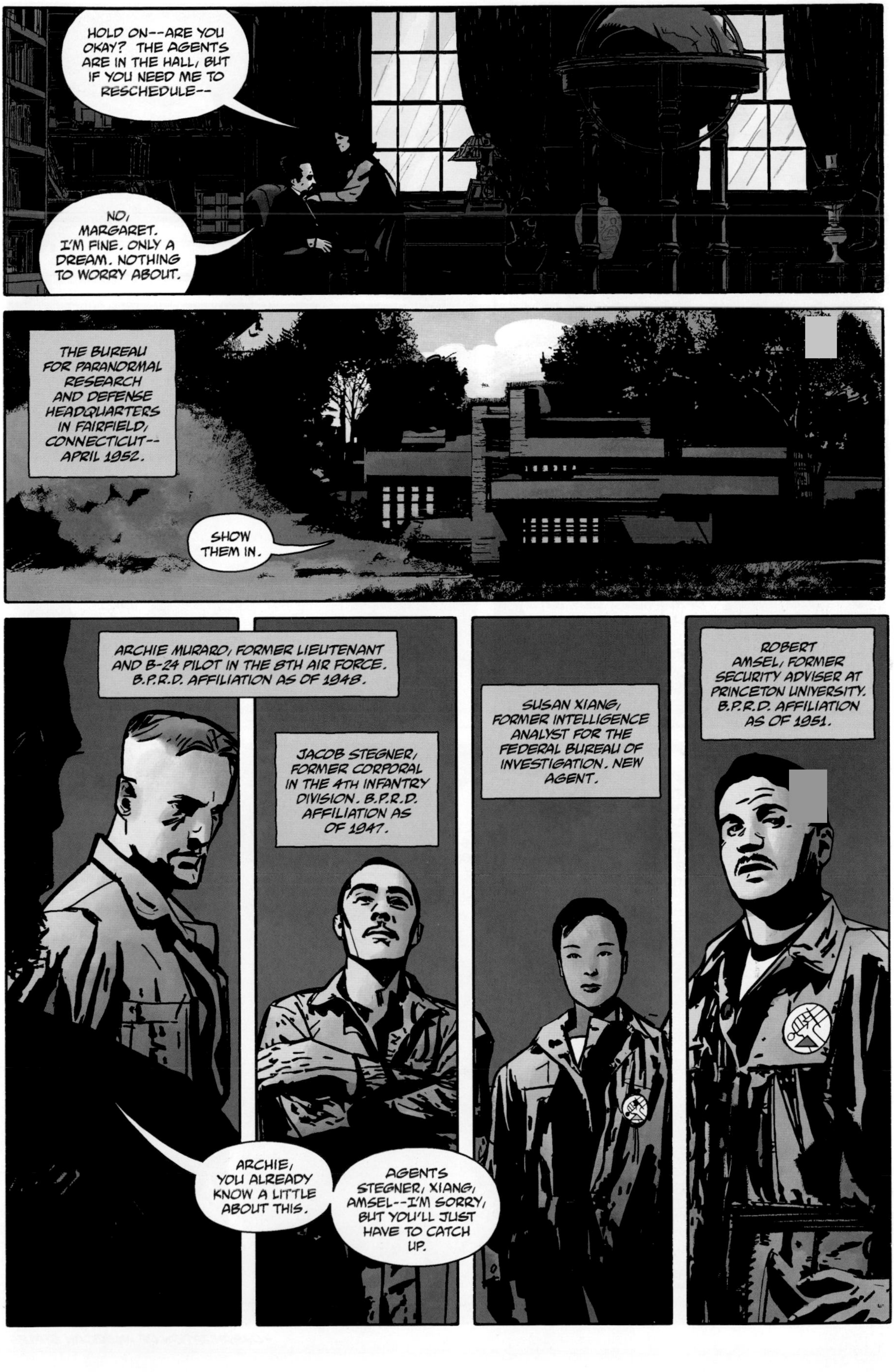
HOLD ON--ARE YOU OKAY? THE AGENTS ARE IN THE HALL, BUT IF YOU NEED ME TO RESCHEDULE--
NO, MARGARET. I'M FINE. ONLY A DREAM. NOTHING TO WORRY ABOUT.
THE BUREAU FOR PARANORMAL RESEARCH AND DEFENSE HEADQUARTERS IN FAIRFIELD, CONNECTICUT-- APRIL 1952.
SHOW THEM IN.
ARCHIE MURARO, FORMER LIEUTENANT AND B-24 PILOT IN THE 8TH AIR FORCE. B.P.R.D. AFFILIATION AS OF 1948.
JACOB STEGNER, FORMER CORPORAL IN THE 4TH INFANTRY DIVISION. B.P.R.D. AFFILIATION AS OF 1947.
SUSAN XIANG, FORMER INTELLIGENCE ANALYST FOR THE FEDERAL BUREAU OF INVESTIGATION. NEW AGENT.
ROBERT AMSEL, FORMER SECURITY ADVISER AT PRINCETON UNIVERSITY. B.P.R.D. AFFILIATION AS OF 1951.
ARCHIE, YOU ALREADY KNOW A LITTLE ABOUT THIS.
AGENTS STEGNER, XIANG, AMSEL--I'M SORRY, BUT YOU'LL JUST HAVE TO CATCH UP.

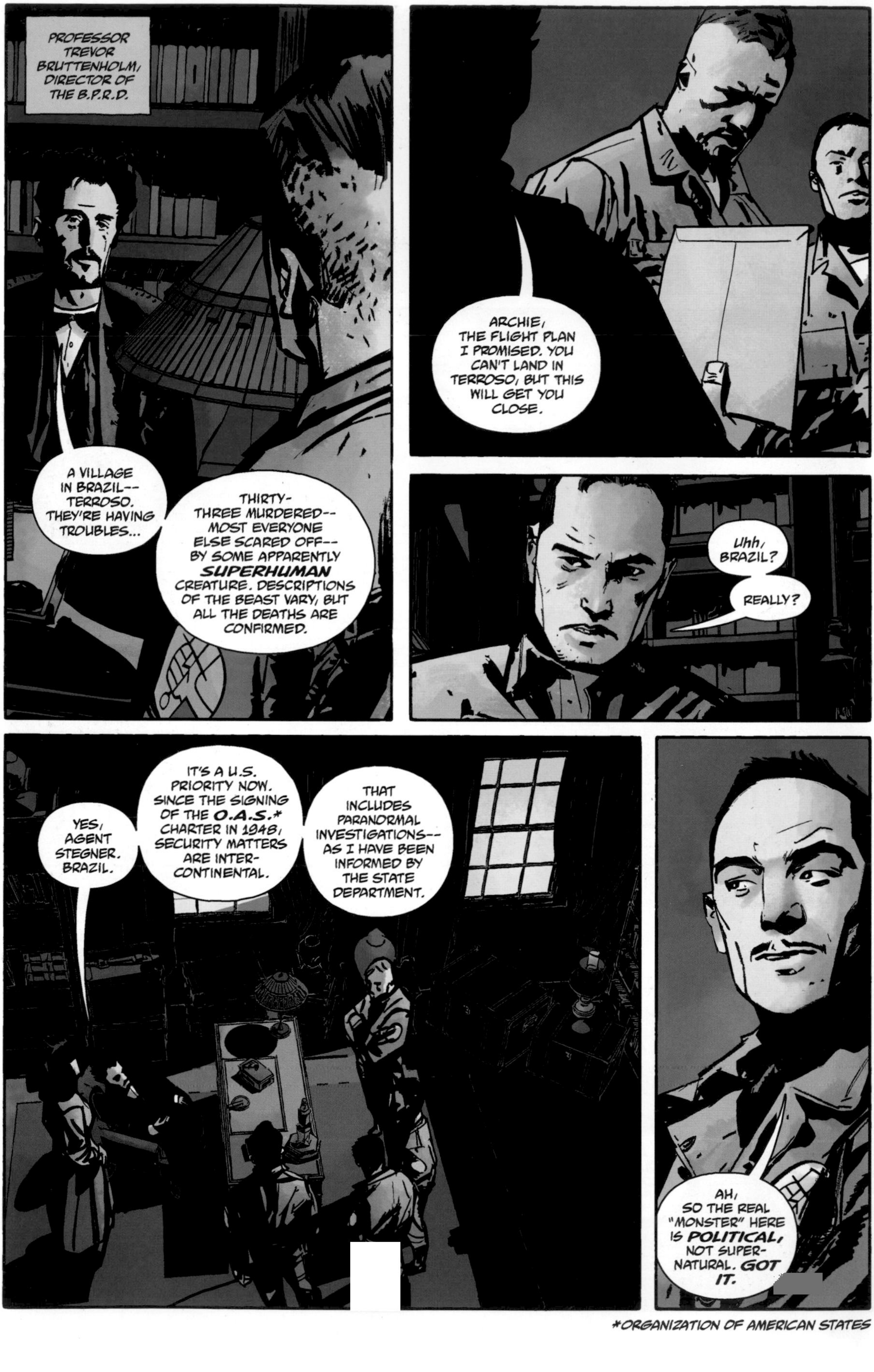
PROFESSOR TREVOR BRUTTENHOLM, DIRECTOR OF THE B.P.R.D.
A VILLAGE IN BRAZIL-- TERROSO. THEY'RE HAVING TROUBLES...
THIRTY-THREE MURDERED-- MOST EVERYONE ELSE SCARED OFF-- BY SOME APPARENTLY SUPERHUMAN CREATURE. DESCRIPTIONS OF THE BEAST VARY, BUT ALL THE DEATHS ARE CONFIRMED.
ARCHIE, THE FLIGHT PLAN I PROMISED. YOU CAN'T LAND IN TERROSO, BUT THIS WILL GET YOU CLOSE.
UHH, BRAZIL?
REALLY?
YES, AGENT STEGNER. BRAZIL.
IT'S A U.S. PRIORITY NOW. SINCE THE SIGNING OF THE O.A.S.* CHARTER IN 1948, SECURITY MATTERS ARE INTER-CONTINENTAL.
THAT INCLUDES PARANORMAL INVESTIGATIONS-- AS I HAVE BEEN INFORMED BY THE STATE DEPARTMENT.
AH, SO THE REAL "MONSTER" HERE IS POLITICAL, NOT SUPER-NATURAL. GOT IT.

*ORGANIZATION OF AMERICAN STATES

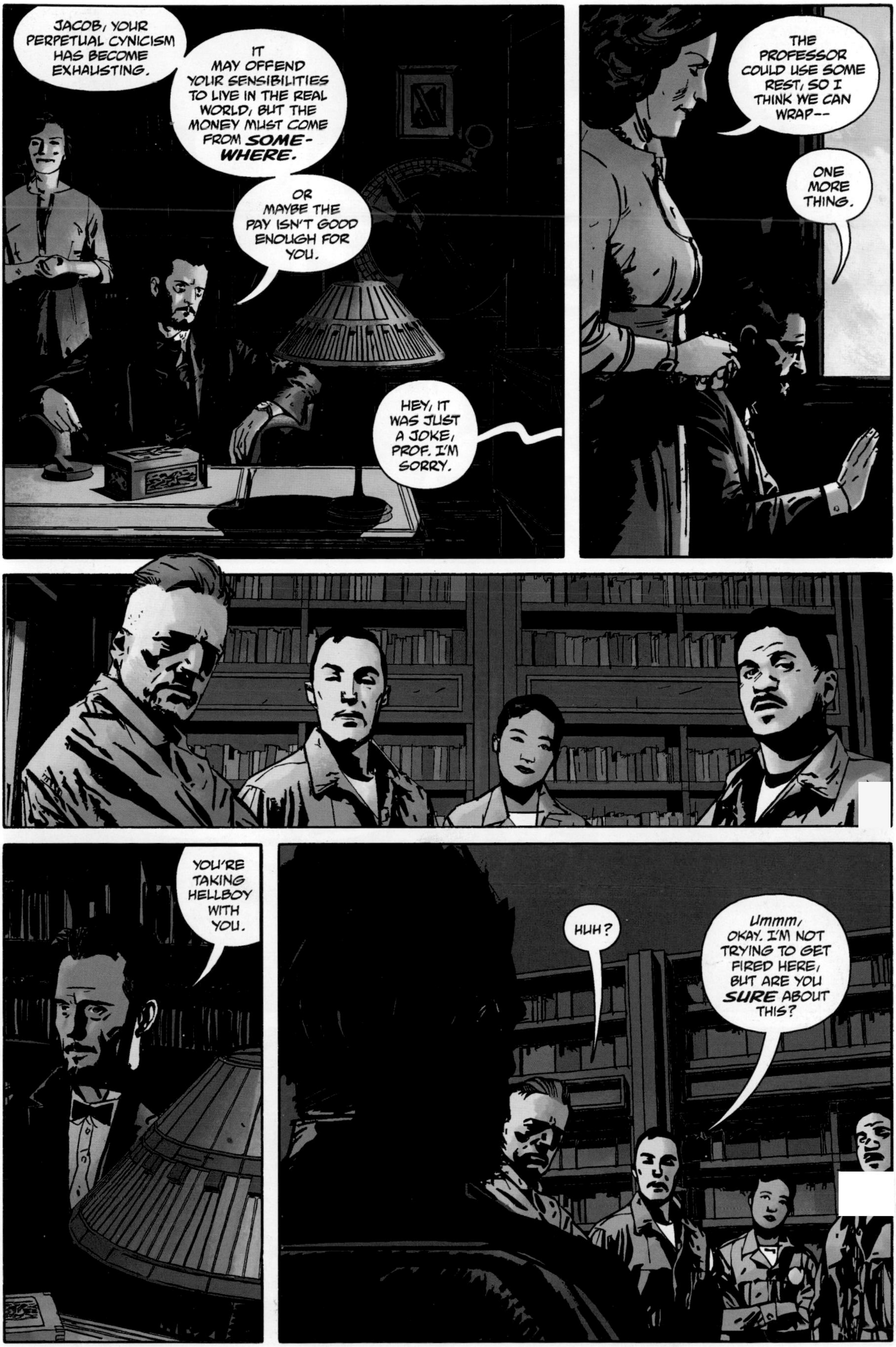
JACOB, YOUR PERPETUAL CYNICISM HAS BECOME EXHAUSTING.
IT MAY OFFEND YOUR SENSIBILITIES TO LIVE IN THE REAL WORLD, BUT THE MONEY MUST COME FROM SOME-WHERE.
OR MAYBE THE PAY ISN'T GOOD ENOUGH FOR YOU.
HEY, IT WAS JUST A JOKE, PROF. I'M SORRY.
THE PROFESSOR COULD USE SOME REST, SO I THINK WE CAN WRAP--
ONE MORE THING.
YOU'RE TAKING HELLBOY WITH YOU.
HUH?
Ummm, OKAY. I'M NOT TRYING TO GET FIRED HERE, BUT ARE YOU SURE ABOUT THIS?

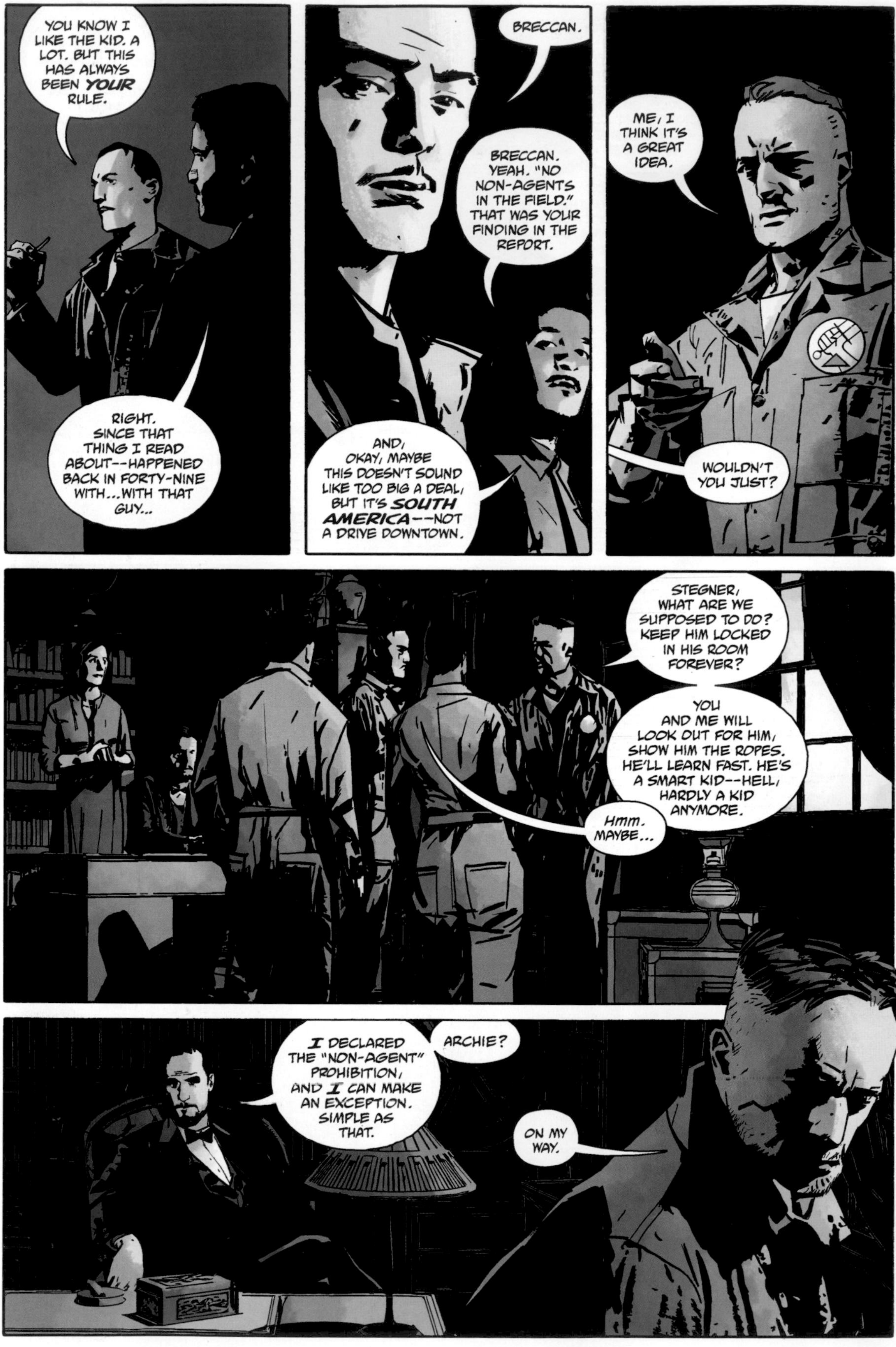
YOU KNOW I LIKE THE KID. A LOT. BUT THIS HAS ALWAYS BEEN YOUR RULE.
RIGHT. SINCE THAT THING I READ ABOUT--HAPPENED BACK IN FORTY-NINE WITH...WITH THAT GUY...
BRECCAN.
BRECCAN. YEAH. "NO NON-AGENTS IN THE FIELD." THAT WAS YOUR FINDING IN THE REPORT.
AND, OKAY, MAYBE THIS DOESN'T SOUND LIKE TOO BIG A DEAL, BUT IT'S SOUTH AMERICA--NOT A DRIVE DOWNTOWN.
ME, I THINK IT'S A GREAT IDEA.
WOULDN'T YOU JUST?
STEGNER, WHAT ARE WE SUPPOSED TO DO? KEEP HIM LOCKED IN HIS ROOM FOREVER?
YOU AND ME WILL LOOK OUT FOR HIM, SHOW HIM THE ROPES. HE'LL LEARN FAST. HE'S A SMART KID--HELL, HARDLY A KID ANYMORE.
Hmm. MAYBE...
I DECLARED THE "NON-AGENT" PROHIBITION, AND I CAN MAKE AN EXCEPTION. SIMPLE AS THAT.
ARCHIE?
ON MY WAY.

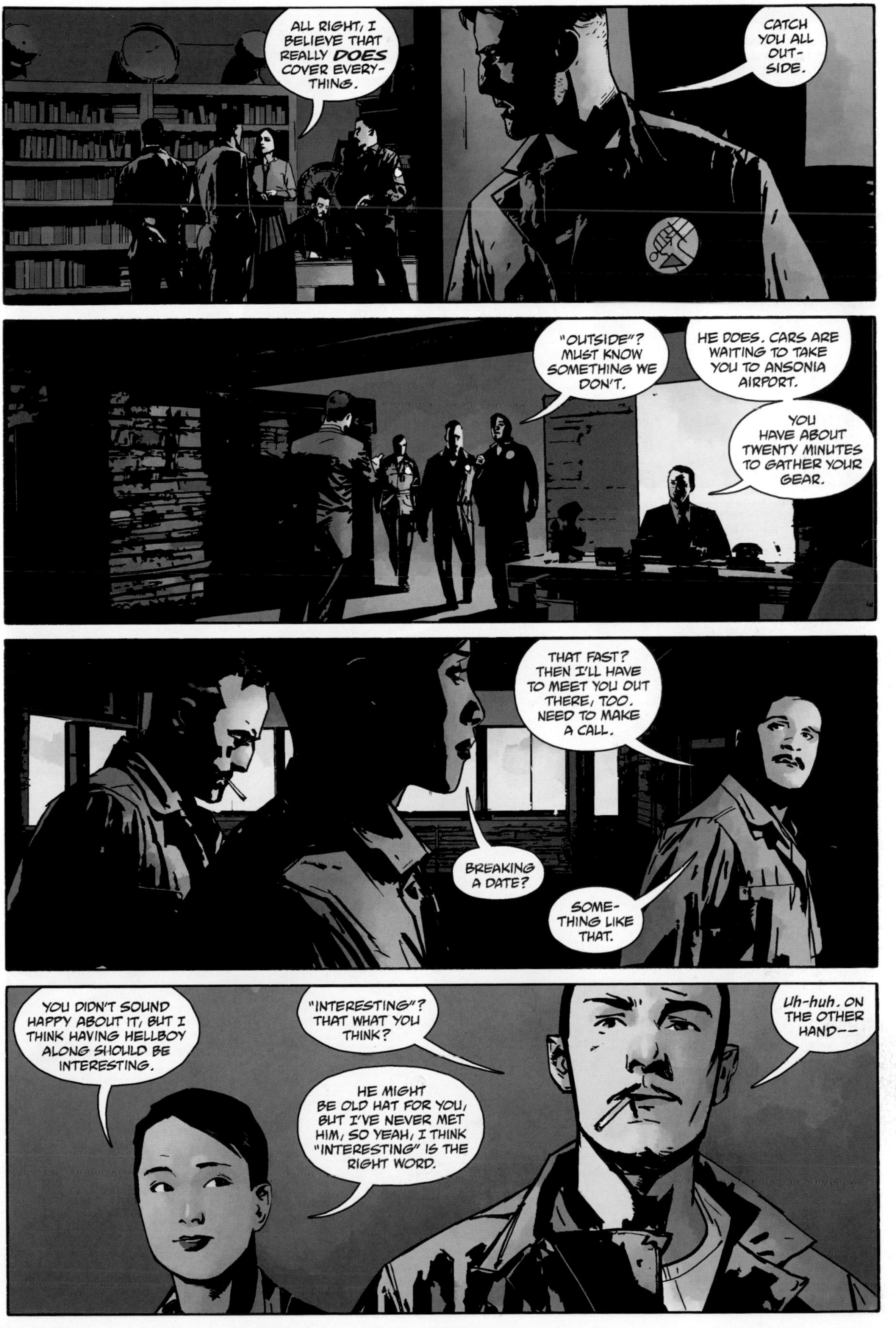
ALL RIGHT, I BELIEVE THAT REALLY DOES COVER EVERY-THING.
CATCH YOU ALL OUT-SIDE.
"OUTSIDE"? MUST KNOW SOMETHING WE DON'T.
HE DOES. CARS ARE WAITING TO TAKE YOU TO ANSONIA AIRPORT.
YOU HAVE ABOUT TWENTY MINUTES TO GATHER YOUR GEAR.
THAT FAST? THEN I'LL HAVE TO MEET YOU OUT THERE, TOO. NEED TO MAKE A CALL.
BREAKING A DATE?
SOME-THING LIKE THAT.
YOU DIDN'T SOUND HAPPY ABOUT IT, BUT I THINK HAVING HELLBOY ALONG SHOULD BE INTERESTING.
"INTERESTING"? THAT WHAT YOU THINK?
HE MIGHT BE OLD HAT FOR YOU, BUT I'VE NEVER MET HIM, SO YEAH, I THINK "INTERESTING" IS THE RIGHT WORD.
Uh-huh. ON THE OTHER HAND--

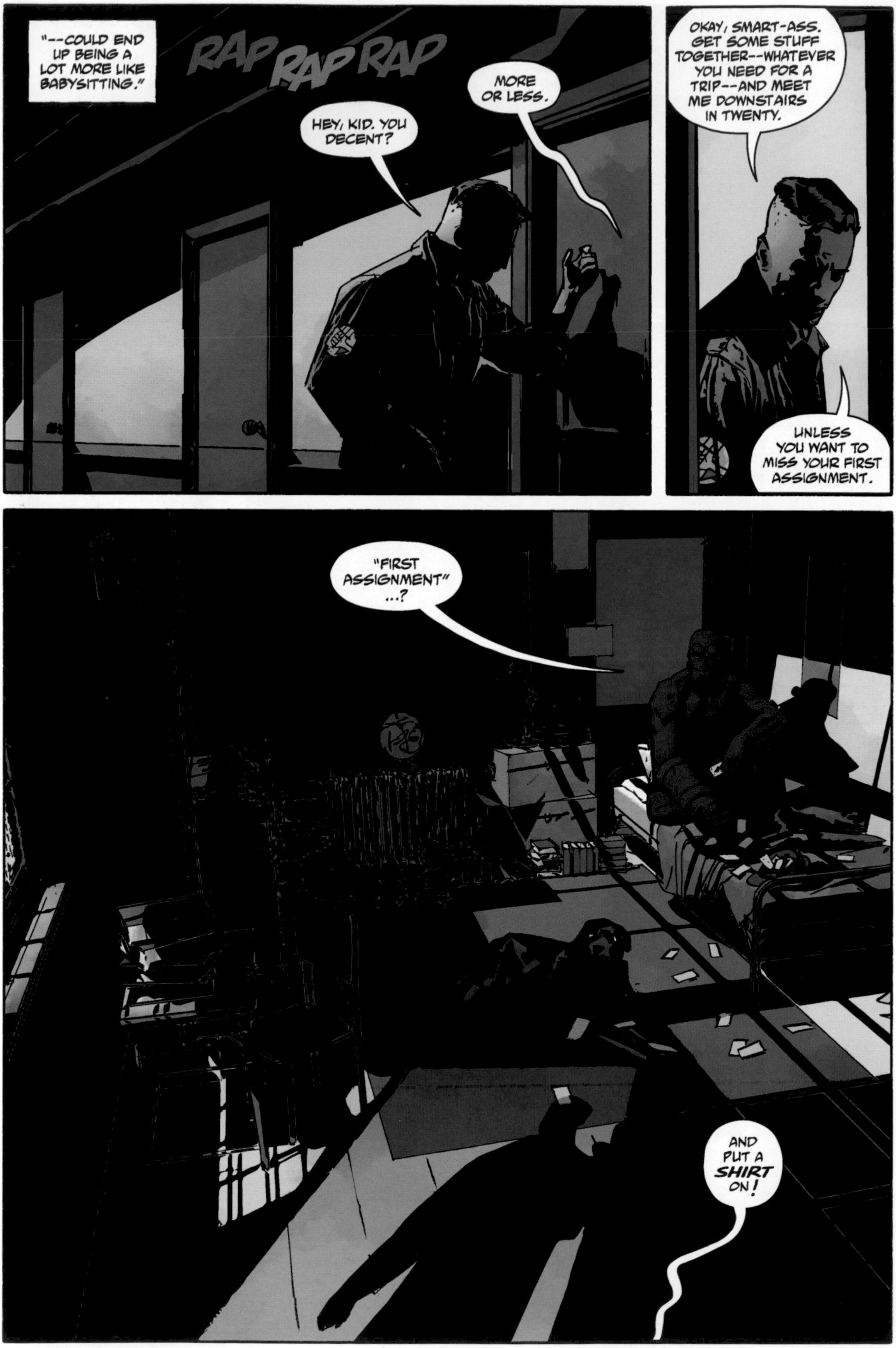
"--COULD END UP BEING A LOT MORE LIKE BABYSITTING."
RAP RAP RAP
HEY, KID. YOU DECENT?
MORE OR LESS.
OKAY, SMART-ASS. GET SOME STUFF TOGETHER--WHATEVER YOU NEED FOR A TRIP--AND MEET ME DOWNSTAIRS IN TWENTY.
UNLESS YOU WANT TO MISS YOUR FIRST ASSIGNMENT.
"FIRST ASSIGNMENT" ...?
AND PUT A SHIRT ON!

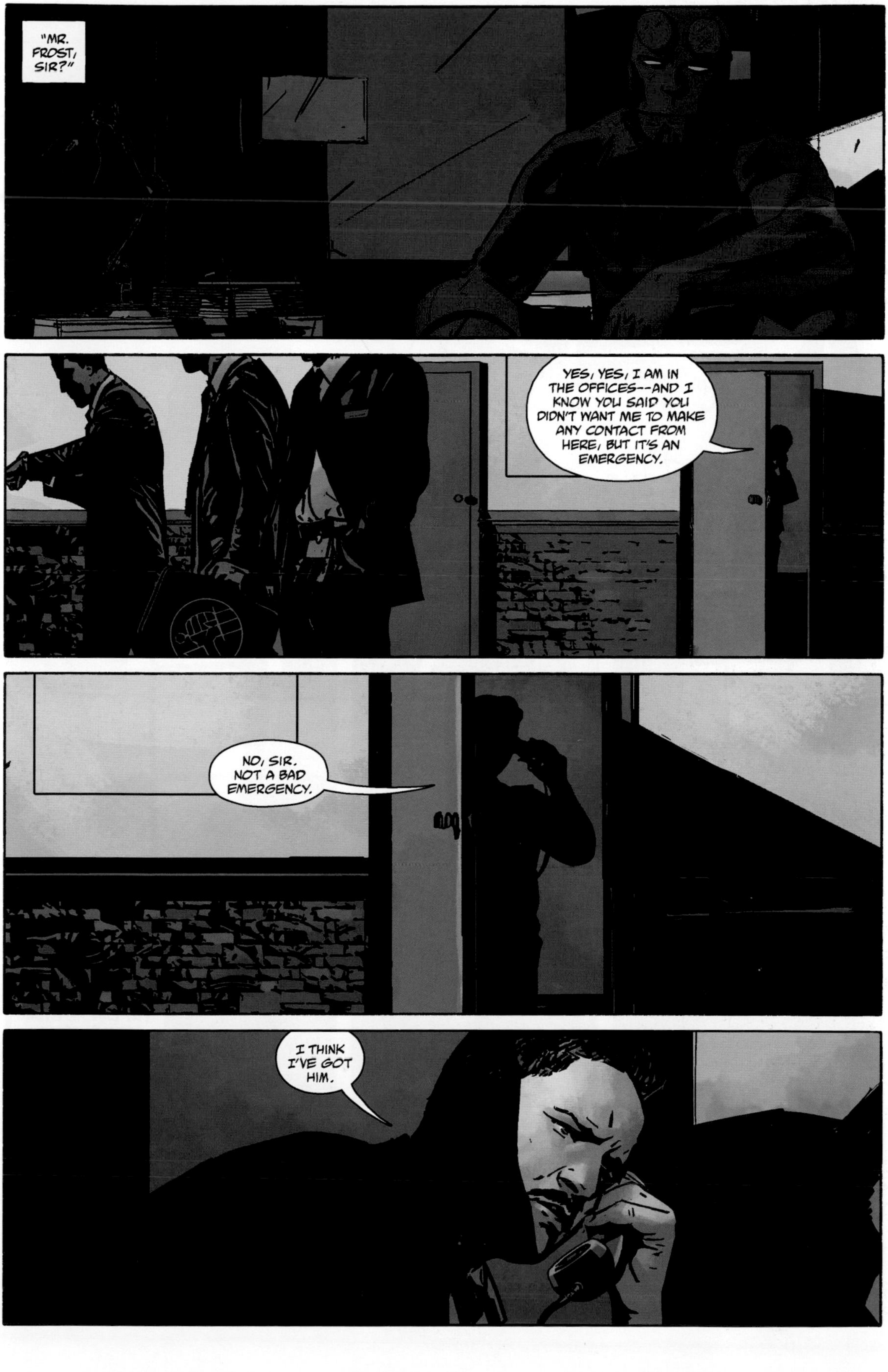
"MR. FROST, SIR?"
YES, YES, I AM IN THE OFFICES--AND I KNOW YOU SAID YOU DIDN'T WANT ME TO MAKE ANY CONTACT FROM HERE, BUT IT'S AN EMERGENCY.
NO, SIR. NOT A BAD EMERGENCY.
I THINK I'VE GOT HIM.

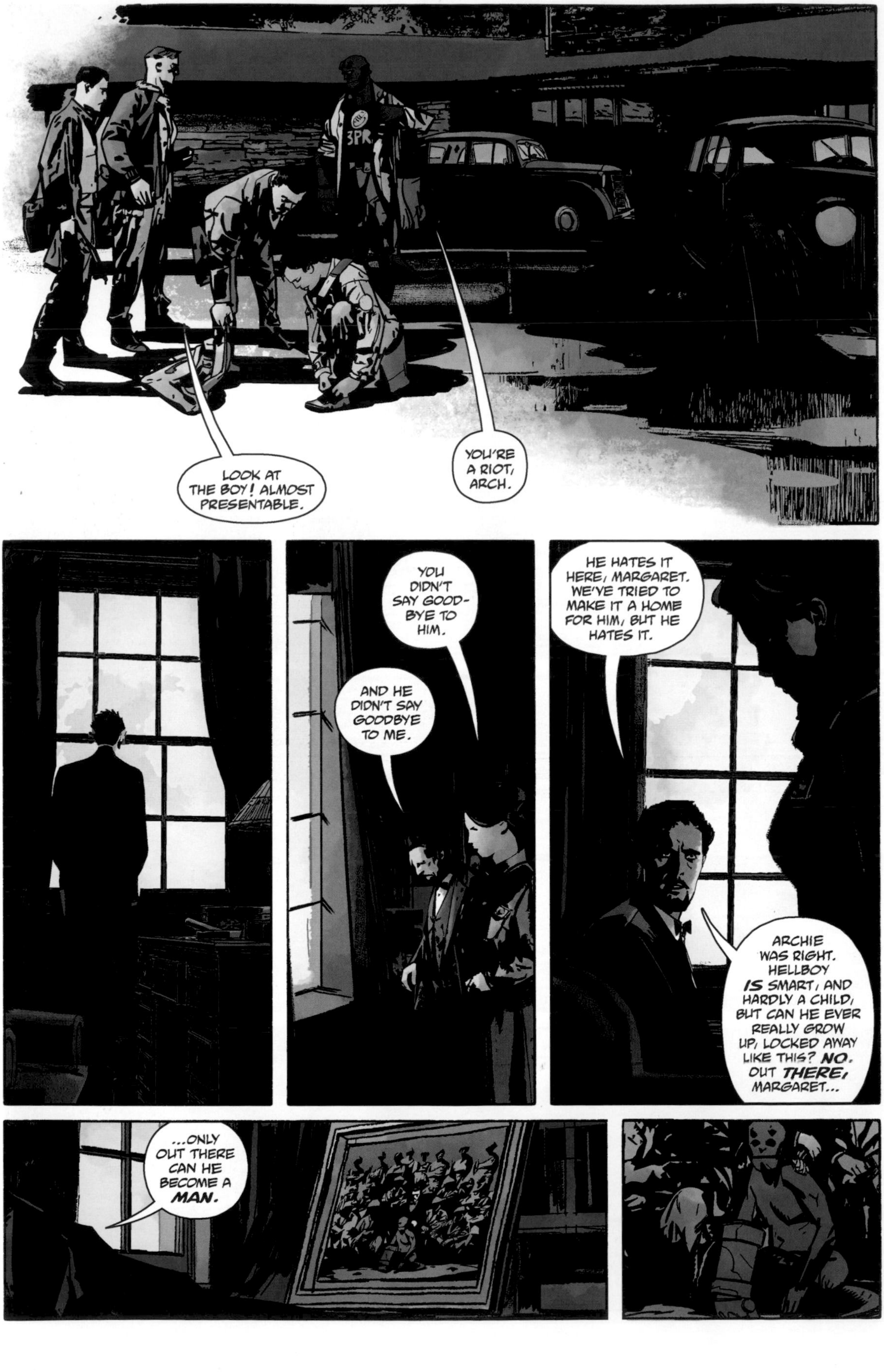
LOOK AT THE BOY! ALMOST PRESENTABLE.
YOU'RE A RIOT, ARCH.
YOU DIDN'T SAY GOOD-BYE TO HIM.
AND HE DIDN'T SAY GOODBYE TO ME.
HE HATES IT HERE, MARGARET. WE'VE TRIED TO MAKE IT A HOME FOR HIM, BUT HE HATES IT.
ARCHIE WAS RIGHT. HELLBOY IS SMART, AND HARDLY A CHILD, BUT CAN HE EVER REALLY GROW UP, LOCKED AWAY LIKE THIS? NO. OUT THERE, MARGARET...
...ONLY OUT THERE CAN HE BECOME A MAN.

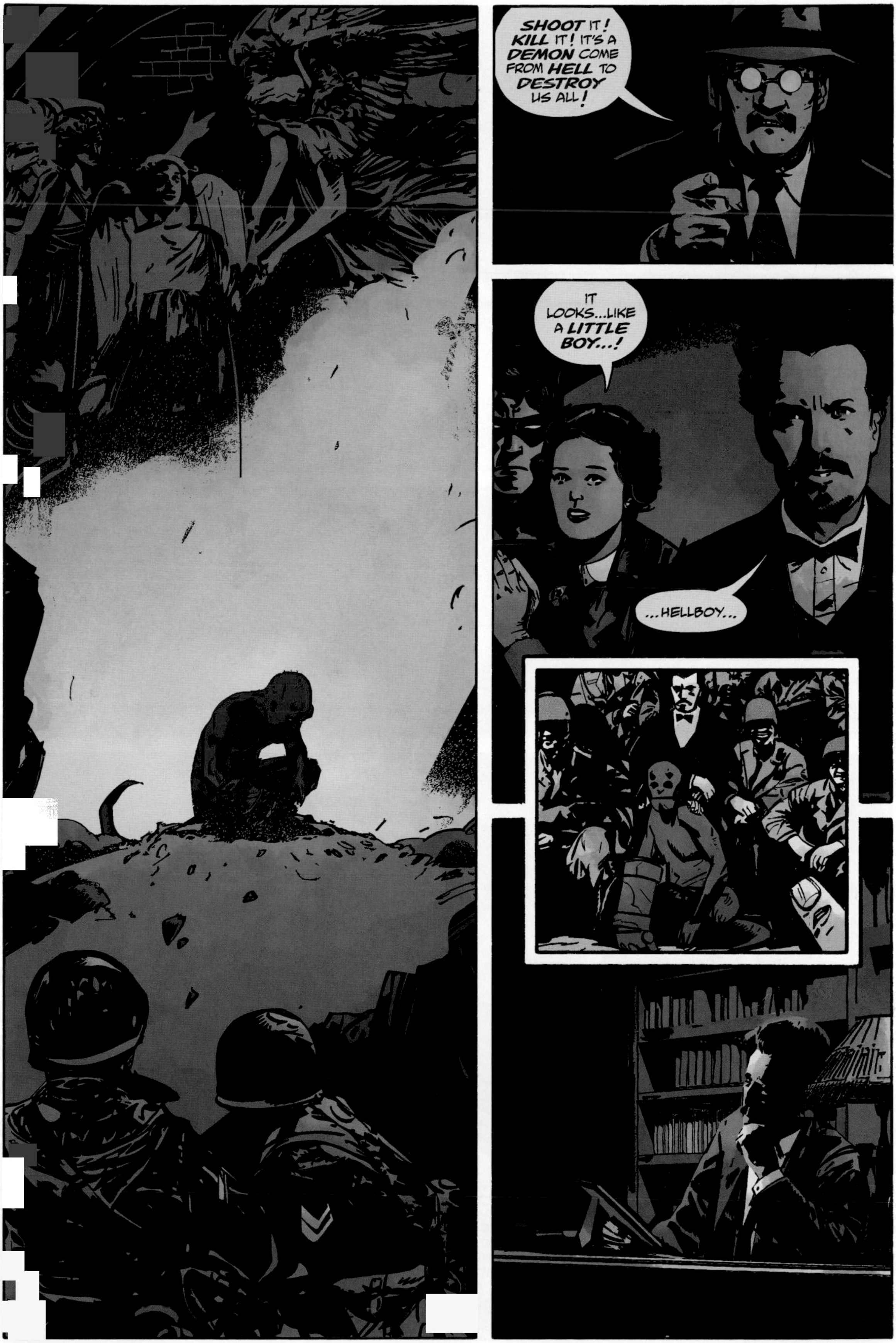
SHOOT IT! KILL IT! IT'S A DEMON COME FROM HELL TO DESTROY US ALL!
IT LOOKS...LIKE A LITTLE BOY...!
...HELLBOY...

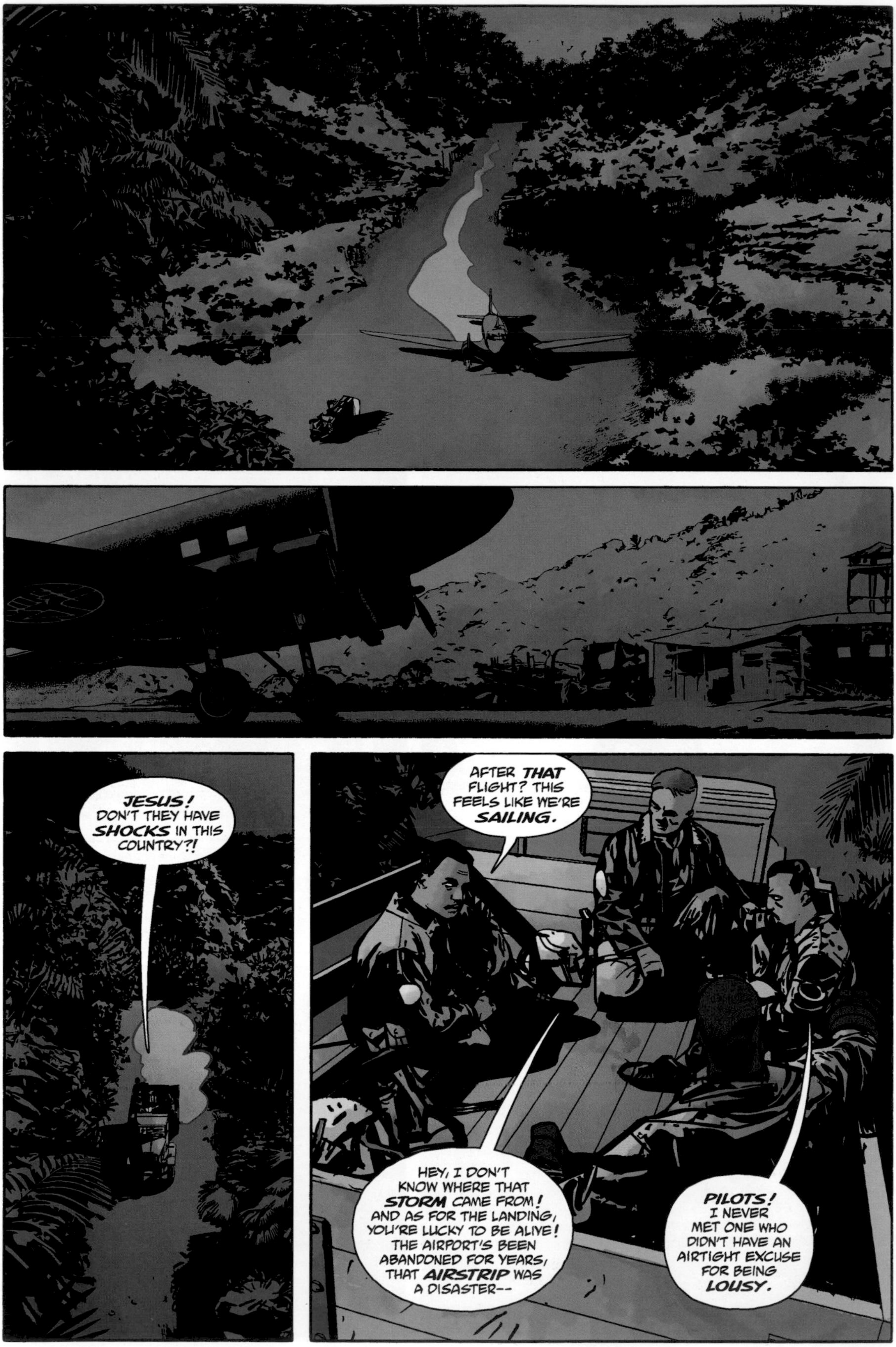
JESUS! DON'T THEY HAVE SHOCKS IN THIS COUNTRY?!
AFTER THAT FLIGHT? THIS FEELS LIKE WE'RE SAILING.
HEY, I DON'T KNOW WHERE THAT STORM CAME FROM! AND AS FOR THE LANDING, YOU'RE LUCKY TO BE ALIVE! THE AIRPORT'S BEEN ABANDONED FOR YEARS, THAT AIRSTRIP WAS A DISASTER--
PILOTS! I NEVER MET ONE WHO DIDN'T HAVE AN AIRTIGHT EXCUSE FOR BEING LOUSY.

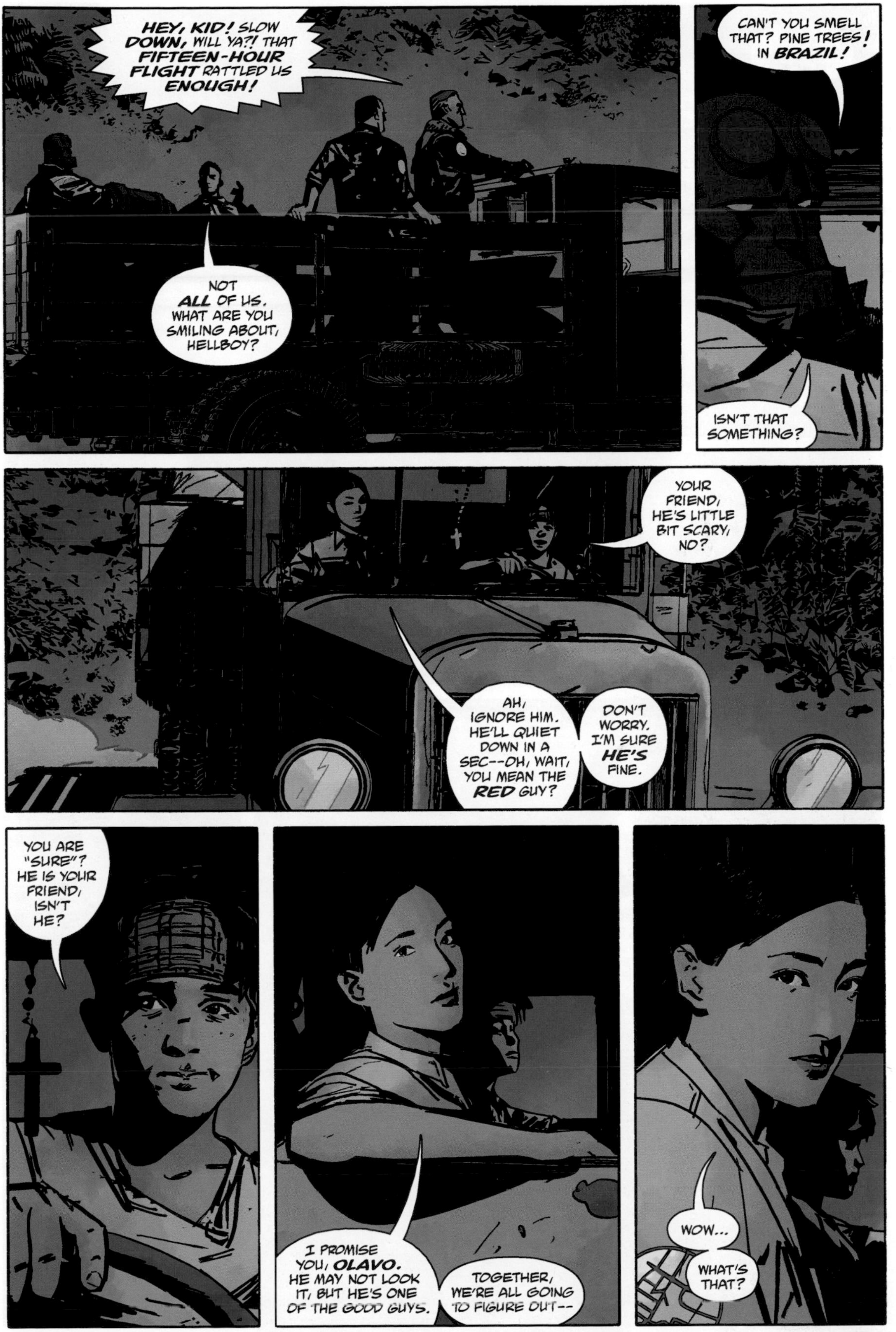
HEY, KID! SLOW DOWN, WILL YA?! THAT FIFTEEN-HOUR FLIGHT RATTLED US ENOUGH!
NOT ALL OF US. WHAT ARE YOU SMILING ABOUT, HELLBOY?
CAN'T YOU SMELL THAT? PINE TREES! IN BRAZIL!
ISN'T THAT SOMETHING?
YOUR FRIEND, HE'S LITTLE BIT SCARY, NO?
AH, IGNORE HIM. HE'LL QUIET DOWN IN A SEC--OH, WAIT, YOU MEAN THE RED GUY?
DON'T WORRY. I'M SURE HE'S FINE.
YOU ARE "SURE"? HE IS YOUR FRIEND, ISN'T HE?
I PROMISE YOU, OLAVO. HE MAY NOT LOOK IT, BUT HE'S ONE OF THE GOOD GUYS.
TOGETHER, WE'RE ALL GOING TO FIGURE OUT--
WOW...
WHAT'S THAT?

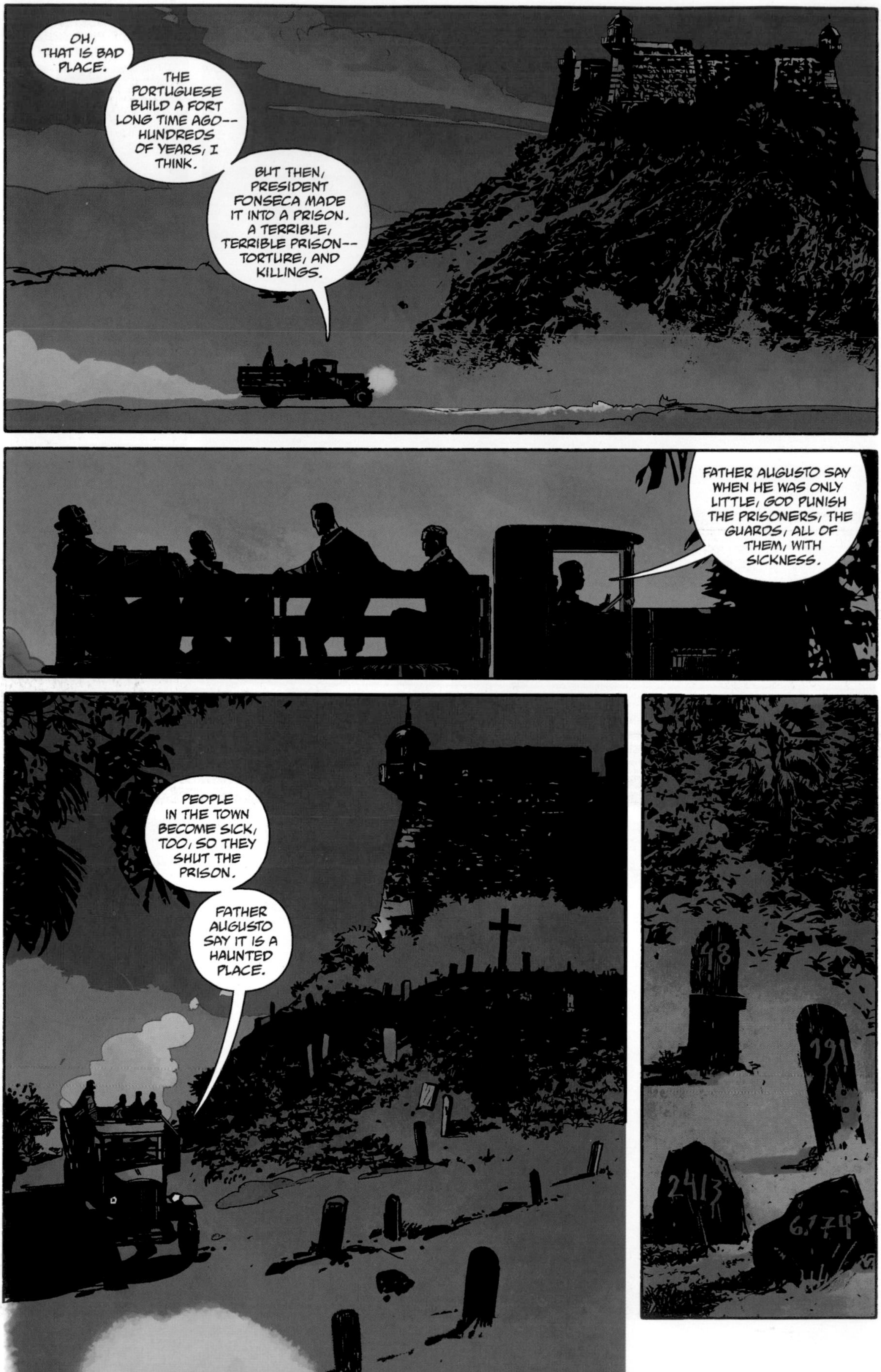
OH, THAT IS BAD PLACE.
THE PORTUGUESE BUILD A FORT LONG TIME AGO-- HUNDREDS OF YEARS, I THINK.
BUT THEN, PRESIDENT FONSECA MADE IT INTO A PRISON. A TERRIBLE, TERRIBLE PRISON-- TORTURE, AND KILLINGS.
FATHER AUGUSTO SAY WHEN HE WAS ONLY LITTLE, GOD PUNISH THE PRISONERS, THE GUARDS, ALL OF THEM, WITH SICKNESS.
PEOPLE IN THE TOWN BECOME SICK, TOO, SO THEY SHUT THE PRISON.
FATHER AUGUSTO SAY IT IS A HAUNTED PLACE.

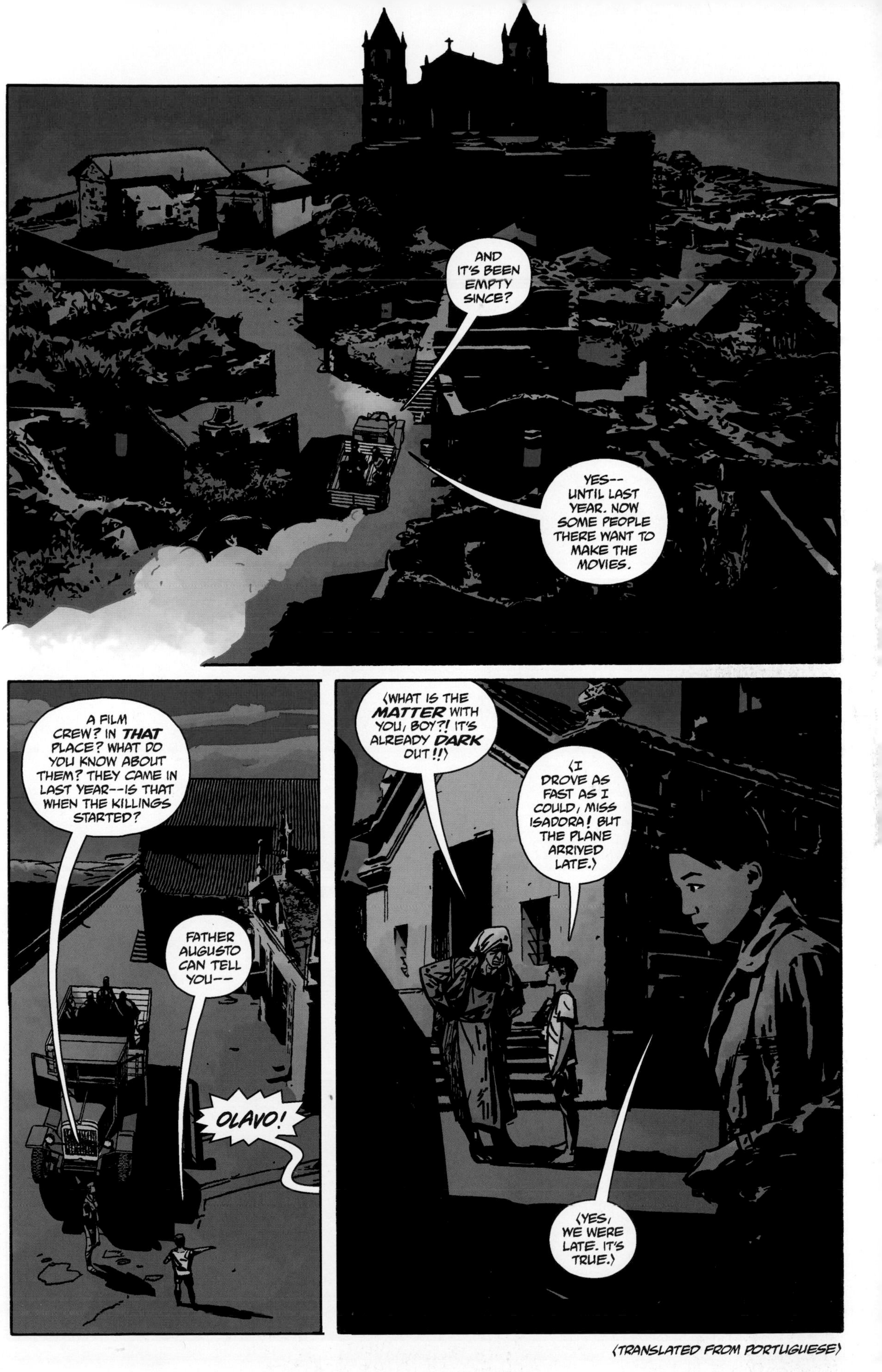
AND IT'S BEEN EMPTY SINCE?
YES-- UNTIL LAST YEAR. NOW SOME PEOPLE THERE WANT TO MAKE THE MOVIES.
A FILM CREW? IN THAT PLACE? WHAT DO YOU KNOW ABOUT THEM? THEY CAME IN LAST YEAR--IS THAT WHEN THE KILLINGS STARTED?
FATHER AUGUSTO CAN TELL YOU--
OLAVO!
⟨WHAT IS THE MATTER WITH YOU, BOY?! IT'S ALREADY DARK OUT!!⟩
⟨I DROVE AS FAST AS I COULD, MISS ISADORA! BUT THE PLANE ARRIVED LATE.⟩
⟨YES, WE WERE LATE. IT'S TRUE.⟩
⟨TRANSLATED FROM PORTUGUESE⟩

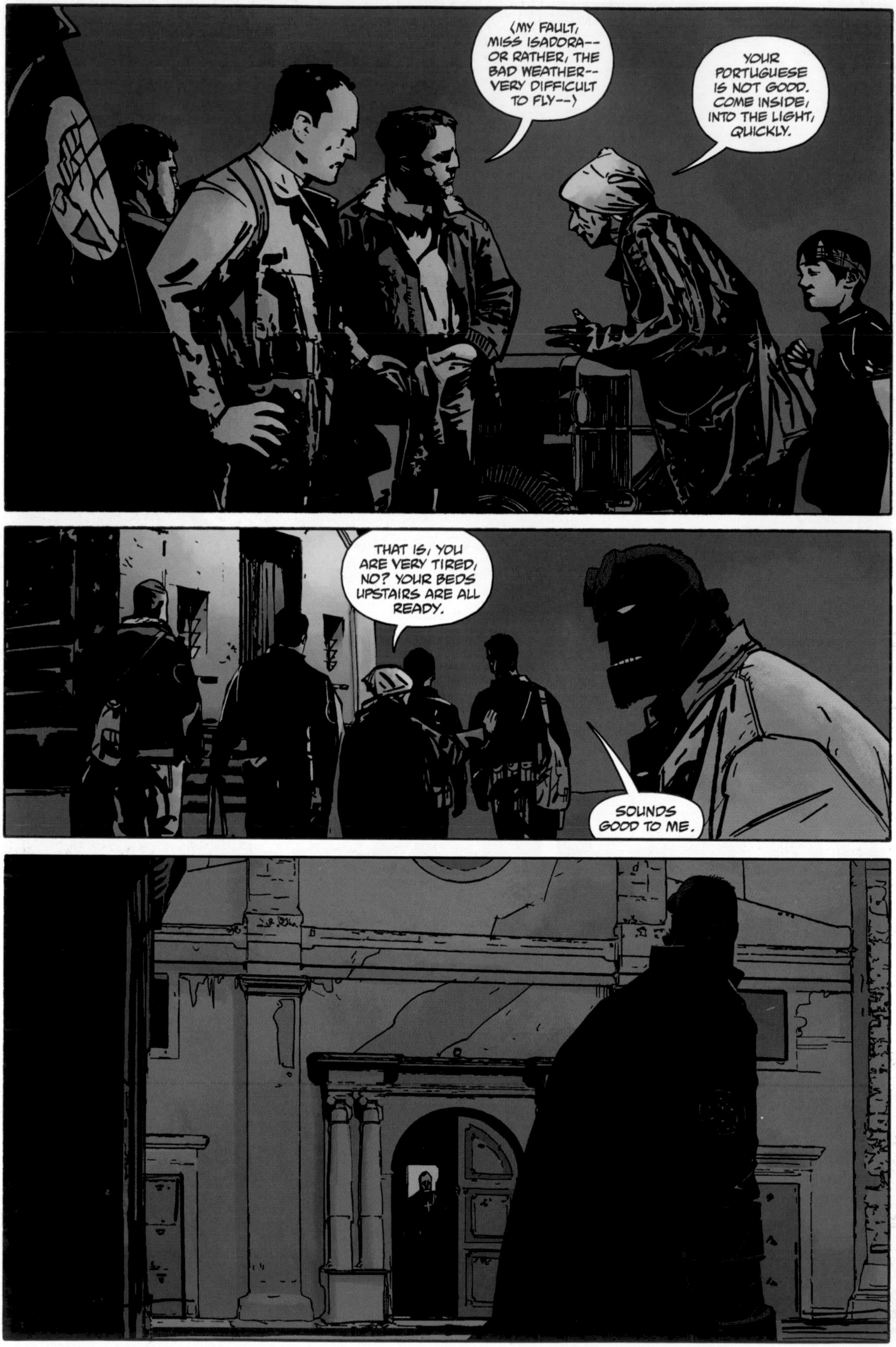

⟨MY FAULT, MISS ISADORA-- OR RATHER, THE BAD WEATHER-- VERY DIFFICULT TO FLY--⟩
YOUR PORTUGUESE IS NOT GOOD. COME INSIDE, INTO THE LIGHT, QUICKLY.
THAT IS, YOU ARE VERY TIRED, NO? YOUR BEDS UPSTAIRS ARE ALL READY.
SOUNDS GOOD TO ME.

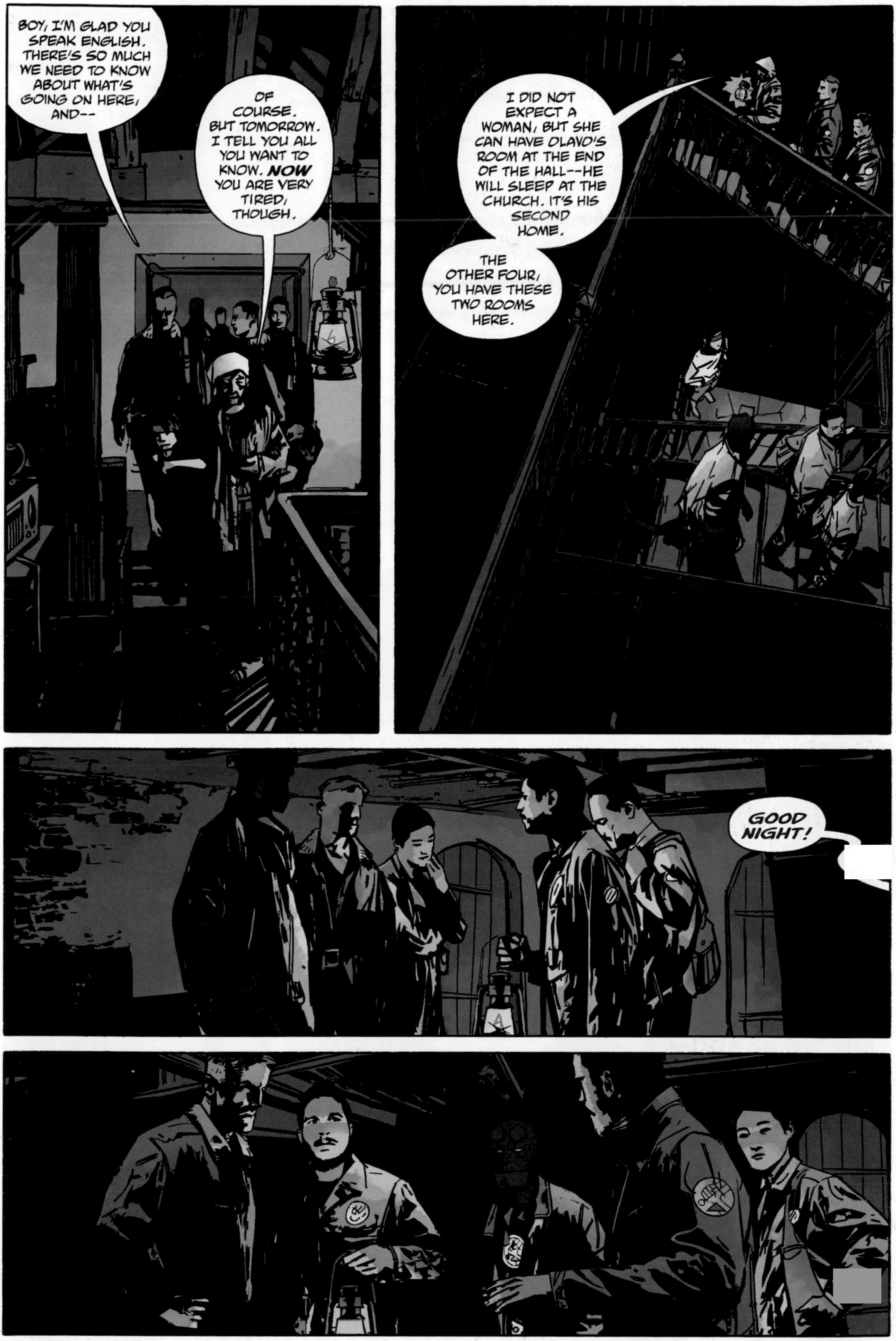
BOY, I'M GLAD YOU SPEAK ENGLISH. THERE'S SO MUCH WE NEED TO KNOW ABOUT WHAT'S GOING ON HERE, AND--
OF COURSE. BUT TOMORROW. I TELL YOU ALL YOU WANT TO KNOW. **NOW** YOU ARE VERY TIRED, THOUGH.
I DID NOT EXPECT A WOMAN, BUT SHE CAN HAVE OLAVO'S ROOM AT THE END OF THE HALL--HE WILL SLEEP AT THE CHURCH. IT'S HIS SECOND HOME.
THE OTHER FOUR, YOU HAVE THESE TWO ROOMS HERE.
GOOD NIGHT!

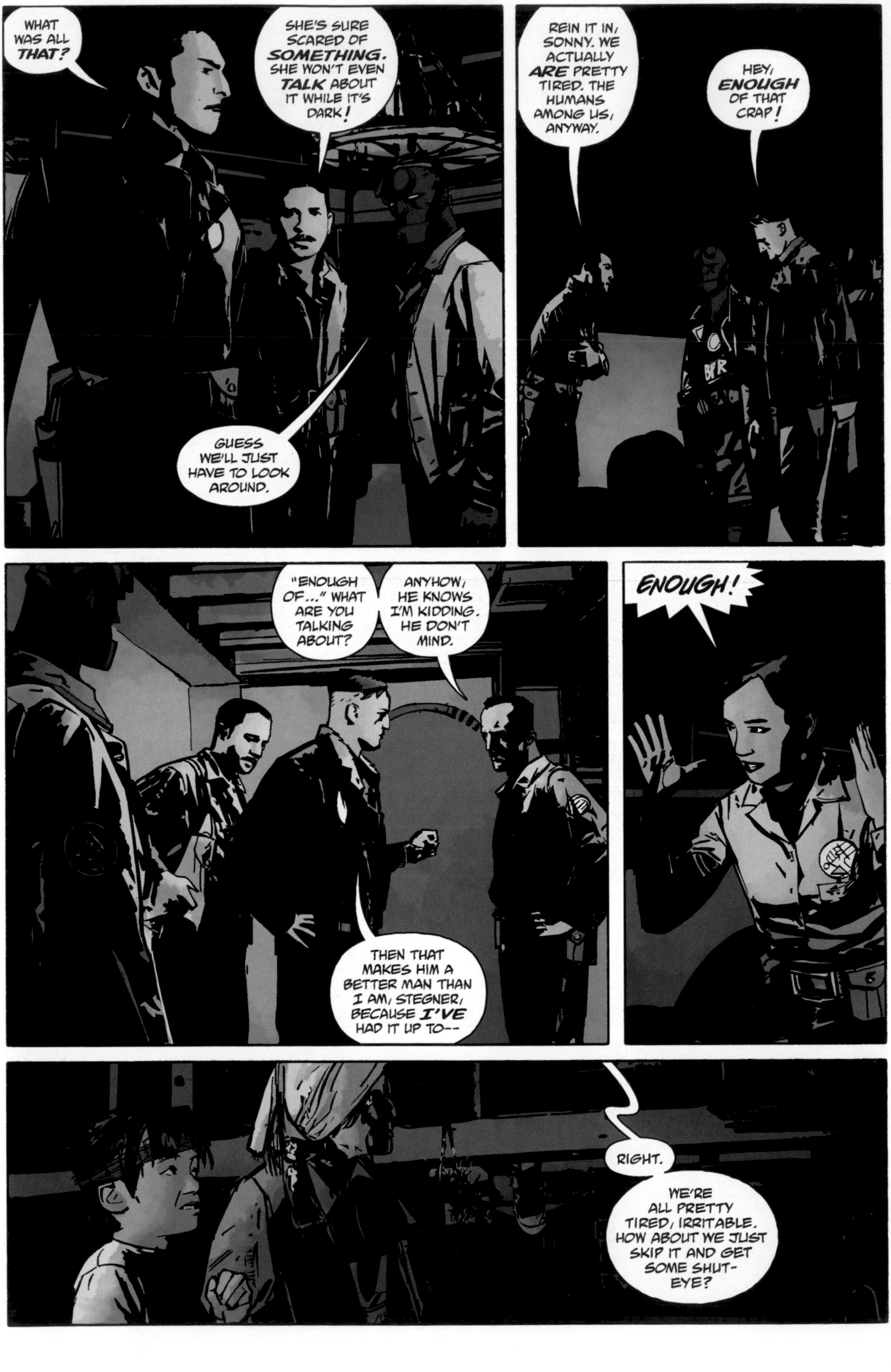
WHAT WAS ALL THAT?
SHE'S SURE SCARED OF SOMETHING. SHE WON'T EVEN TALK ABOUT IT WHILE IT'S DARK!
GUESS WE'LL JUST HAVE TO LOOK AROUND.
REIN IT IN, SONNY. WE ACTUALLY ARE PRETTY TIRED. THE HUMANS AMONG US, ANYWAY.
HEY, ENOUGH OF THAT CRAP!
"ENOUGH OF..." WHAT ARE YOU TALKING ABOUT?
ANYHOW, HE KNOWS I'M KIDDING. HE DON'T MIND.
THEN THAT MAKES HIM A BETTER MAN THAN I AM, STEGNER, BECAUSE I'VE HAD IT UP TO--
ENOUGH!
RIGHT.
WE'RE ALL PRETTY TIRED, IRRITABLE. HOW ABOUT WE JUST SKIP IT AND GET SOME SHUT-EYE?

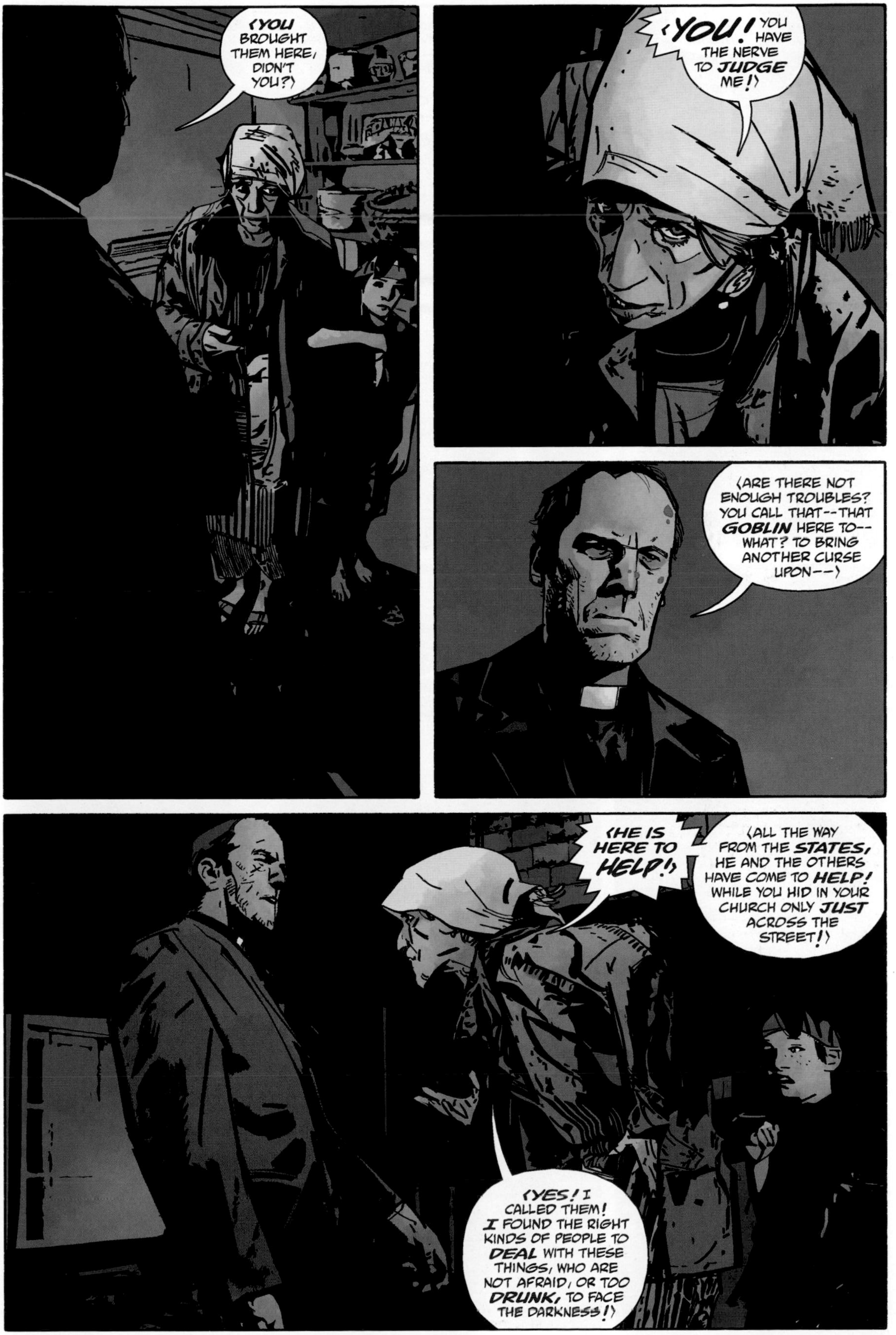
‹YOU BROUGHT THEM HERE, DIDN'T YOU?›
‹YOU! YOU HAVE THE NERVE TO JUDGE ME!›
‹ARE THERE NOT ENOUGH TROUBLES? YOU CALL THAT--THAT GOBLIN HERE TO-- WHAT? TO BRING ANOTHER CURSE UPON--›
‹HE IS HERE TO HELP!›
‹ALL THE WAY FROM THE STATES, HE AND THE OTHERS HAVE COME TO HELP! WHILE YOU HID IN YOUR CHURCH ONLY JUST ACROSS THE STREET!›
‹YES! I CALLED THEM! I FOUND THE RIGHT KINDS OF PEOPLE TO DEAL WITH THESE THINGS, WHO ARE NOT AFRAID, OR TOO DRUNK, TO FACE THE DARKNESS!›

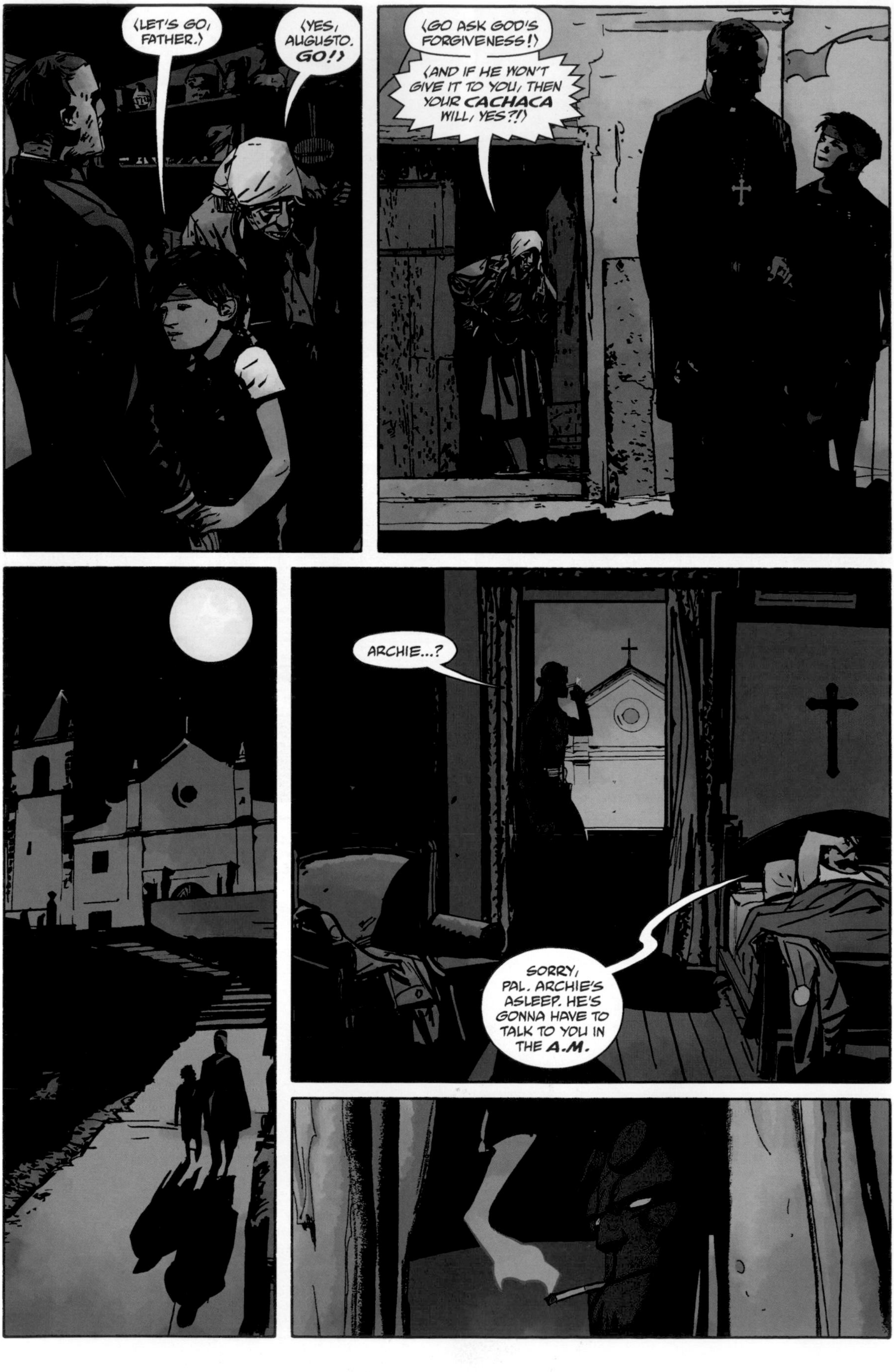

‹LET'S GO, FATHER.›
‹YES, AUGUSTO. GO!›
‹GO ASK GOD'S FORGIVENESS!›
‹AND IF HE WON'T GIVE IT TO YOU, THEN YOUR CACHACA WILL, YES?!›
ARCHIE...?
SORRY, PAL. ARCHIE'S ASLEEP. HE'S GONNA HAVE TO TALK TO YOU IN THE A.M.

Chapter Two

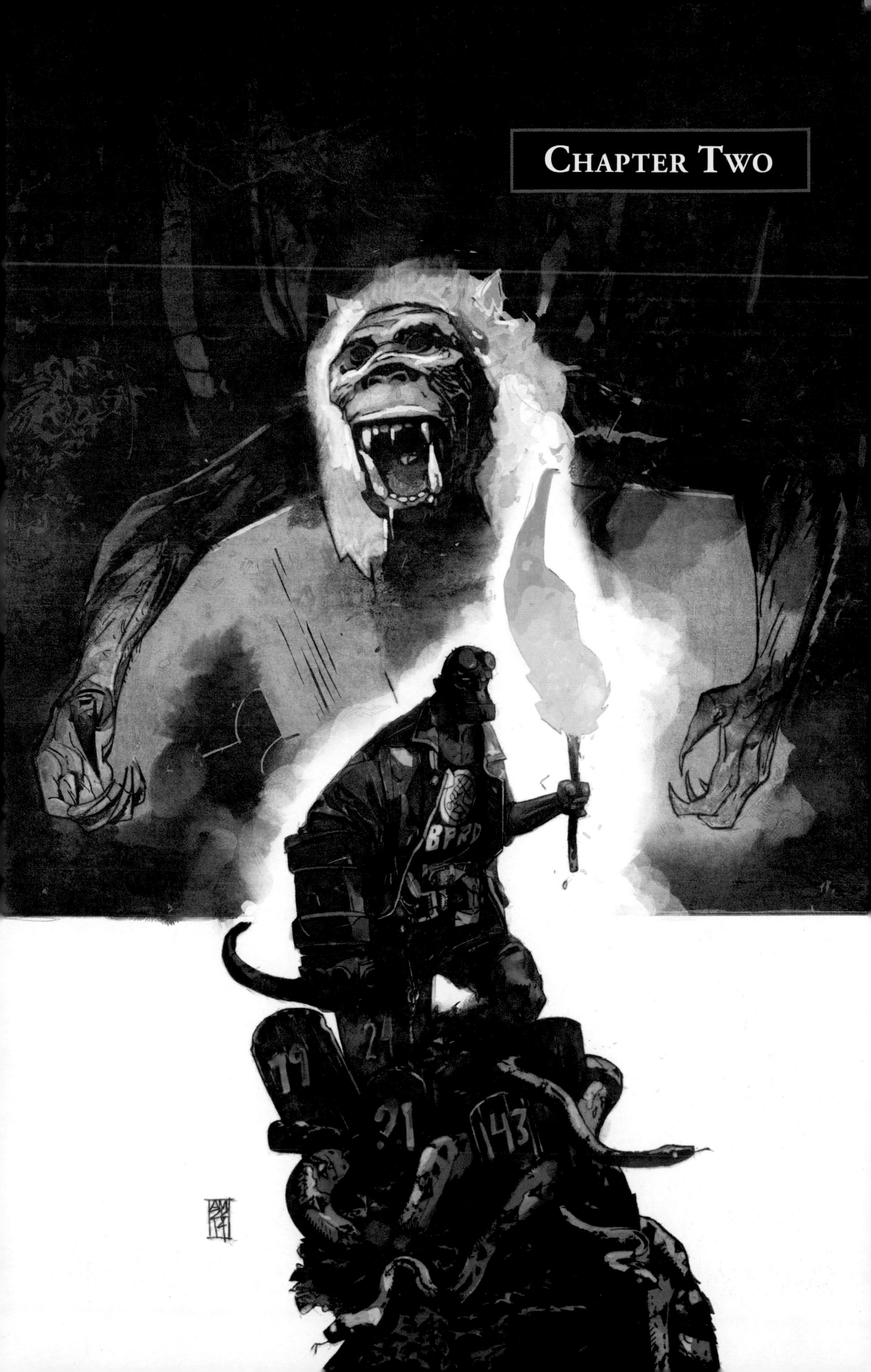

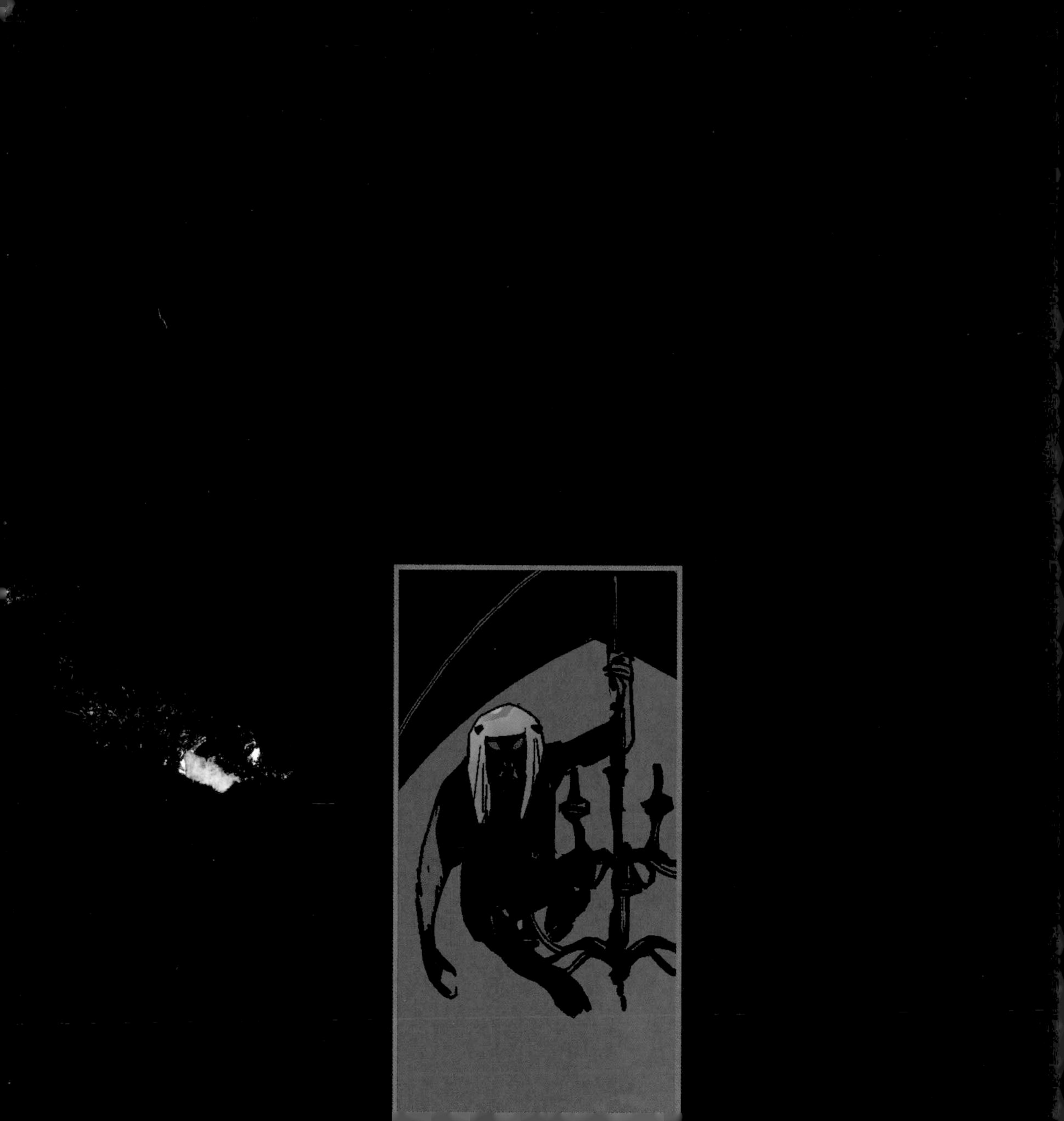

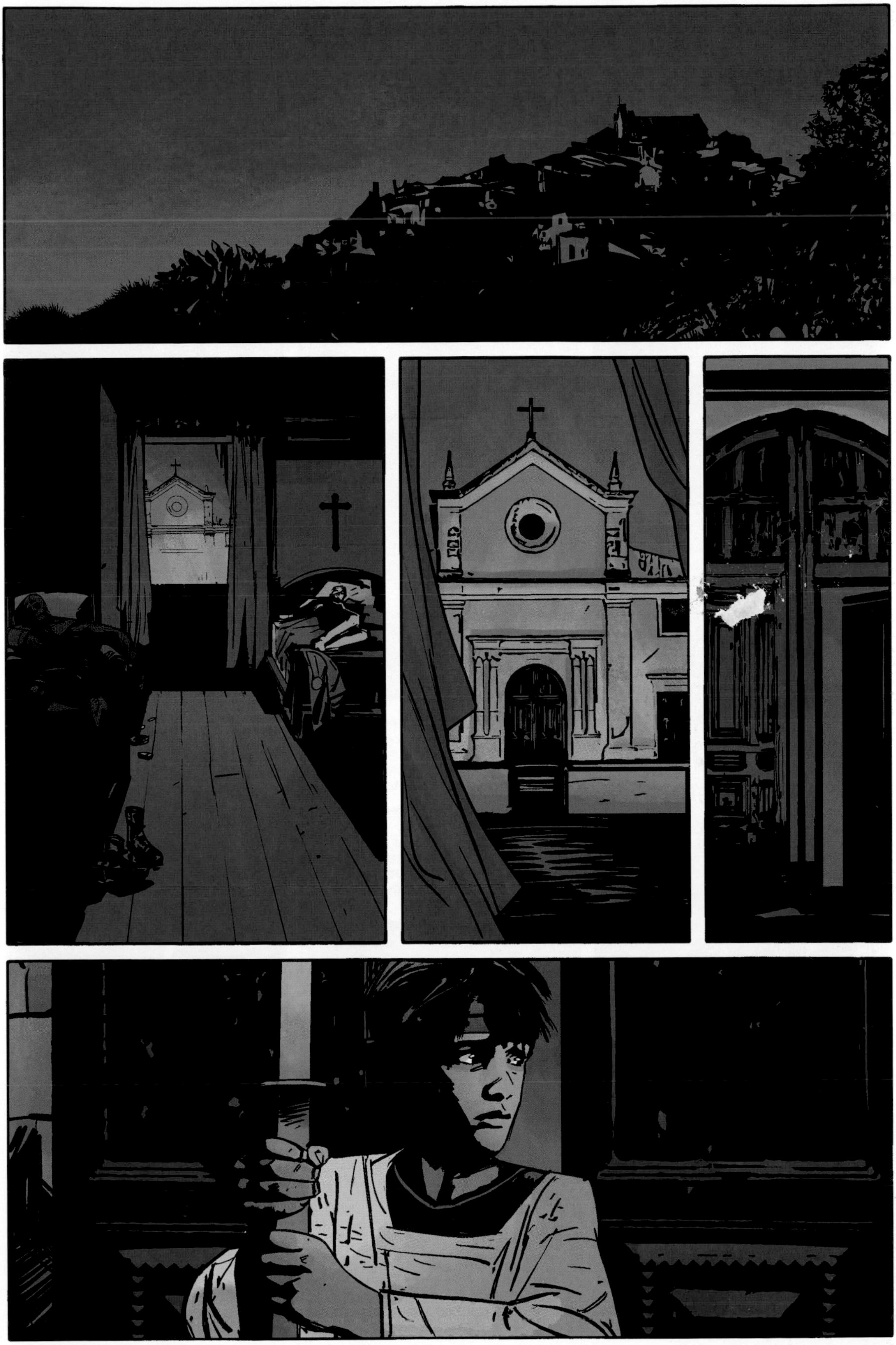

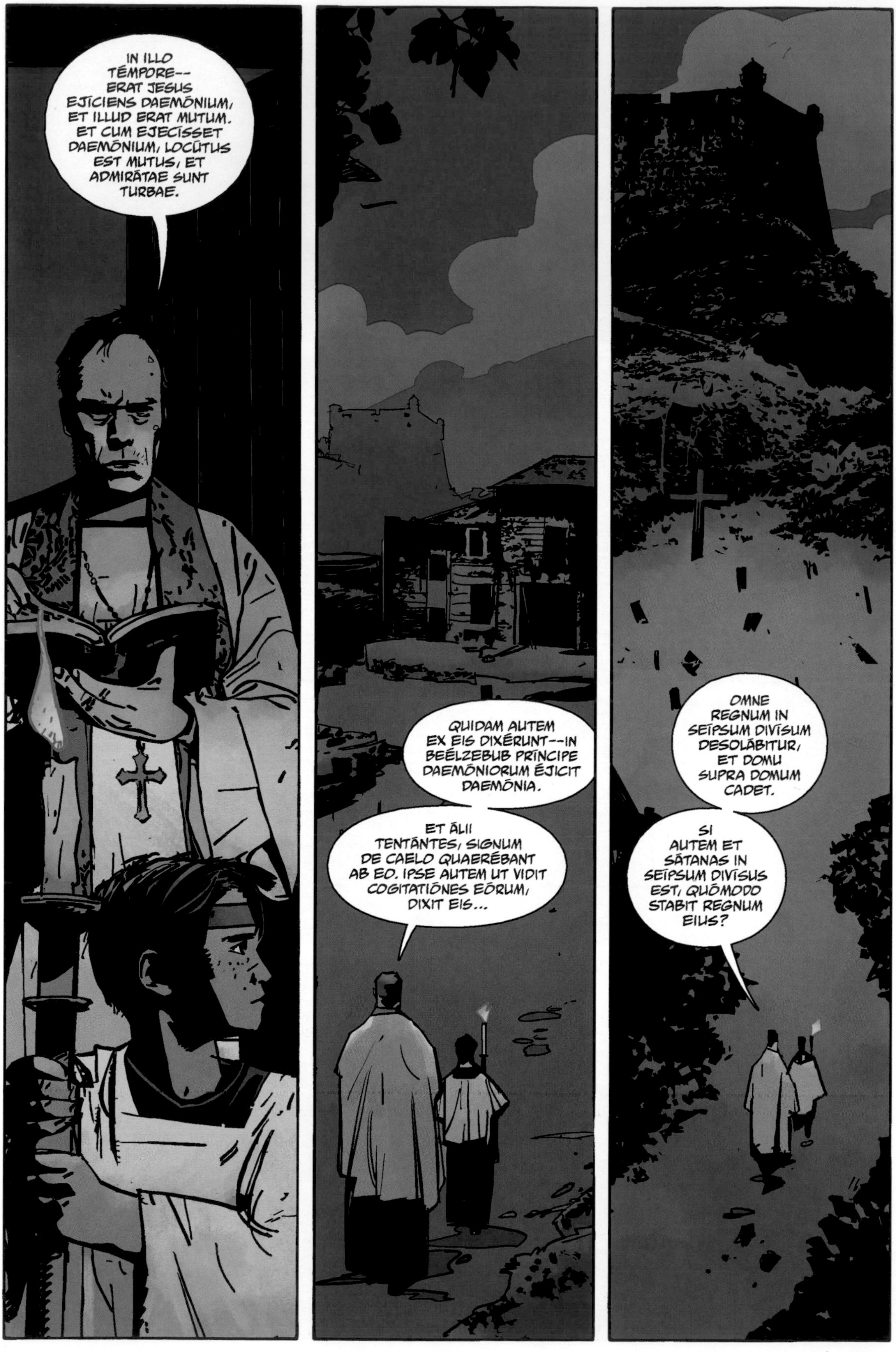
IN ILLO TÉMPORE--ERAT JESUS EJÍCIENS DAEMŌNIUM, ET ILLUD ERAT MUTUM. ET CUM EJECÍSSET DAEMŌNIUM, LOCŪTUS EST MUTUS, ET ADMIRĀTAE SUNT TURBAE.
QUIDAM AUTEM EX EIS DIXÉRUNT--IN BEÉLZEBUB PRÍNCIPE DAEMŌNIORUM ÉJICIT DAEMŌNIA.
ET ĀLII TENTĀNTES, SIGNUM DE CAELO QUAERÉBANT AB EO. IPSE AUTEM UT VIDIT COGITATIŌNES EŌRUM, DIXIT EIS...
OMNE REGNUM IN SEÍPSUM DIVÍSUM DESOLĀBITUR, ET DOMU SUPRA DOMUM CADET.
SI AUTEM ET SĀTANAS IN SEÍPSUM DIVÍSUS EST, QUŌMODO STABIT REGNUM EIUS?

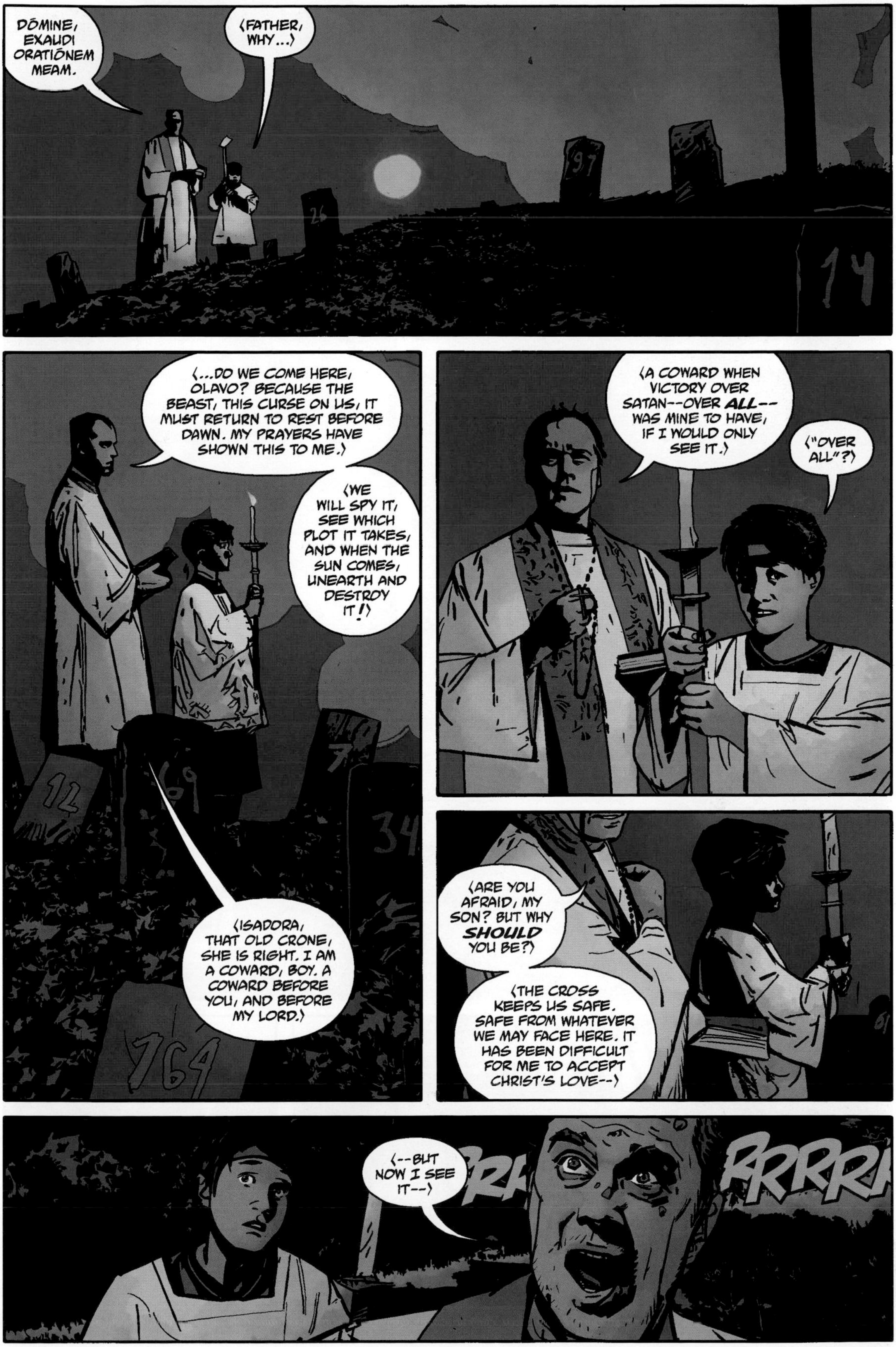
DŌMINE, EXAUDI ORATIŌNEM MEAM.
⟨FATHER, WHY...⟩
⟨...DO WE COME HERE, OLAVO? BECAUSE THE BEAST, THIS CURSE ON US, IT MUST RETURN TO REST BEFORE DAWN. MY PRAYERS HAVE SHOWN THIS TO ME.⟩
⟨WE WILL SPY IT, SEE WHICH PLOT IT TAKES, AND WHEN THE SUN COMES, UNEARTH AND DESTROY IT!⟩
⟨ISADORA, THAT OLD CRONE, SHE IS RIGHT. I AM A COWARD, BOY. A COWARD BEFORE YOU, AND BEFORE MY LORD.⟩
⟨A COWARD WHEN VICTORY OVER SATAN--OVER ALL--WAS MINE TO HAVE, IF I WOULD ONLY SEE IT.⟩
⟨"OVER ALL"?⟩
⟨ARE YOU AFRAID, MY SON? BUT WHY SHOULD YOU BE?⟩
⟨THE CROSS KEEPS US SAFE. SAFE FROM WHATEVER WE MAY FACE HERE. IT HAS BEEN DIFFICULT FOR ME TO ACCEPT CHRIST'S LOVE--⟩
⟨--BUT NOW I SEE IT--⟩
RRRRR

⟨TRANSLATED FROM PORTUGUESE⟩

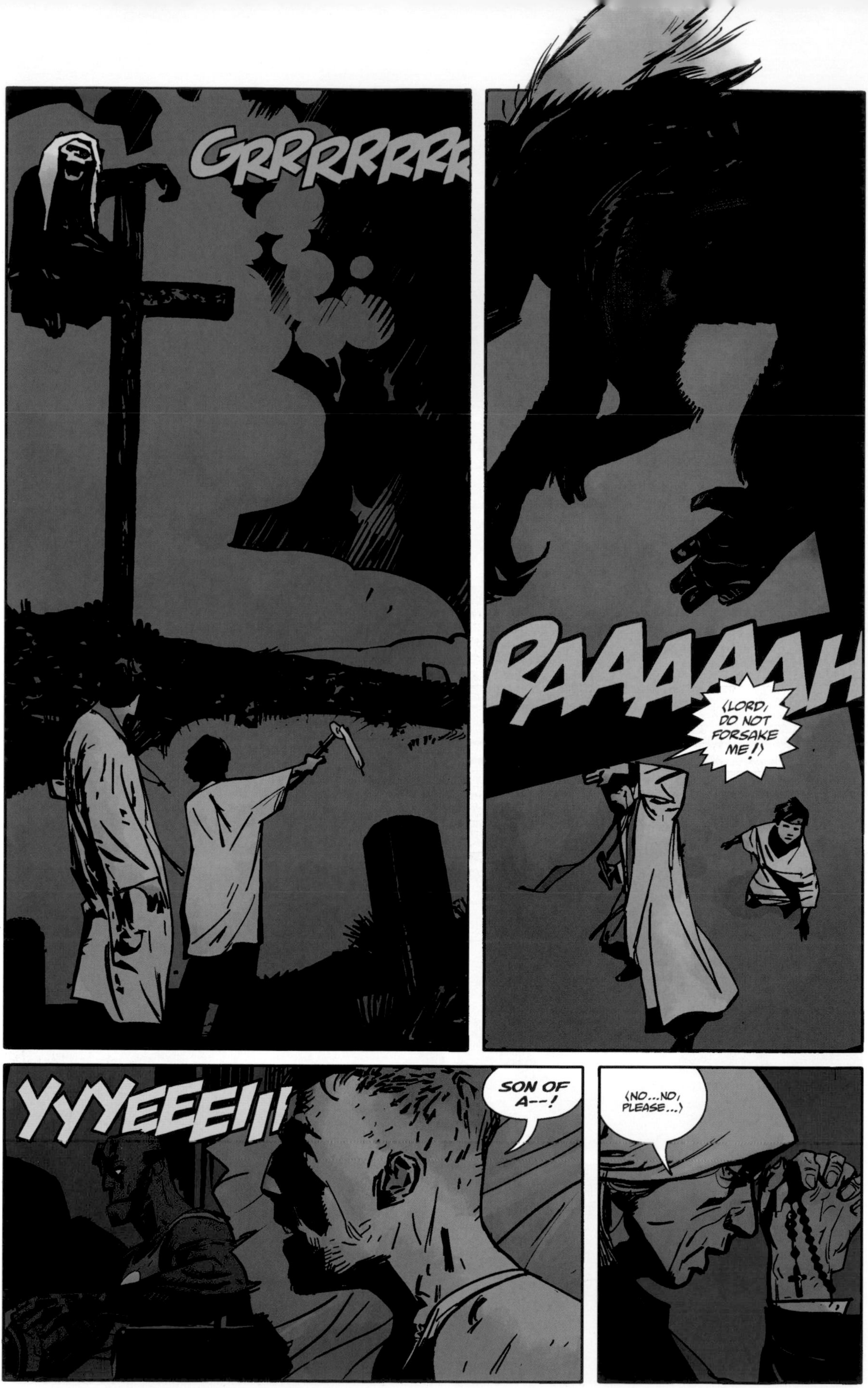
GRRRRRRR
RAAAAAH
⟨LORD, DO NOT FORSAKE ME!⟩
YYYEEEIII
SON OF A--!
⟨NO...NO, PLEASE...⟩

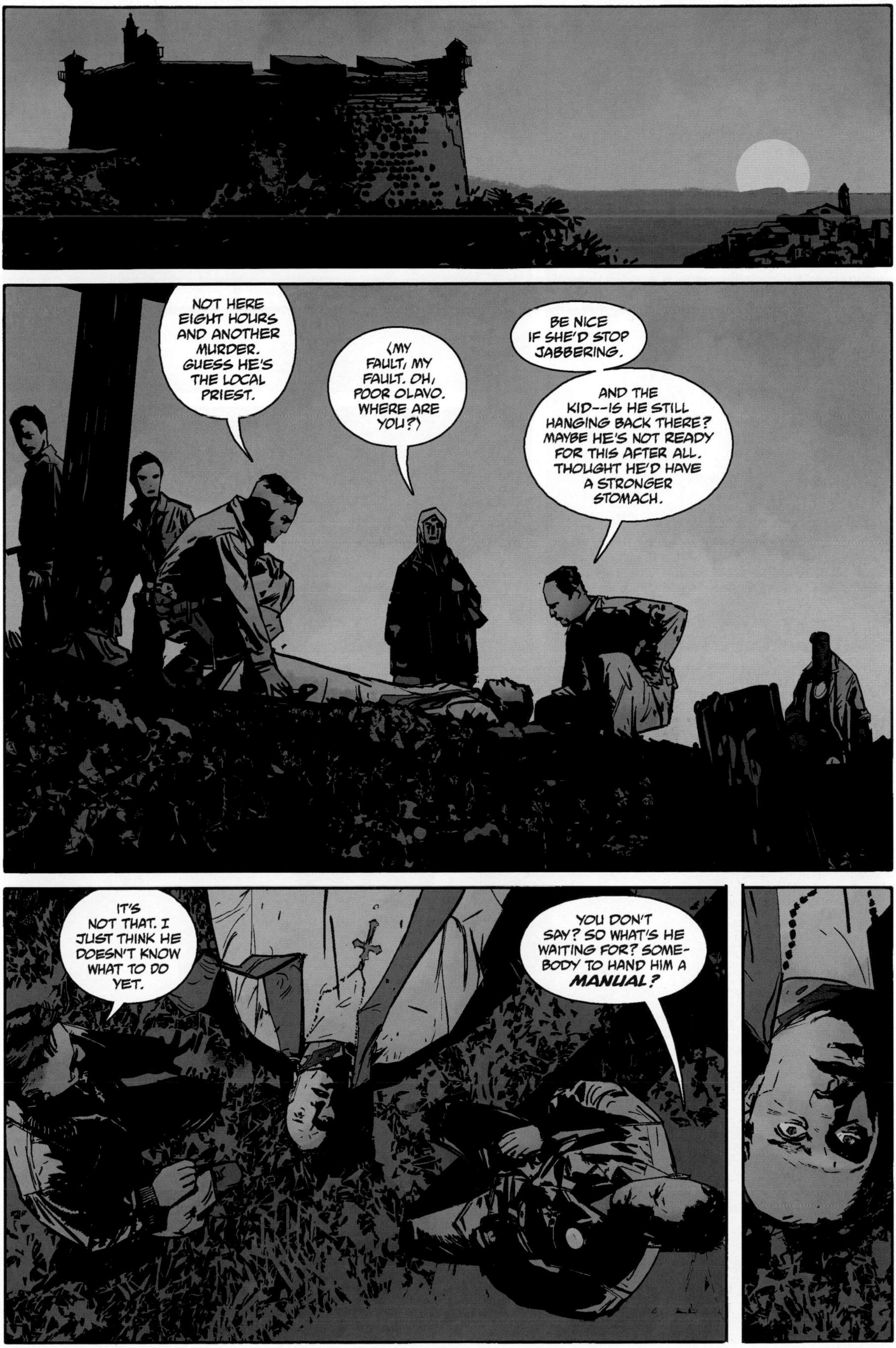
NOT HERE EIGHT HOURS AND ANOTHER MURDER. GUESS HE'S THE LOCAL PRIEST.
⟨MY FAULT, MY FAULT. OH, POOR OLAVO. WHERE ARE YOU?⟩
BE NICE IF SHE'D STOP JABBERING.
AND THE KID--IS HE STILL HANGING BACK THERE? MAYBE HE'S NOT READY FOR THIS AFTER ALL. THOUGHT HE'D HAVE A STRONGER STOMACH.
IT'S NOT THAT. I JUST THINK HE DOESN'T KNOW WHAT TO DO YET.
YOU DON'T SAY? SO WHAT'S HE WAITING FOR? SOME-BODY TO HAND HIM A **MANUAL?**

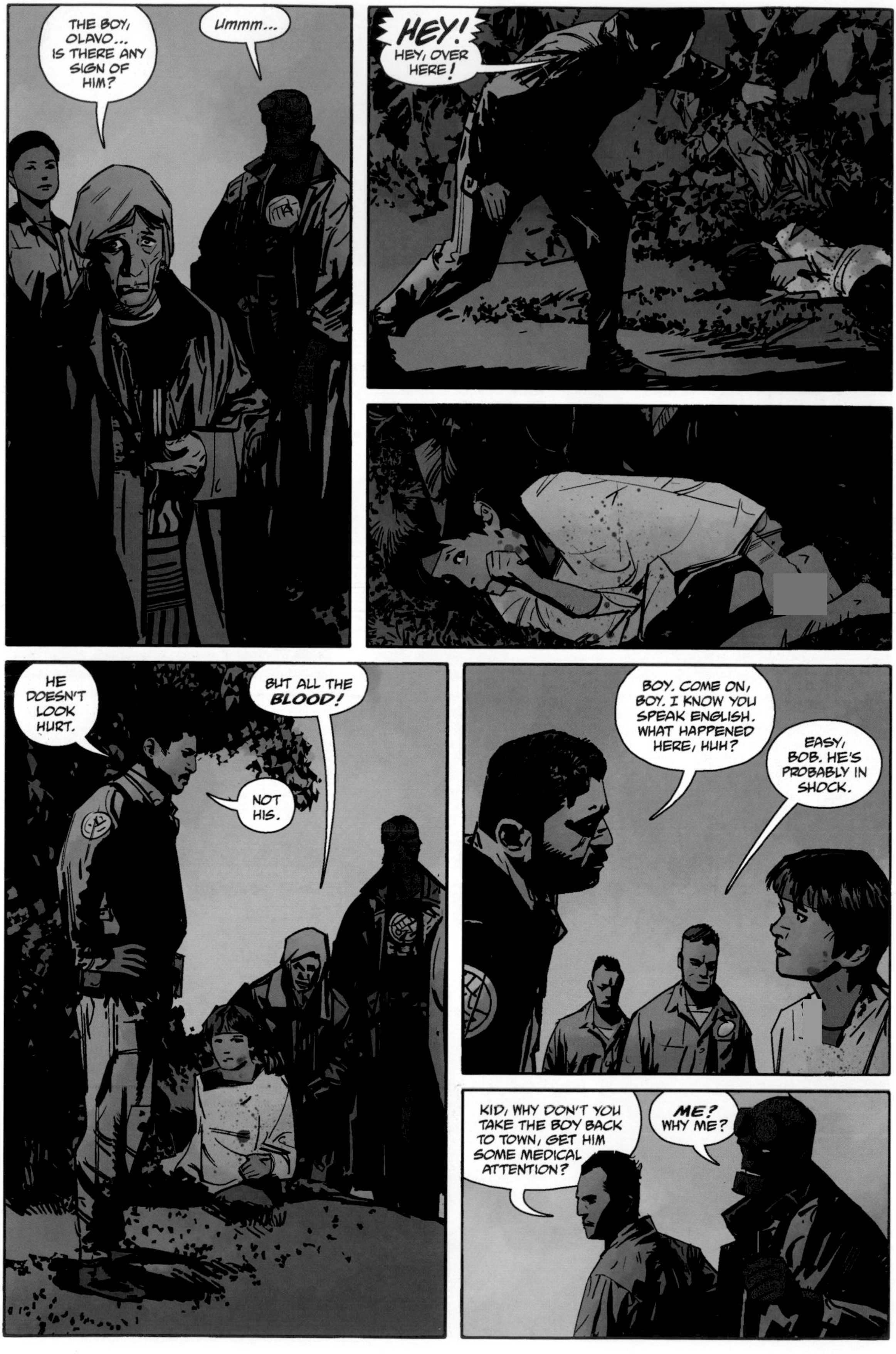
THE BOY, OLAVO... IS THERE ANY SIGN OF HIM?
Ummm...
HEY! HEY, OVER HERE!
HE DOESN'T LOOK HURT.
BUT ALL THE BLOOD!
NOT HIS.
BOY. COME ON, BOY. I KNOW YOU SPEAK ENGLISH. WHAT HAPPENED HERE, HUH?
EASY, BOB. HE'S PROBABLY IN SHOCK.
KID, WHY DON'T YOU TAKE THE BOY BACK TO TOWN, GET HIM SOME MEDICAL ATTENTION?
ME? WHY ME?

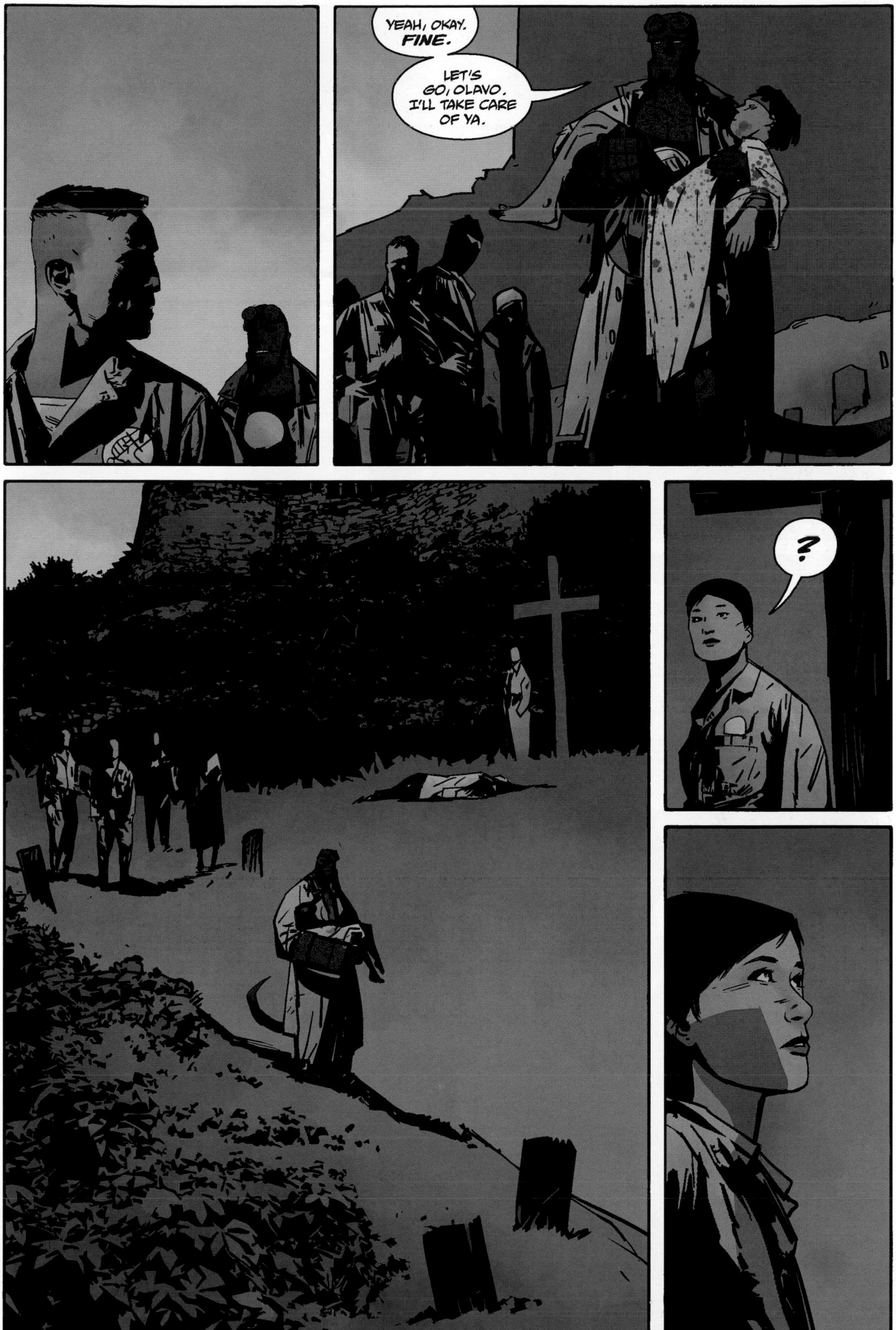
YEAH, OKAY. FINE.
LET'S GO, OLAVO. I'LL TAKE CARE OF YA.
?

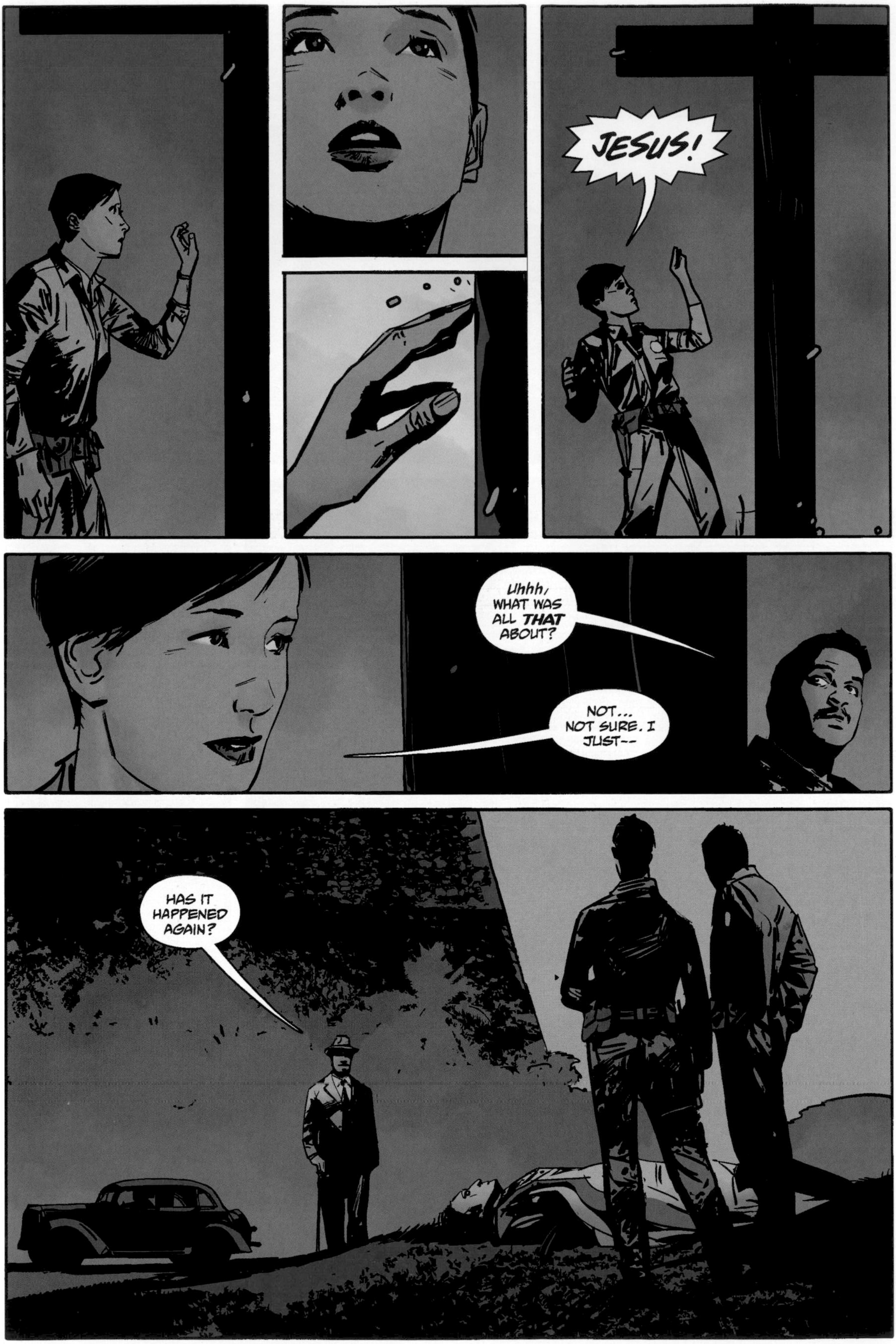
JESUS!
Uhhh, WHAT WAS ALL THAT ABOUT?
NOT... NOT SURE. I JUST--
HAS IT HAPPENED AGAIN?

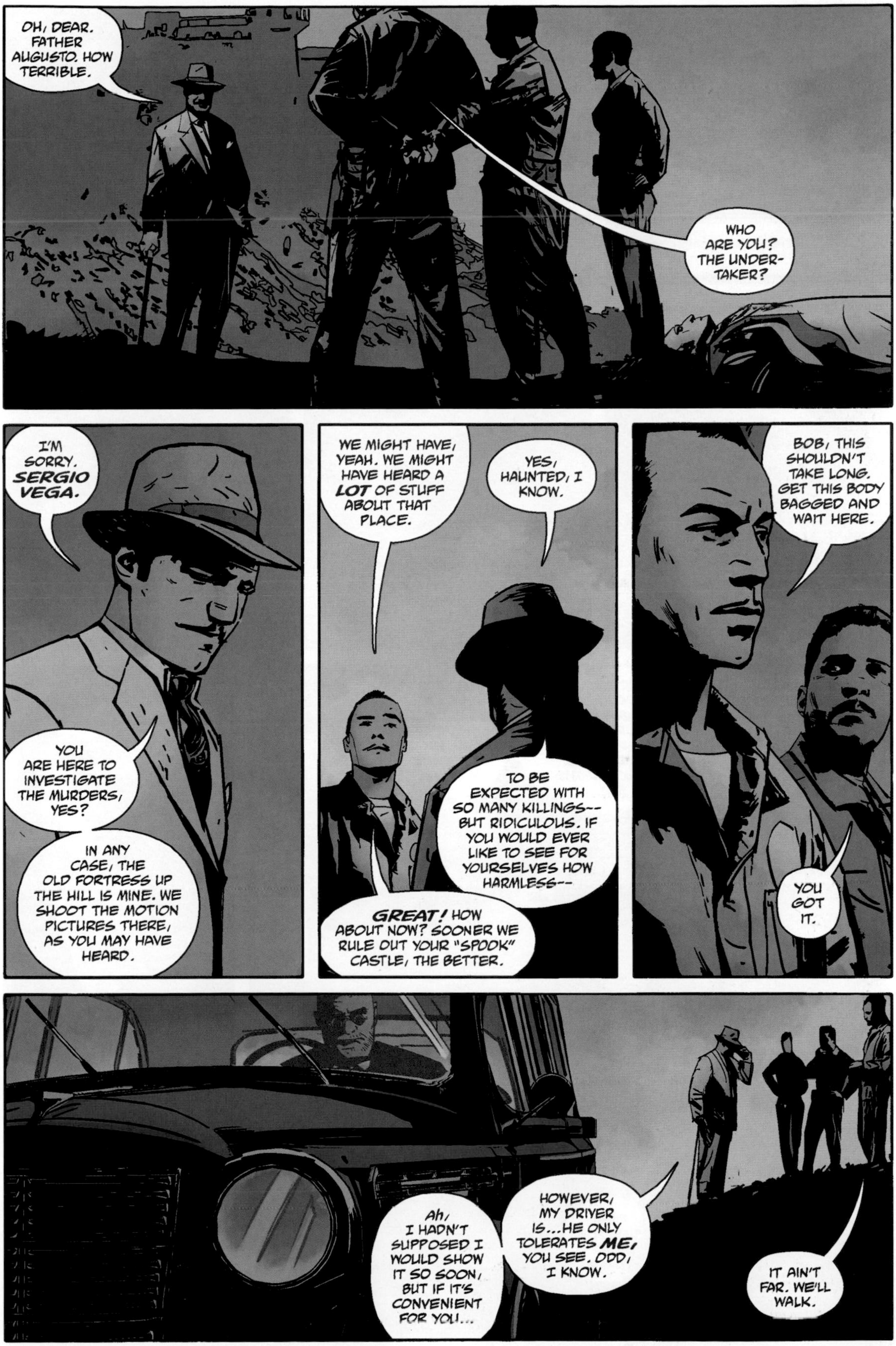
OH, DEAR. FATHER AUGUSTO. HOW TERRIBLE.
WHO ARE YOU? THE UNDER-TAKER?
I'M SORRY. SERGIO VEGA.
YOU ARE HERE TO INVESTIGATE THE MURDERS, YES?
IN ANY CASE, THE OLD FORTRESS UP THE HILL IS MINE. WE SHOOT THE MOTION PICTURES THERE, AS YOU MAY HAVE HEARD.
WE MIGHT HAVE, YEAH. WE MIGHT HAVE HEARD A LOT OF STUFF ABOUT THAT PLACE.
YES, HAUNTED, I KNOW.
TO BE EXPECTED WITH SO MANY KILLINGS-- BUT RIDICULOUS. IF YOU WOULD EVER LIKE TO SEE FOR YOURSELVES HOW HARMLESS--
GREAT! HOW ABOUT NOW? SOONER WE RULE OUT YOUR "SPOOK" CASTLE, THE BETTER.
BOB, THIS SHOULDN'T TAKE LONG. GET THIS BODY BAGGED AND WAIT HERE.
YOU GOT IT.
Ah, I HADN'T SUPPOSED I WOULD SHOW IT SO SOON, BUT IF IT'S CONVENIENT FOR YOU...
HOWEVER, MY DRIVER IS...HE ONLY TOLERATES ME, YOU SEE. ODD, I KNOW.
IT AIN'T FAR. WE'LL WALK.

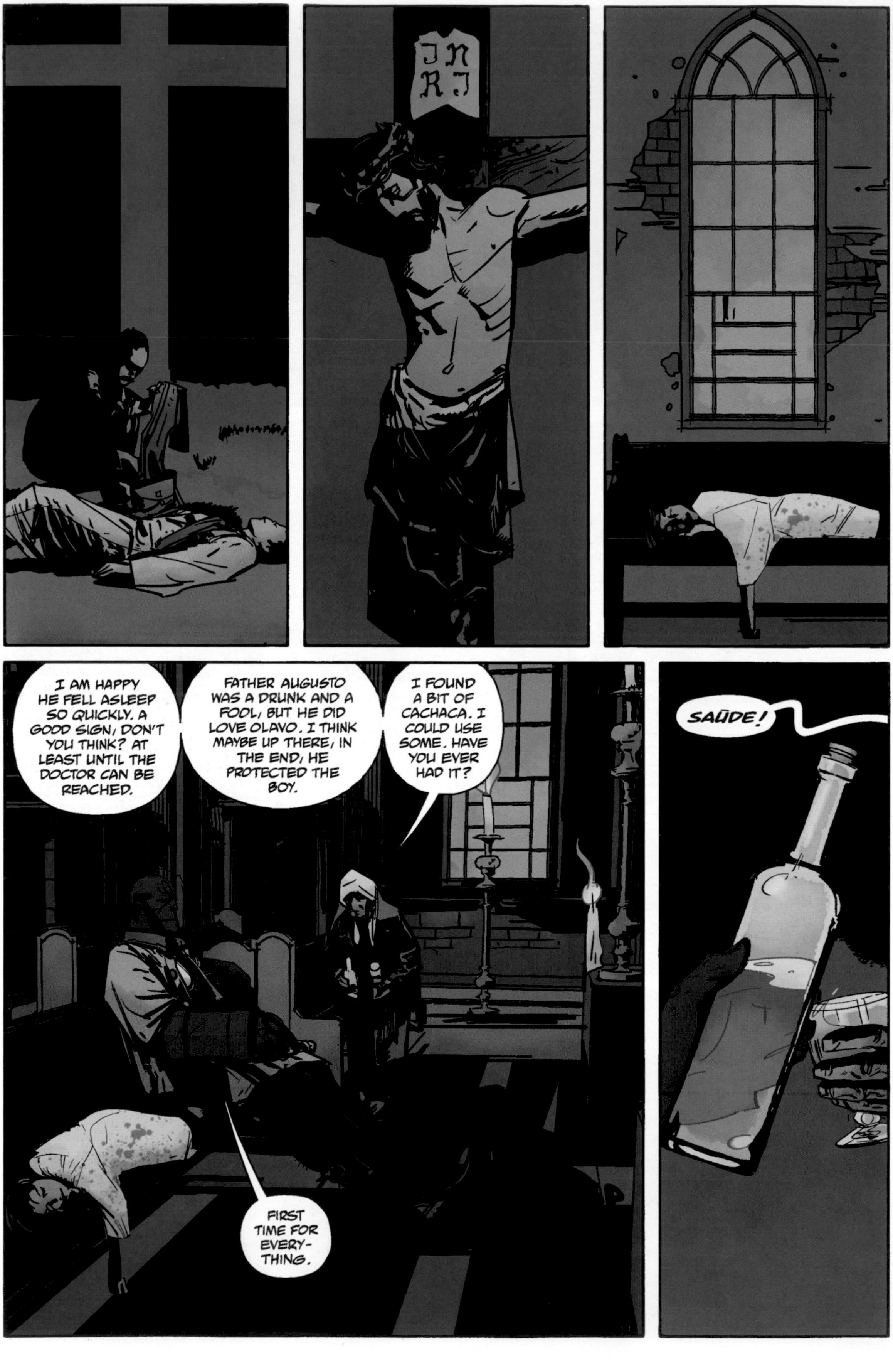
JNRJ
I AM HAPPY HE FELL ASLEEP SO QUICKLY. A GOOD SIGN, DON'T YOU THINK? AT LEAST UNTIL THE DOCTOR CAN BE REACHED.
FATHER AUGUSTO WAS A DRUNK AND A FOOL, BUT HE DID LOVE OLAVO. I THINK MAYBE UP THERE, IN THE END, HE PROTECTED THE BOY.
FIRST TIME FOR EVERY-THING.
I FOUND A BIT OF CACHACA. I COULD USE SOME. HAVE YOU EVER HAD IT?
SAÚDE!

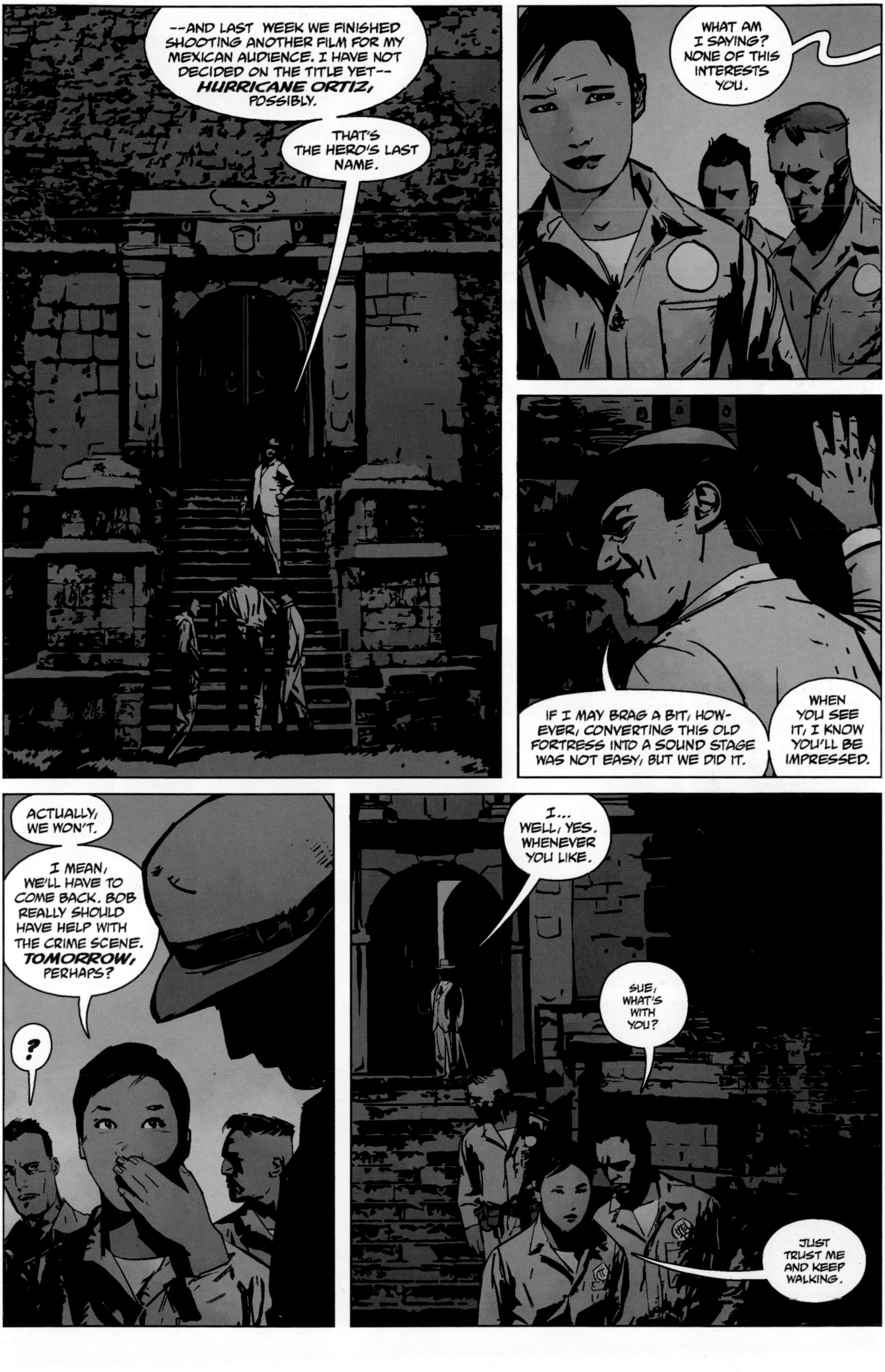
--AND LAST WEEK WE FINISHED SHOOTING ANOTHER FILM FOR MY MEXICAN AUDIENCE. I HAVE NOT DECIDED ON THE TITLE YET-- HURRICANE ORTIZ, POSSIBLY.
THAT'S THE HERO'S LAST NAME.
WHAT AM I SAYING? NONE OF THIS INTERESTS YOU.
IF I MAY BRAG A BIT, HOW-EVER, CONVERTING THIS OLD FORTRESS INTO A SOUND STAGE WAS NOT EASY, BUT WE DID IT.
WHEN YOU SEE IT, I KNOW YOU'LL BE IMPRESSED.
ACTUALLY, WE WON'T.
I MEAN, WE'LL HAVE TO COME BACK. BOB REALLY SHOULD HAVE HELP WITH THE CRIME SCENE. TOMORROW, PERHAPS?
?
I... WELL, YES. WHENEVER YOU LIKE.
SUE, WHAT'S WITH YOU?
JUST TRUST ME AND KEEP WALKING.

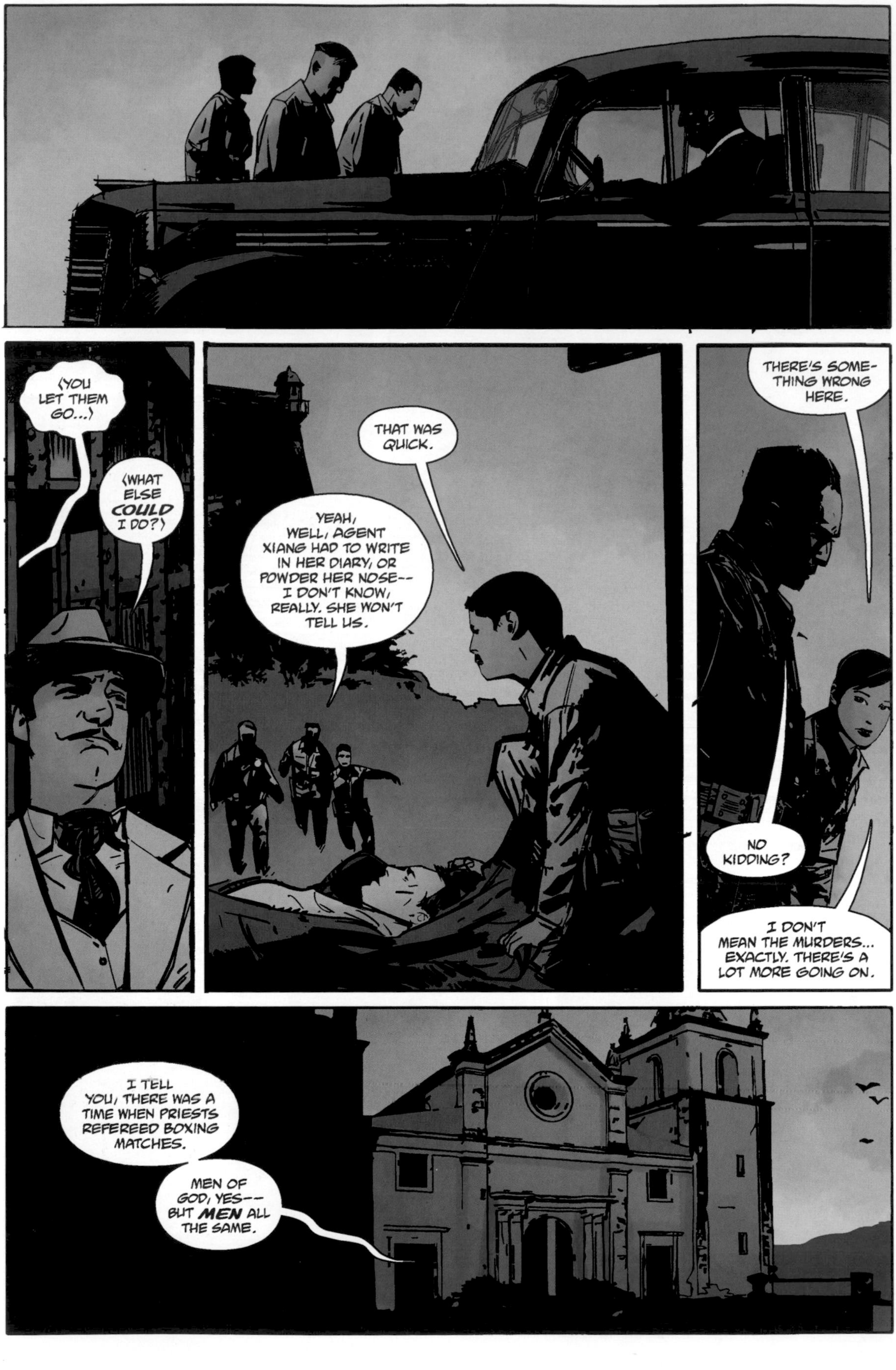

⟨YOU LET THEM GO...⟩
⟨WHAT ELSE COULD I DO?⟩
THAT WAS QUICK.
YEAH, WELL, AGENT XIANG HAD TO WRITE IN HER DIARY, OR POWDER HER NOSE-- I DON'T KNOW, REALLY. SHE WON'T TELL US.
THERE'S SOMETHING WRONG HERE.
NO KIDDING?
I DON'T MEAN THE MURDERS... EXACTLY. THERE'S A LOT MORE GOING ON.
I TELL YOU, THERE WAS A TIME WHEN PRIESTS REFEREED BOXING MATCHES.
MEN OF GOD, YES-- BUT MEN ALL THE SAME.

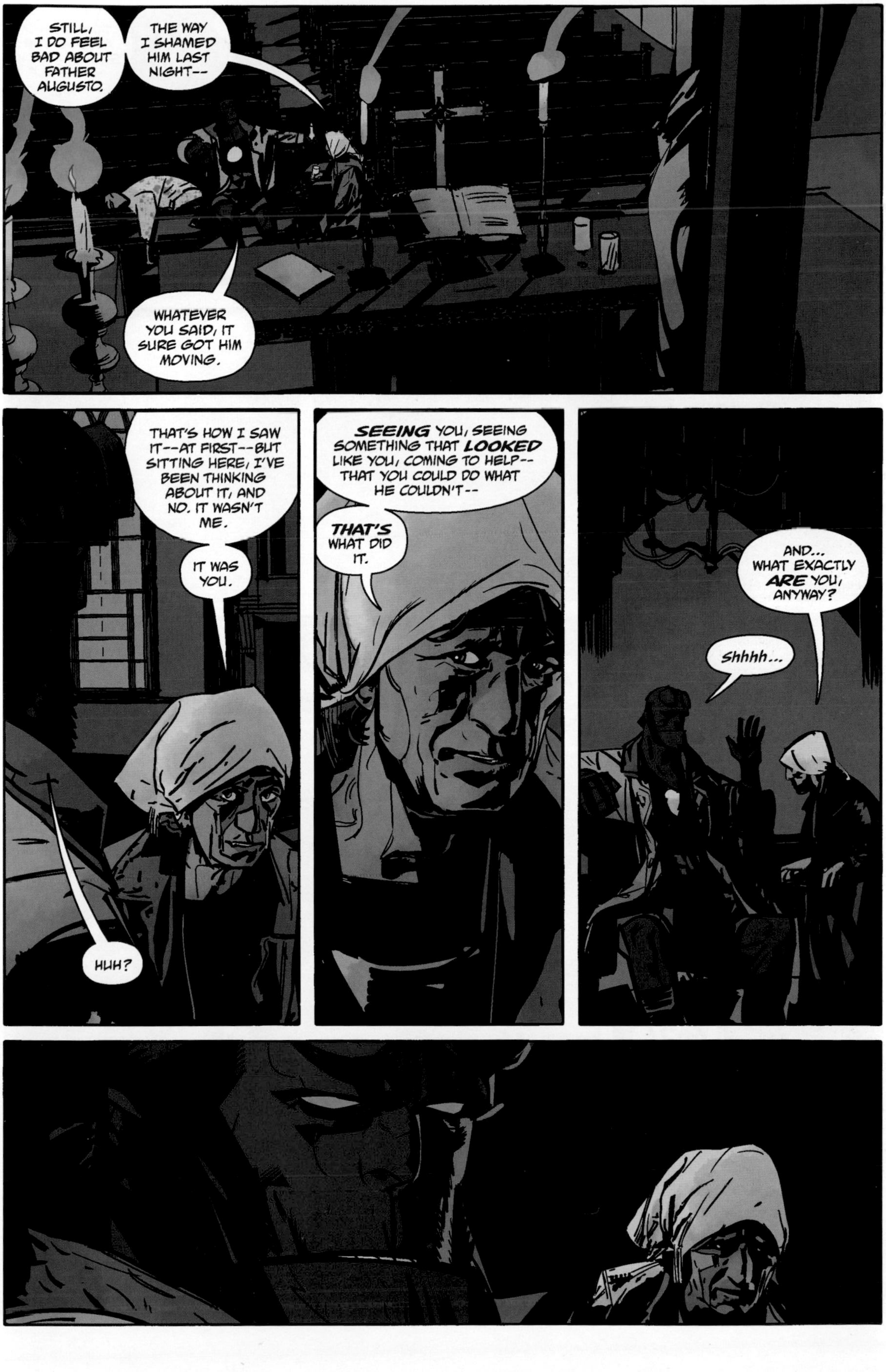
STILL, I DO FEEL BAD ABOUT FATHER AUGUSTO.
THE WAY I SHAMED HIM LAST NIGHT--
WHATEVER YOU SAID, IT SURE GOT HIM MOVING.
THAT'S HOW I SAW IT--AT FIRST--BUT SITTING HERE, I'VE BEEN THINKING ABOUT IT, AND NO. IT WASN'T ME.
IT WAS YOU.
HUH?
SEEING YOU, SEEING SOMETHING THAT LOOKED LIKE YOU, COMING TO HELP--THAT YOU COULD DO WHAT HE COULDN'T--
THAT'S WHAT DID IT.
AND... WHAT EXACTLY ARE YOU, ANYWAY?
Shhhh...

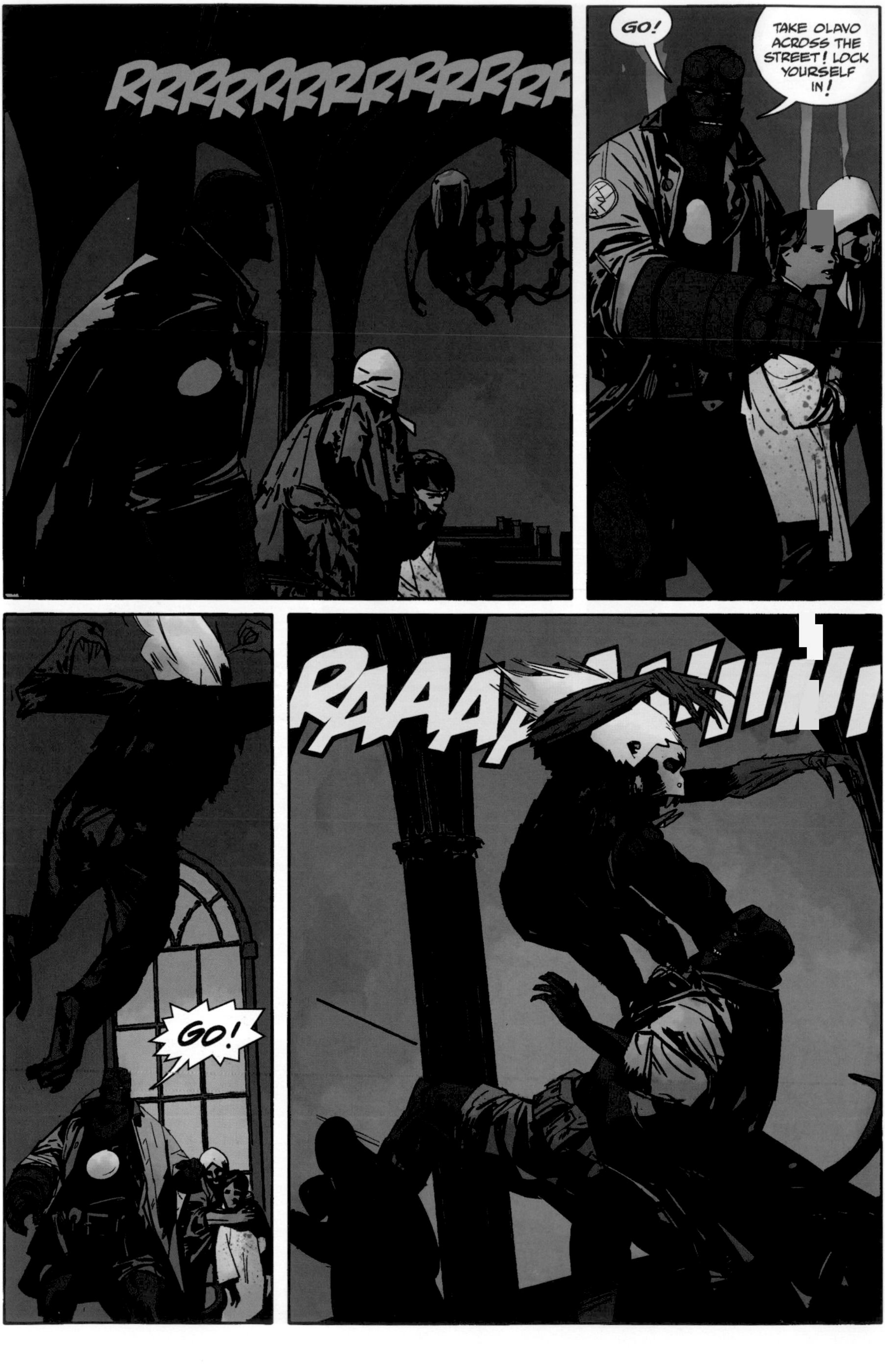
RRRRRRRRRRRRR
GO!
TAKE OLAVO ACROSS THE STREET! LOCK YOURSELF IN!
GO!
RAAA

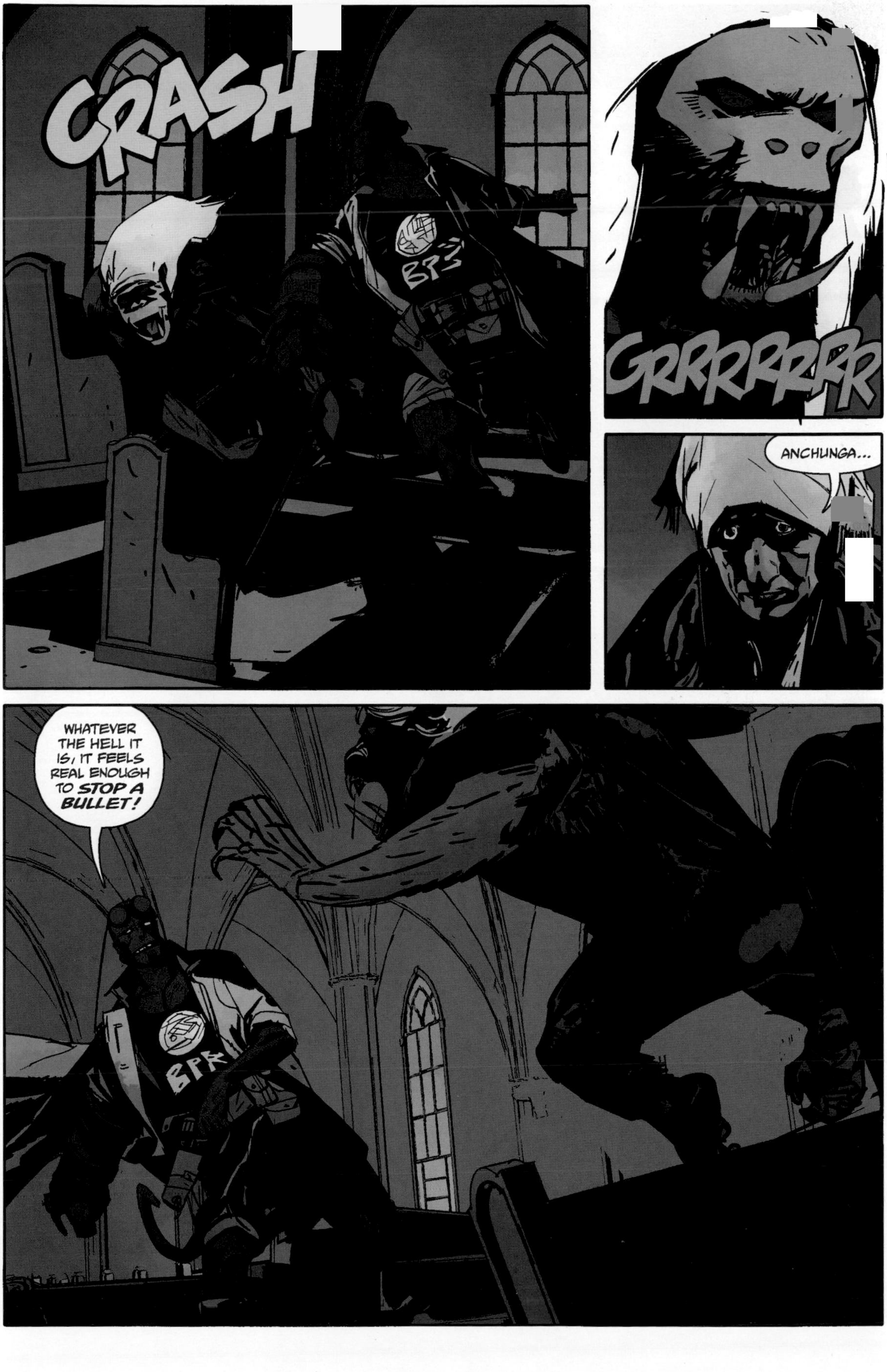
CRASH
GRRRRRRR
ANCHUNGA...
WHATEVER THE HELL IT IS, IT FEELS REAL ENOUGH TO STOP A BULLET!

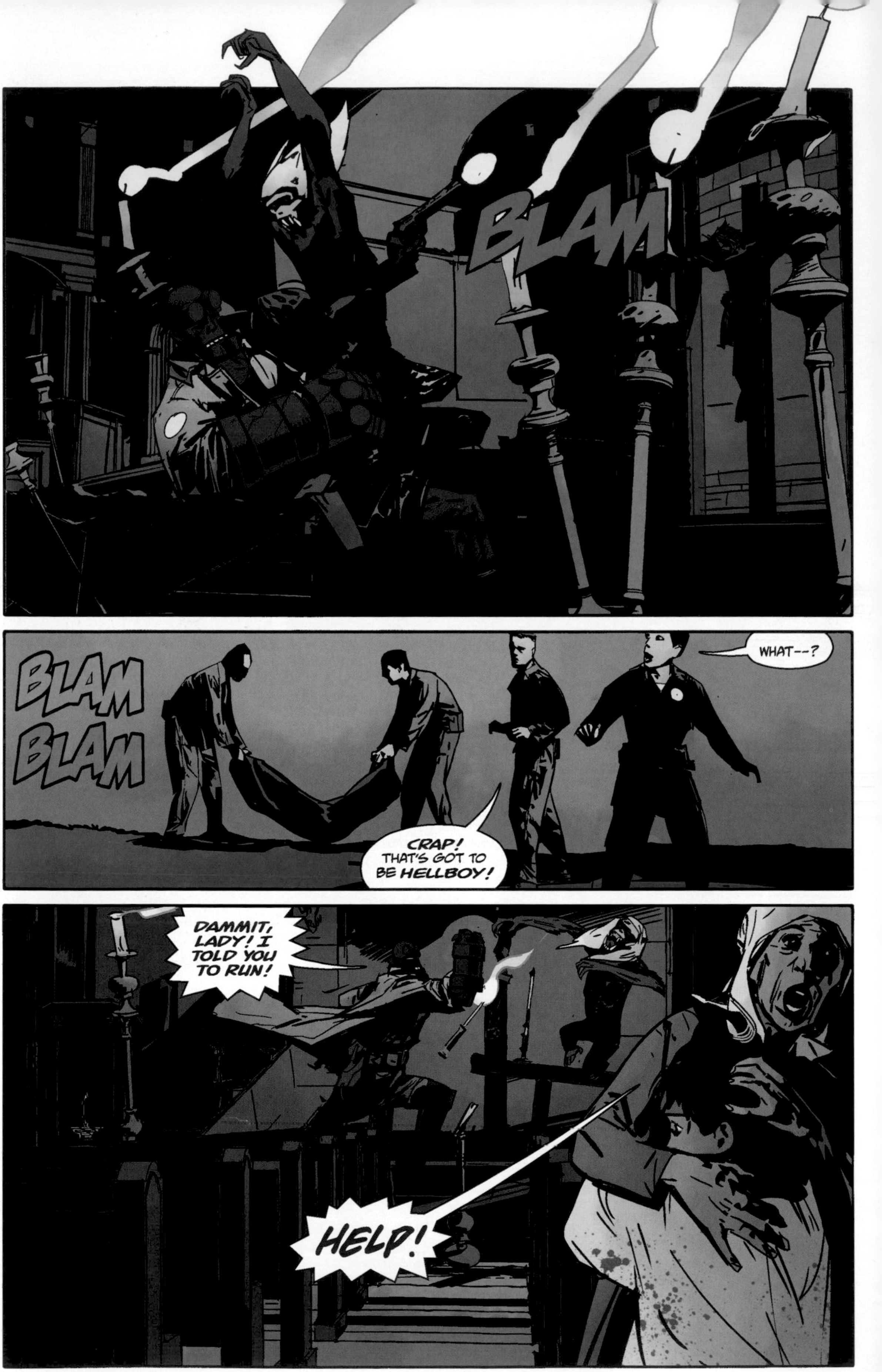
BLAM
BLAM
BLAM
WHAT--?
CRAP! THAT'S GOT TO BE HELLBOY!
DAMMIT, LADY! I TOLD YOU TO RUN!
HELP!

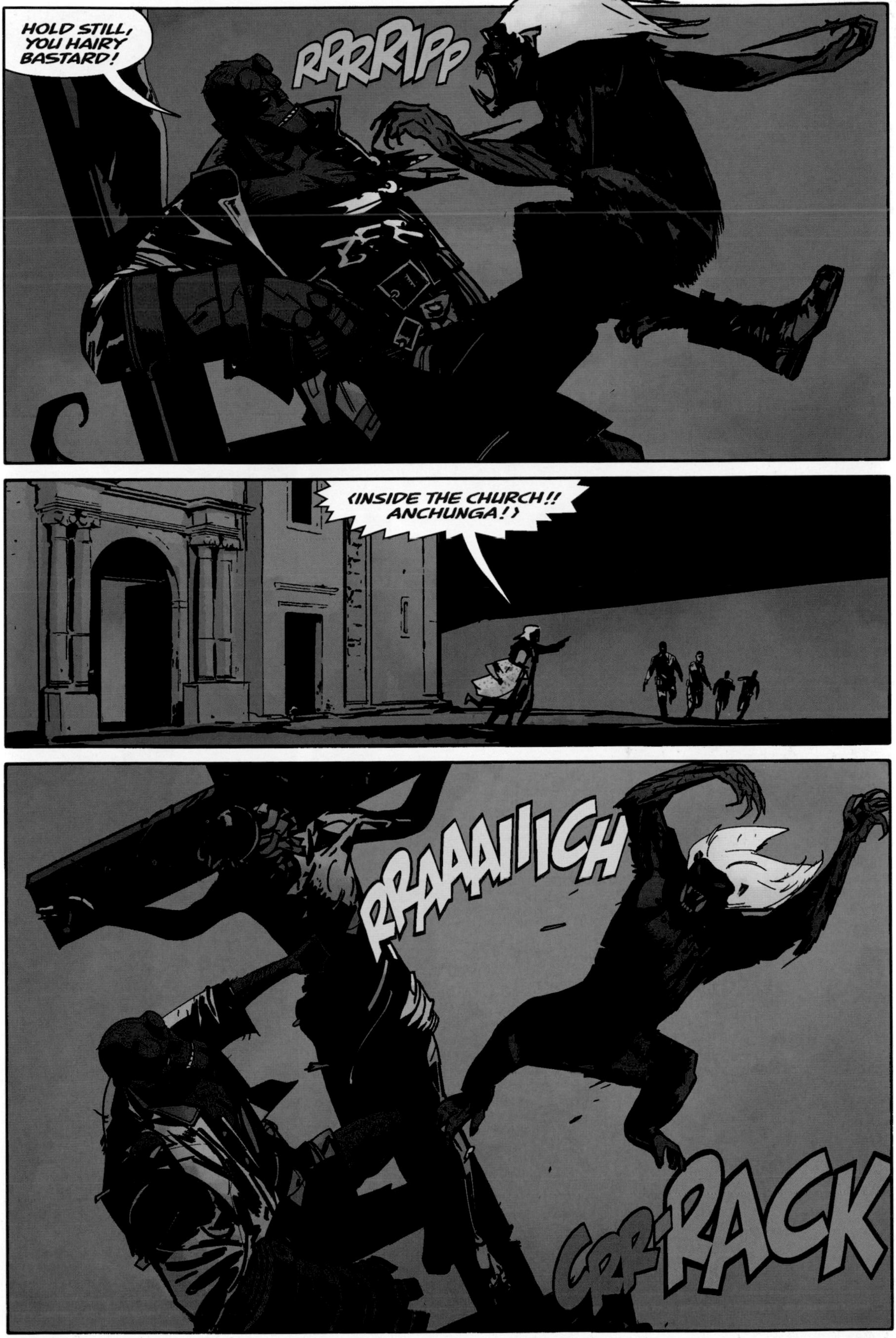
HOLD STILL, YOU HAIRY BASTARD!
RRRRIPP
‹INSIDE THE CHURCH!! ANCHUNGA!›
RRAAAIIICH
CRR-RACK

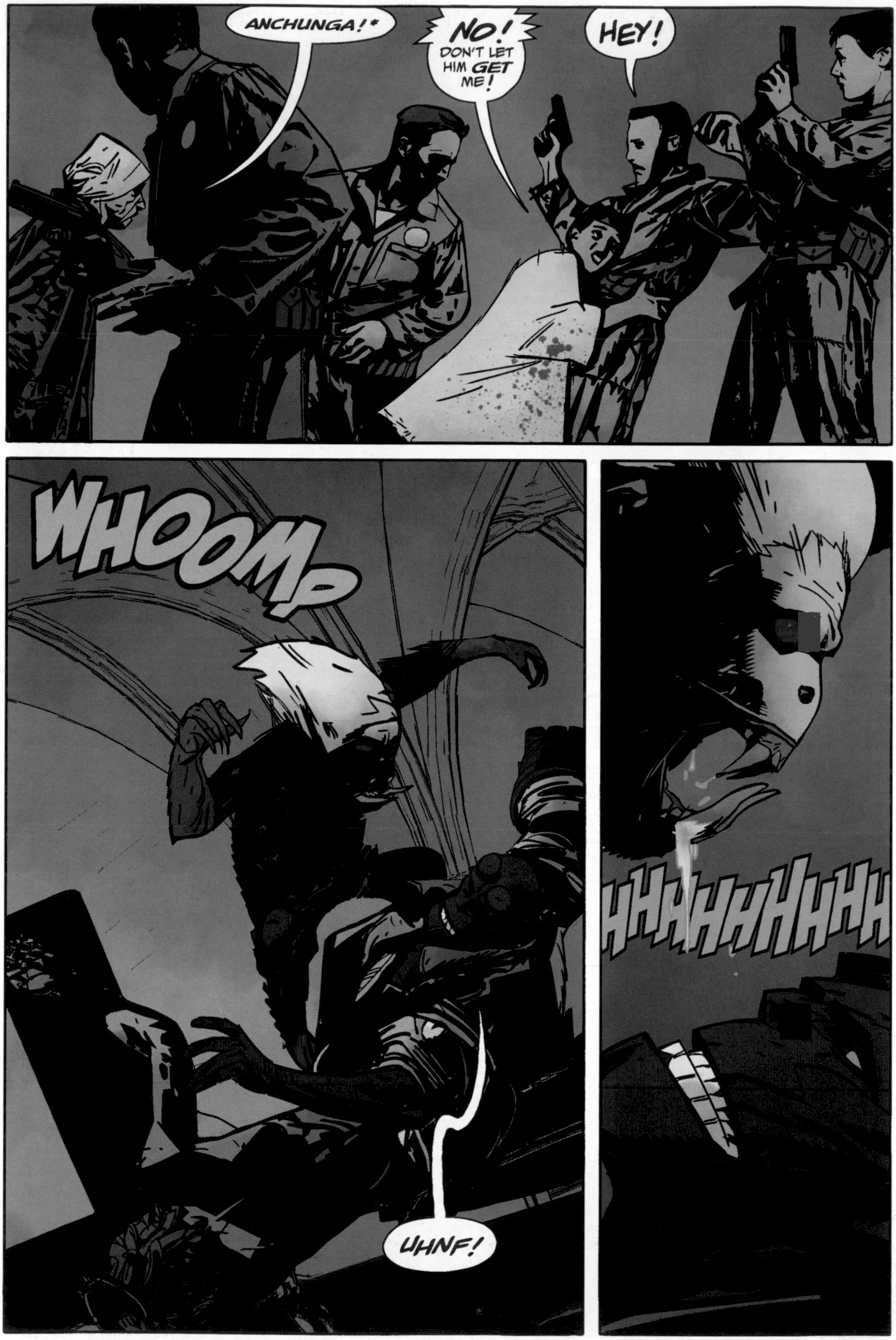
ANCHUNGA!*
NO! DON'T LET HIM GET ME!
HEY!
WHOOMP
UHNF!
HHHHHHHHH

*ACCORDING TO THE TAPIRAPÉ PEOPLE OF CENTRAL BRAZIL, A PARTICULARLY EVIL DEMON

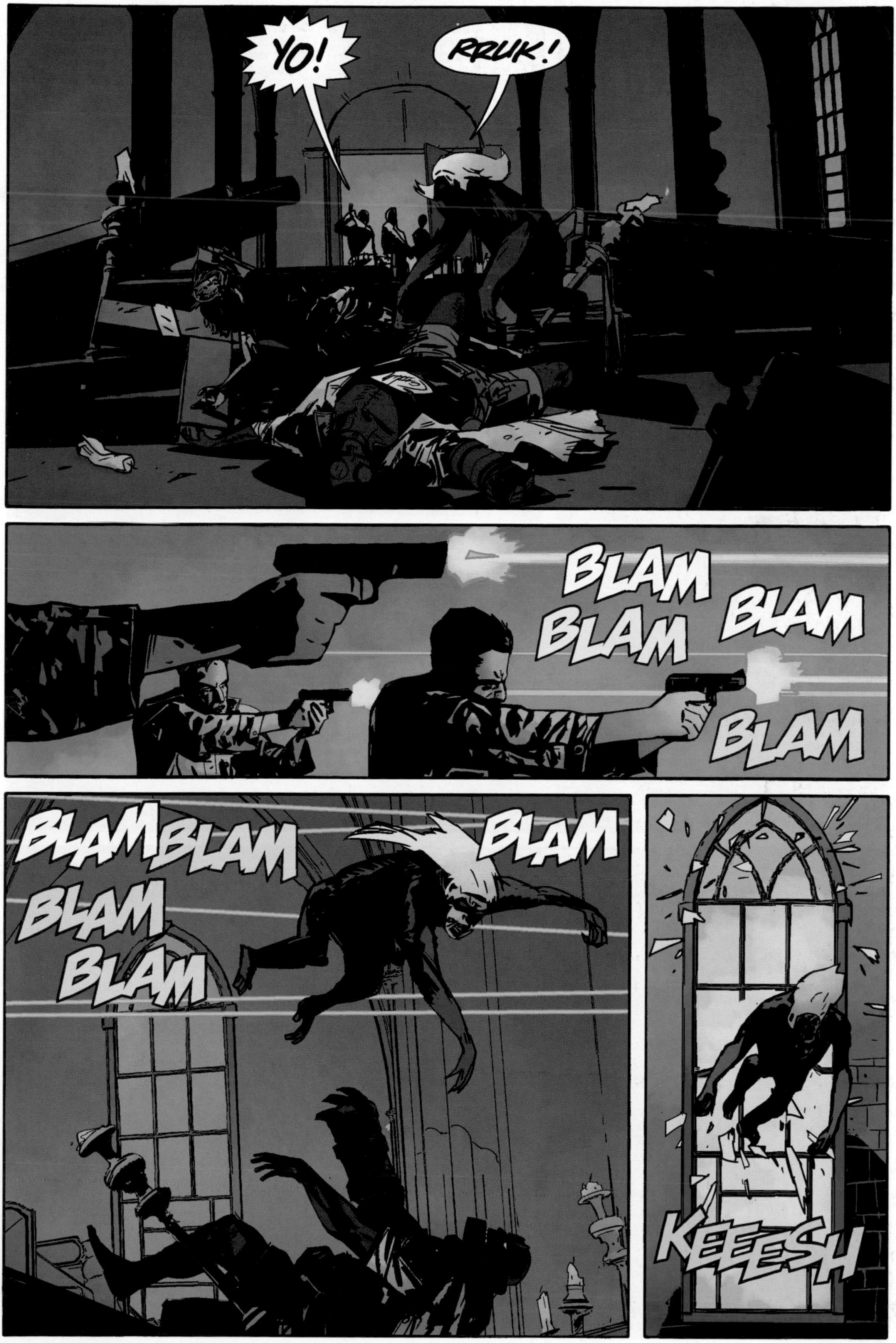
YO!
RRUK!
BLAM
BLAM
BLAM
BLAM
BLAM
BLAM
BLAM
BLAM
BLAM
KEEESH

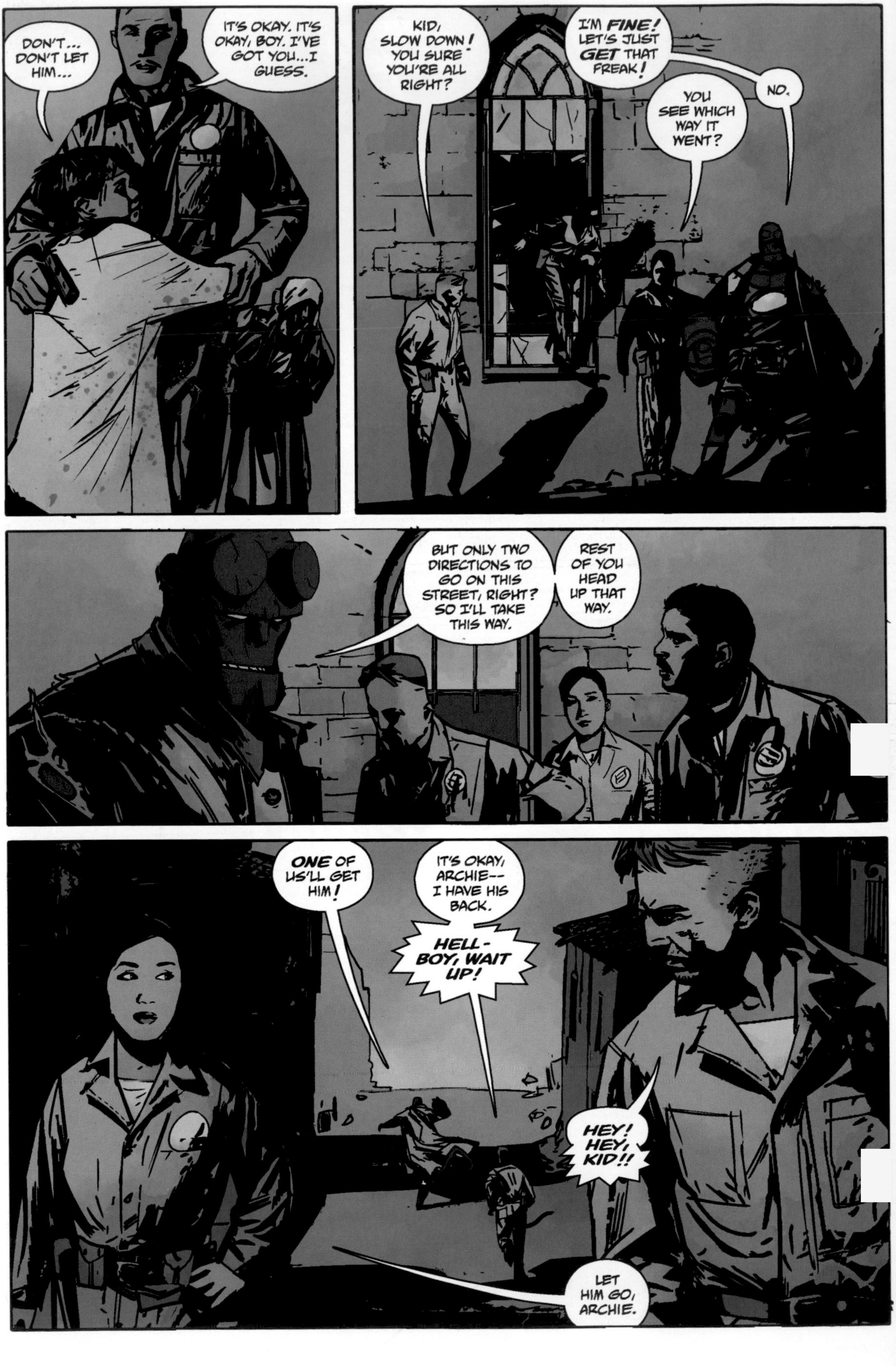
DON'T... DON'T LET HIM...
IT'S OKAY. IT'S OKAY, BOY. I'VE GOT YOU...I GUESS.
KID, SLOW DOWN! YOU SURE YOU'RE ALL RIGHT?
I'M FINE! LET'S JUST GET THAT FREAK!
YOU SEE WHICH WAY IT WENT?
NO.
BUT ONLY TWO DIRECTIONS TO GO ON THIS STREET, RIGHT? SO I'LL TAKE THIS WAY.
REST OF YOU HEAD UP THAT WAY.
ONE OF US'LL GET HIM!
IT'S OKAY, ARCHIE-- I HAVE HIS BACK.
HELL-BOY, WAIT UP!
HEY! HEY, KID!!
LET HIM GO, ARCHIE.

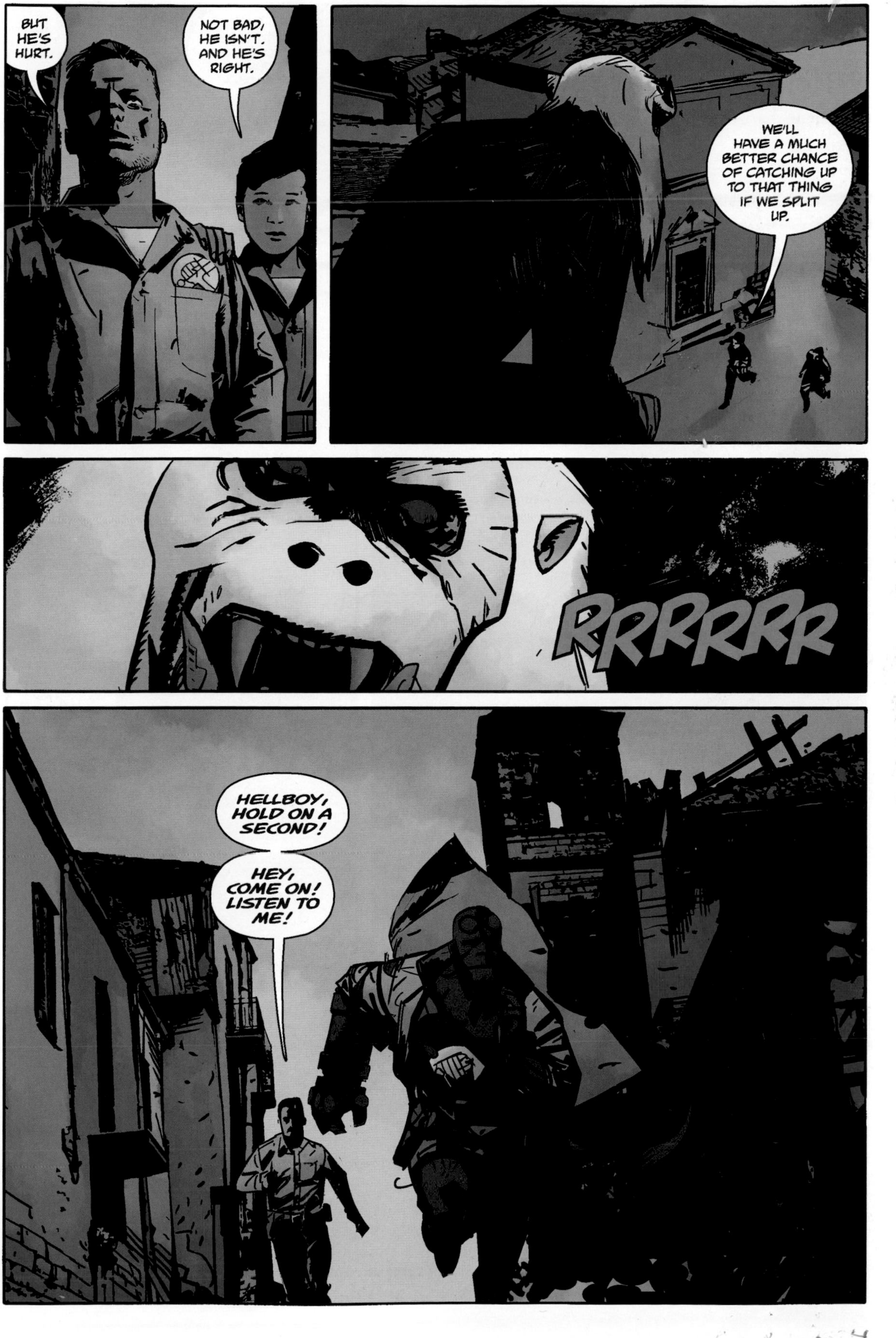
BUT HE'S HURT.
NOT BAD, HE ISN'T. AND HE'S RIGHT.
WE'LL HAVE A MUCH BETTER CHANCE OF CATCHING UP TO THAT THING IF WE SPLIT UP.
RRRRRR
HELLBOY, HOLD ON A SECOND!
HEY, COME ON! LISTEN TO ME!

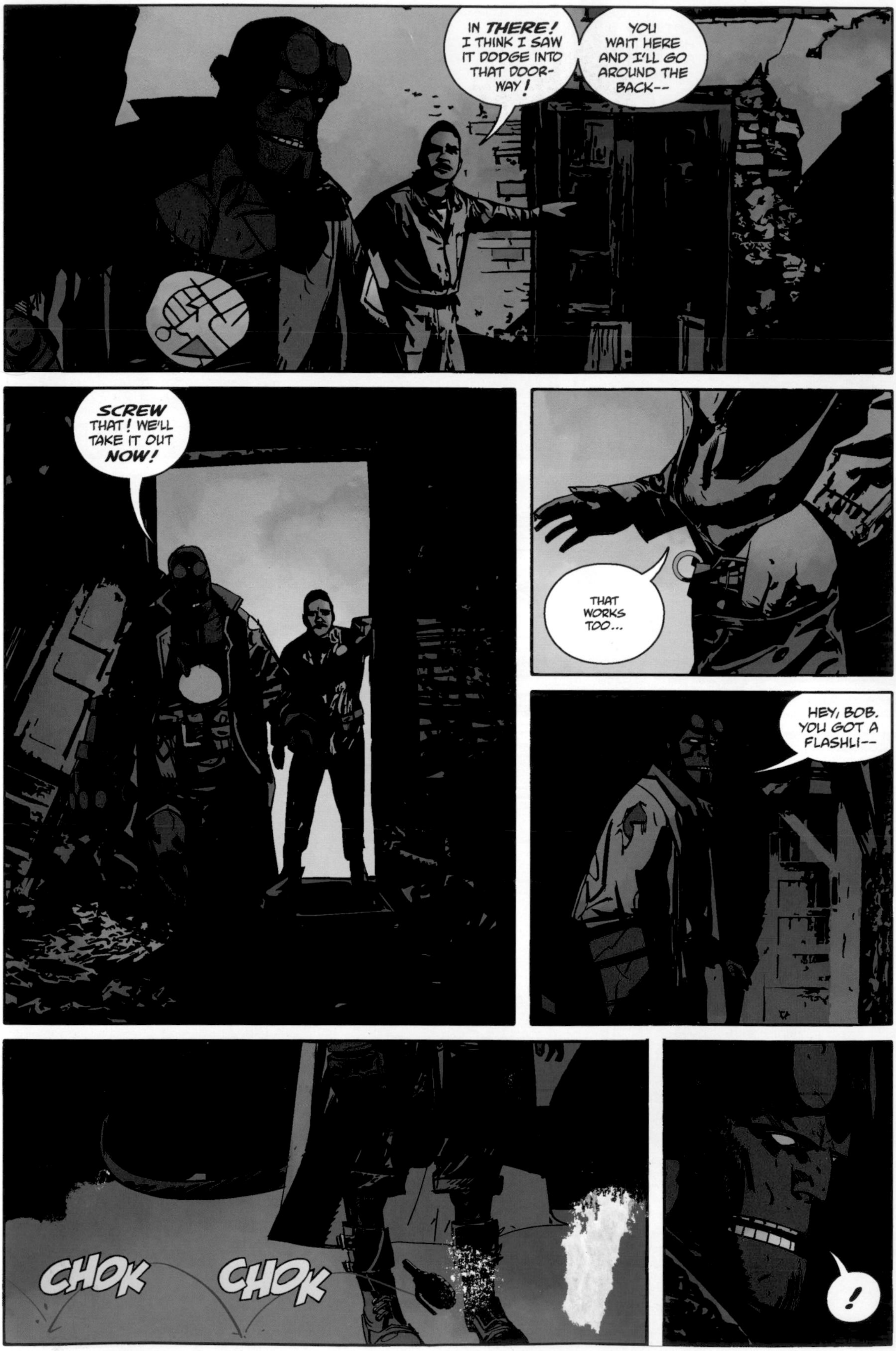
IN THERE! I THINK I SAW IT DODGE INTO THAT DOOR-WAY!
YOU WAIT HERE AND I'LL GO AROUND THE BACK--
SCREW THAT! WE'LL TAKE IT OUT NOW!
THAT WORKS TOO...
HEY, BOB. YOU GOT A FLASHLI--
CHOK
CHOK
!

Chapter Three

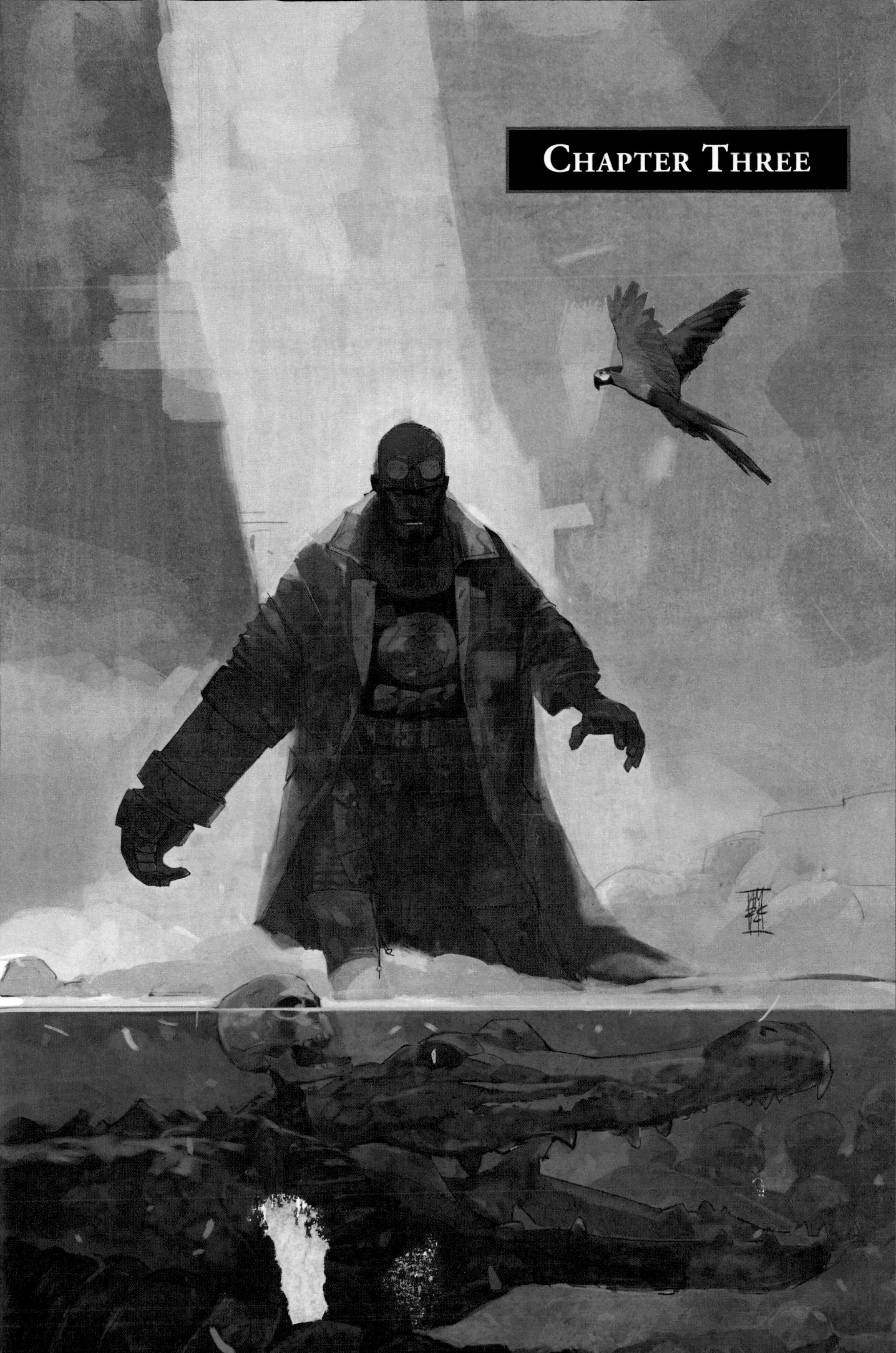

SNAP

CHOK

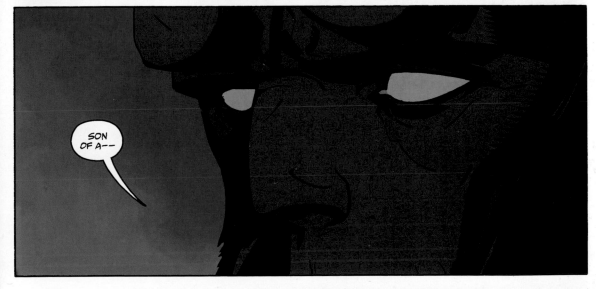

SON OF A--

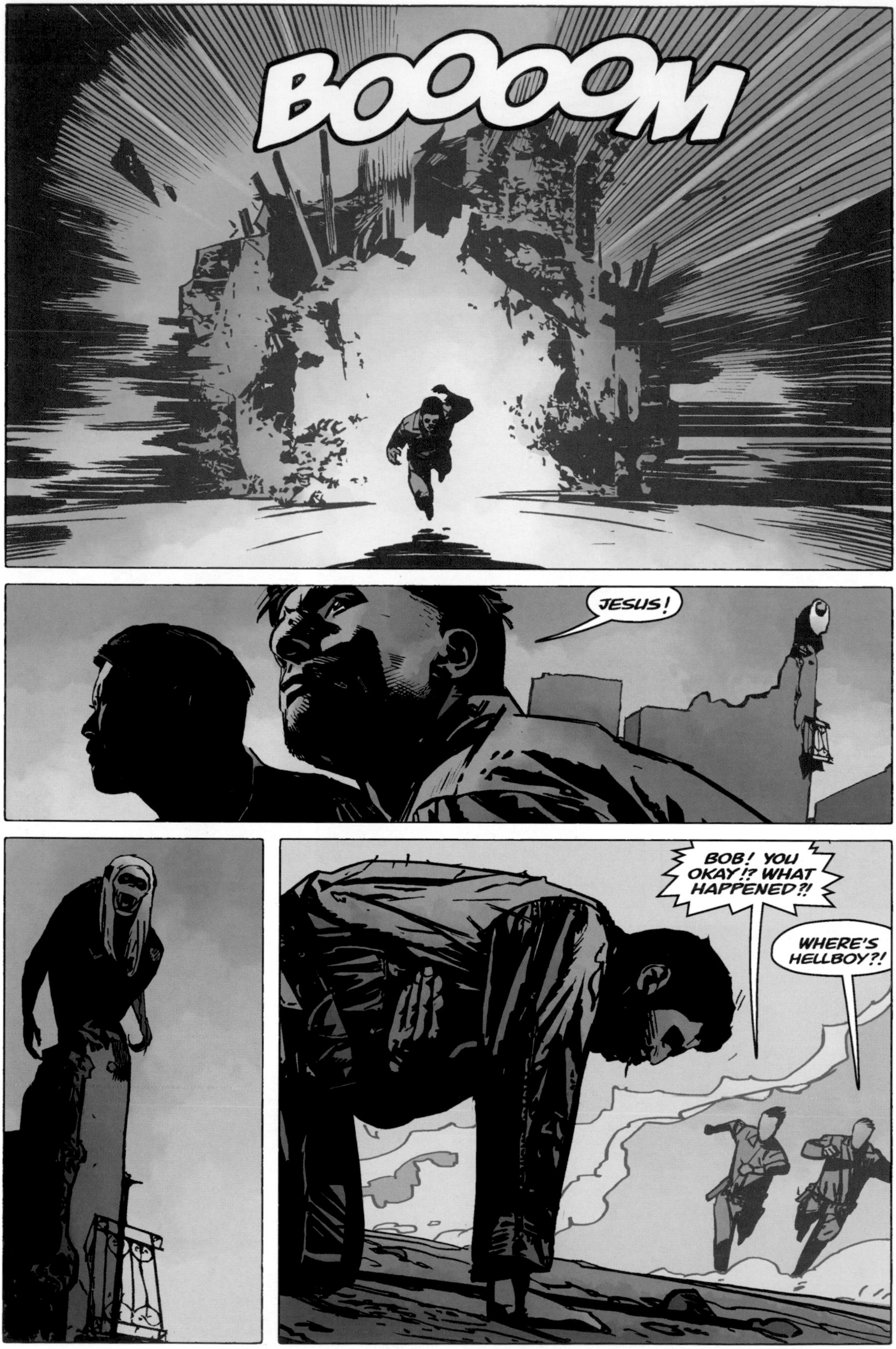
BOOOOM
JESUS!
BOB! YOU OKAY!? WHAT HAPPENED?!
WHERE'S HELLBOY?!

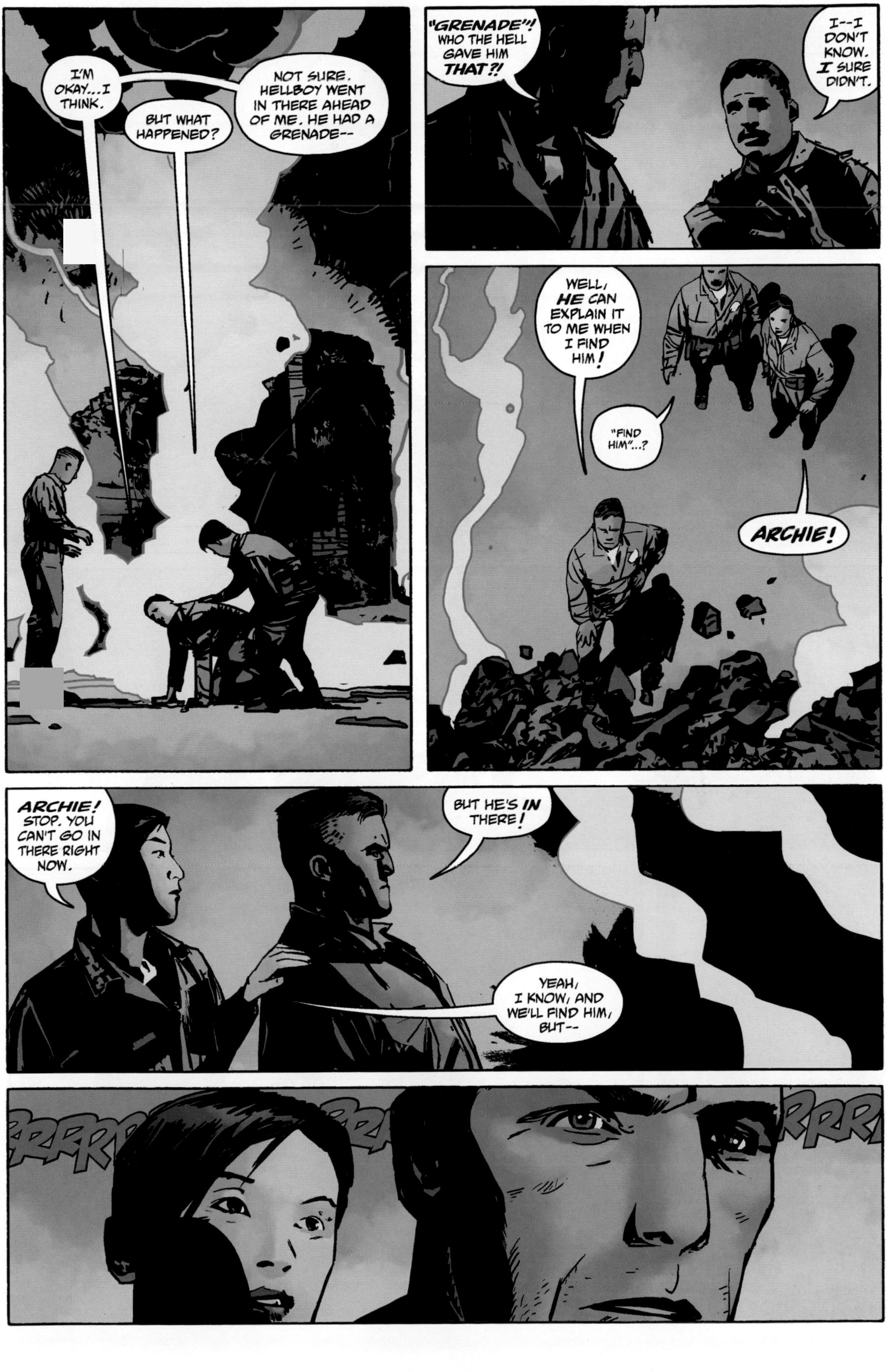
I'M OKAY...I THINK.
BUT WHAT HAPPENED?
NOT SURE. HELLBOY WENT IN THERE AHEAD OF ME. HE HAD A GRENADE--
"GRENADE"! WHO THE HELL GAVE HIM THAT?!
I--I DON'T KNOW. I SURE DIDN'T.
WELL, HE CAN EXPLAIN IT TO ME WHEN I FIND HIM!
"FIND HIM"...?
ARCHIE!
ARCHIE! STOP. YOU CAN'T GO IN THERE RIGHT NOW.
BUT HE'S IN THERE!
YEAH, I KNOW, AND WE'LL FIND HIM, BUT--
RRRRR
RRRR

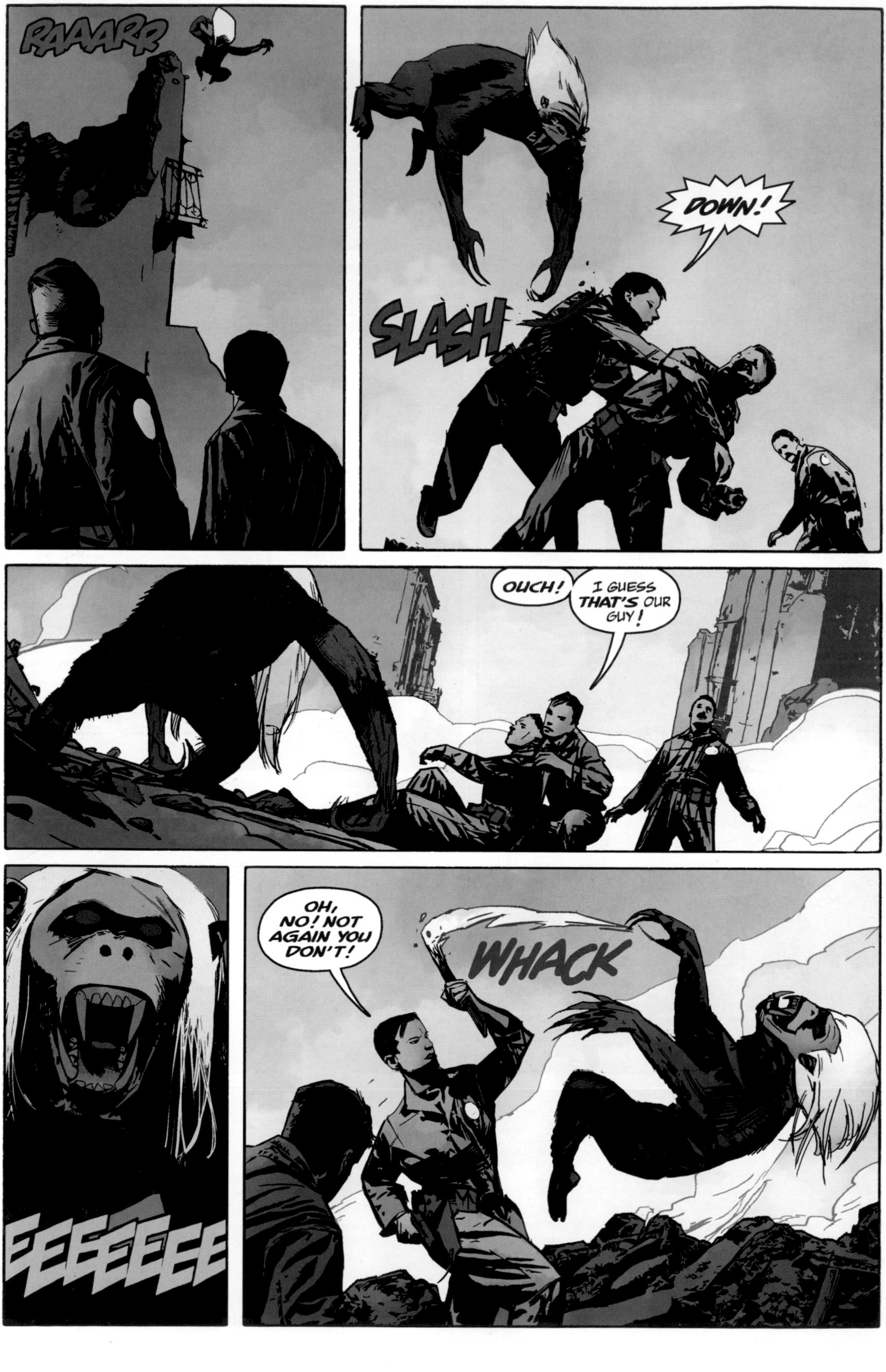
RAAARR
DOWN!
SLASH
OUCH!
I GUESS THAT'S OUR GUY!
EEEEEEEE
OH, NO! NOT AGAIN YOU DON'T!
WHACK

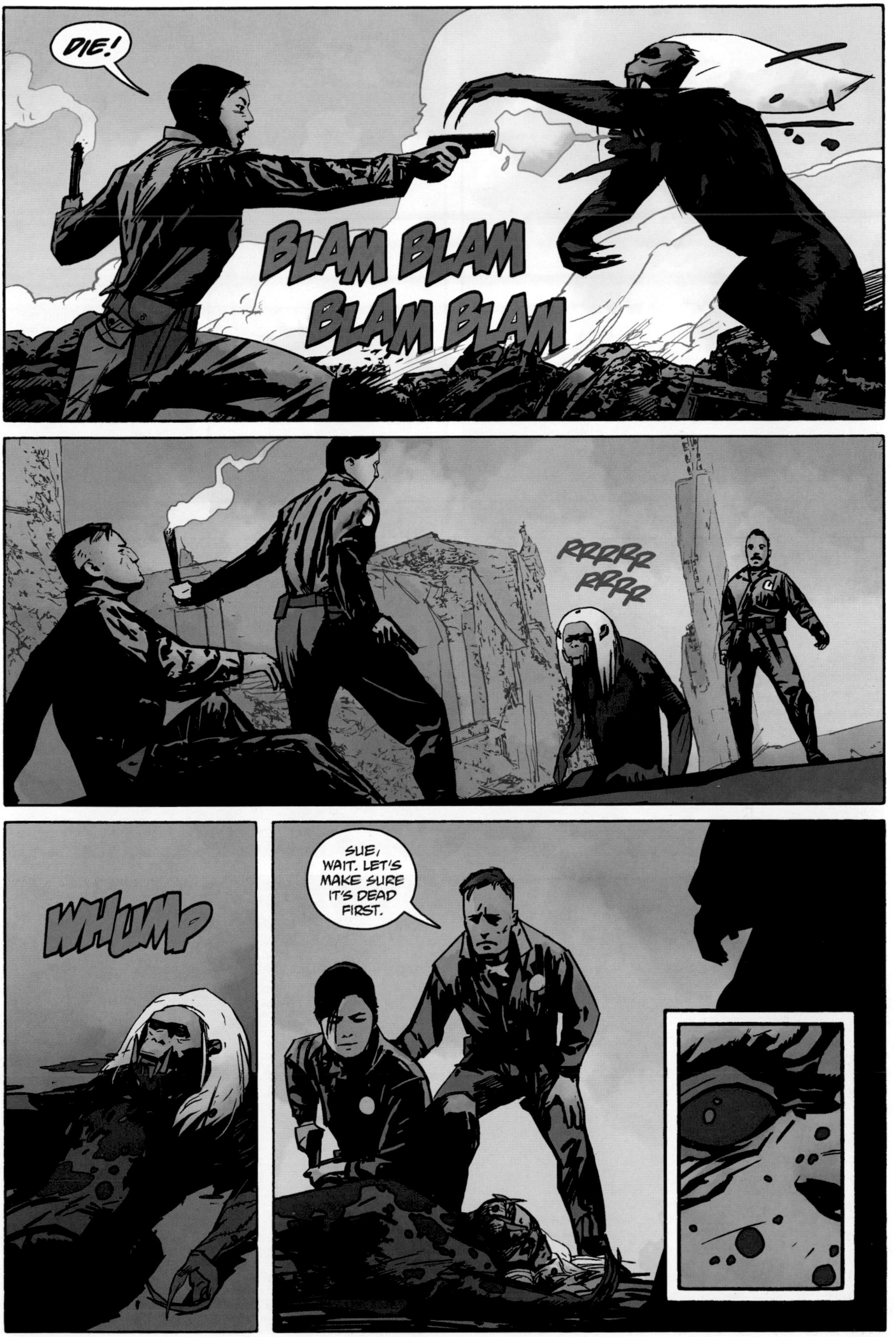
DIE!
BLAM BLAM
BLAM BLAM
RRRRR
RRRR
WHUMP
SUE, WAIT. LET'S MAKE SURE IT'S DEAD FIRST.

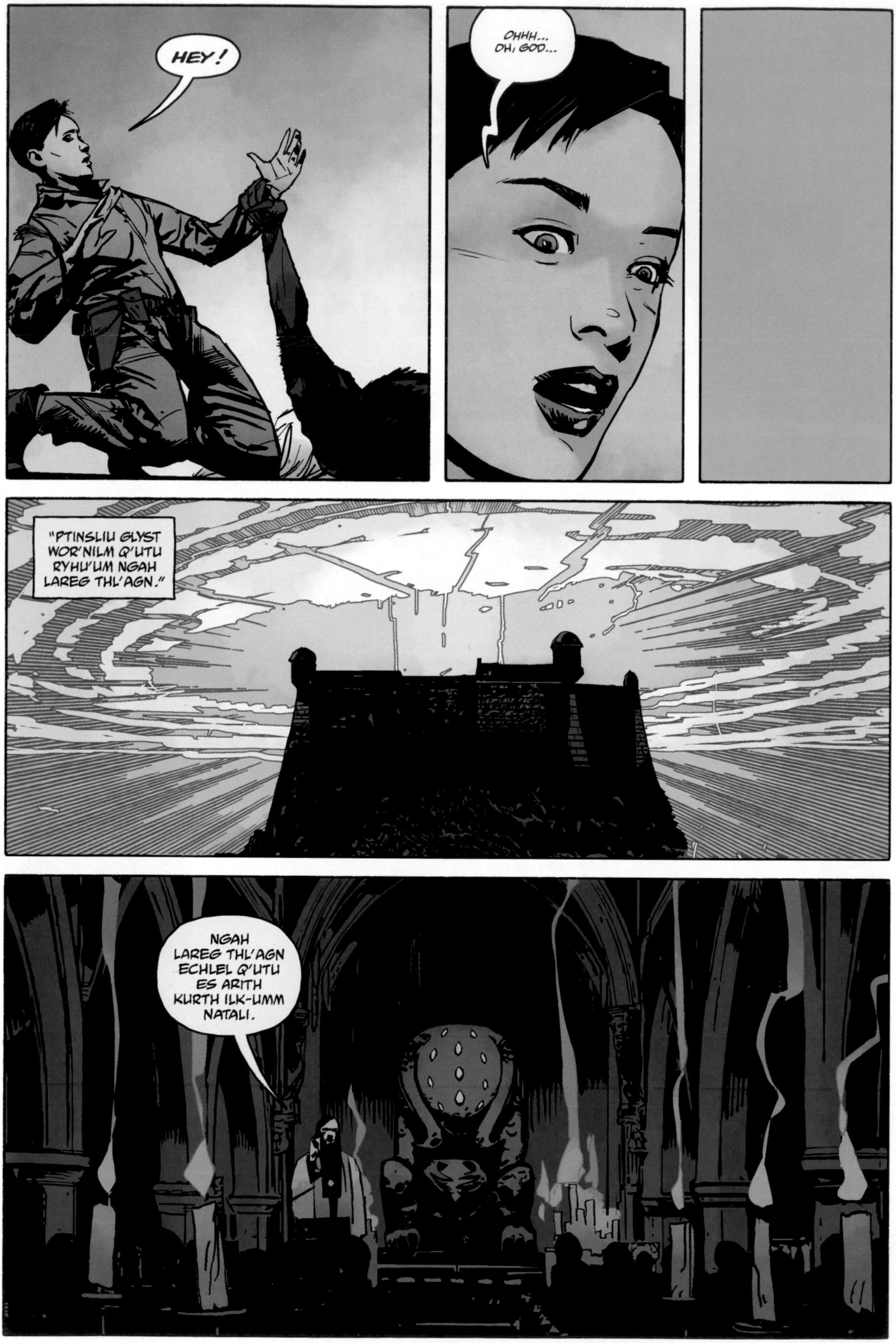
HEY!
OHHH... OH, GOD...
"PTINSLIU GLYST WOR'NILM Q'UTU RYHU'UM NGAH LAREG THL'AGN."
NGAH LAREG THL'AGN ECHLEL Q'UTU ES ARITH KURTH ILK-UMM NATALI.

EPIVAR YTHO NOQ'OAH GOMOA T'OXL URAKH NGAH LAREG.
NGAH LAREG...
NGAH LAREG...
BLAM
BLAM

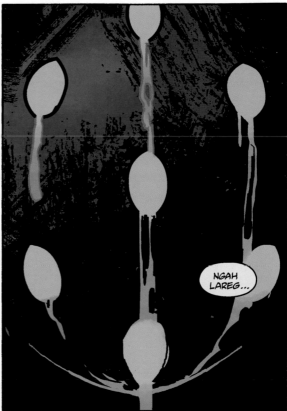

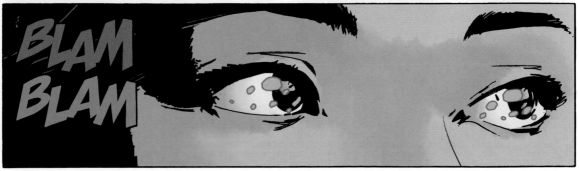

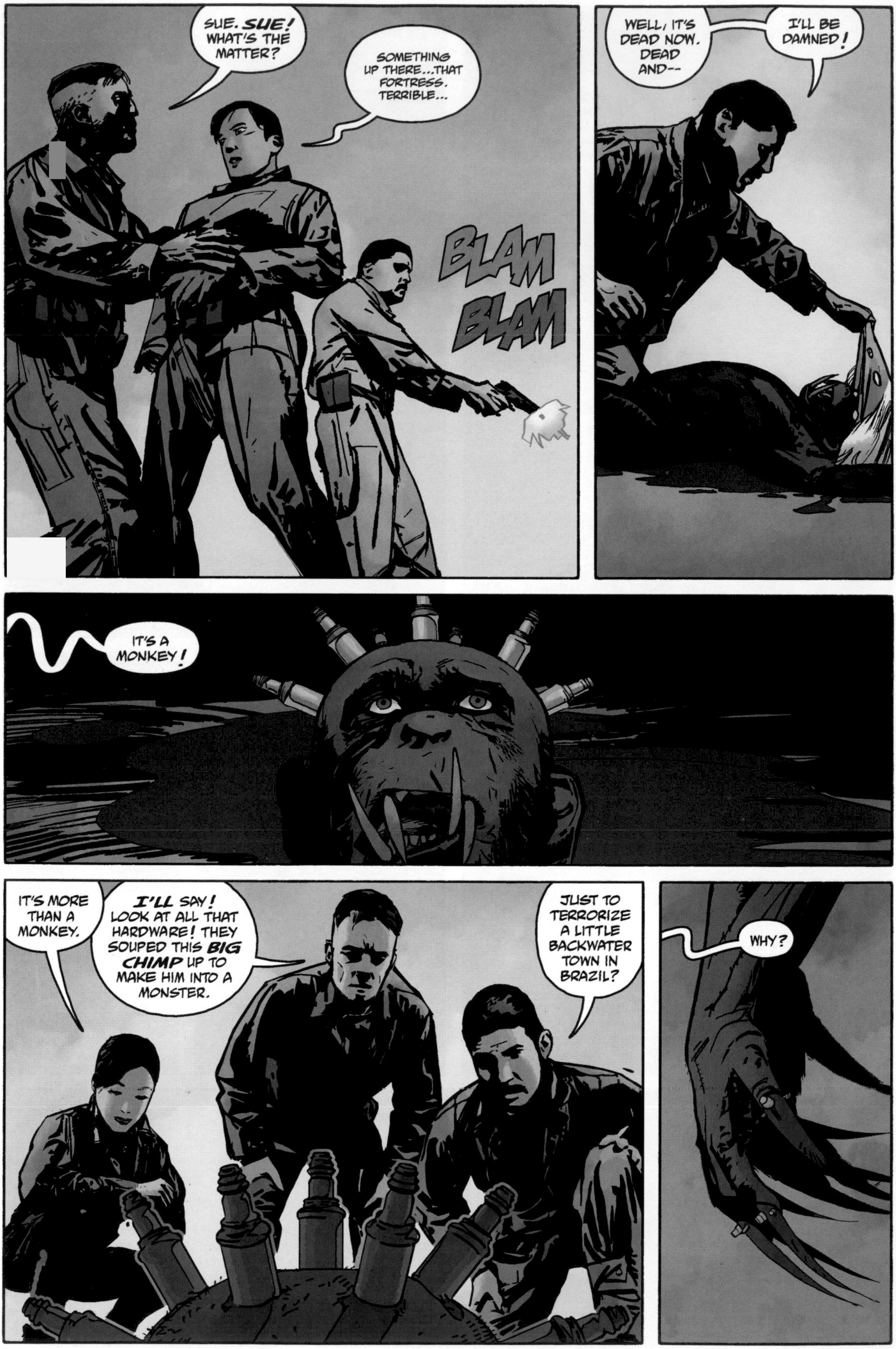
SUE. SUE! WHAT'S THE MATTER?
SOMETHING UP THERE...THAT FORTRESS. TERRIBLE...
BLAM BLAM
WELL, IT'S DEAD NOW. DEAD AND--
I'LL BE DAMNED!
IT'S A MONKEY!
IT'S MORE THAN A MONKEY.
I'LL SAY! LOOK AT ALL THAT HARDWARE! THEY SOUPED THIS BIG CHIMP UP TO MAKE HIM INTO A MONSTER.
JUST TO TERRORIZE A LITTLE BACKWATER TOWN IN BRAZIL?
WHY?

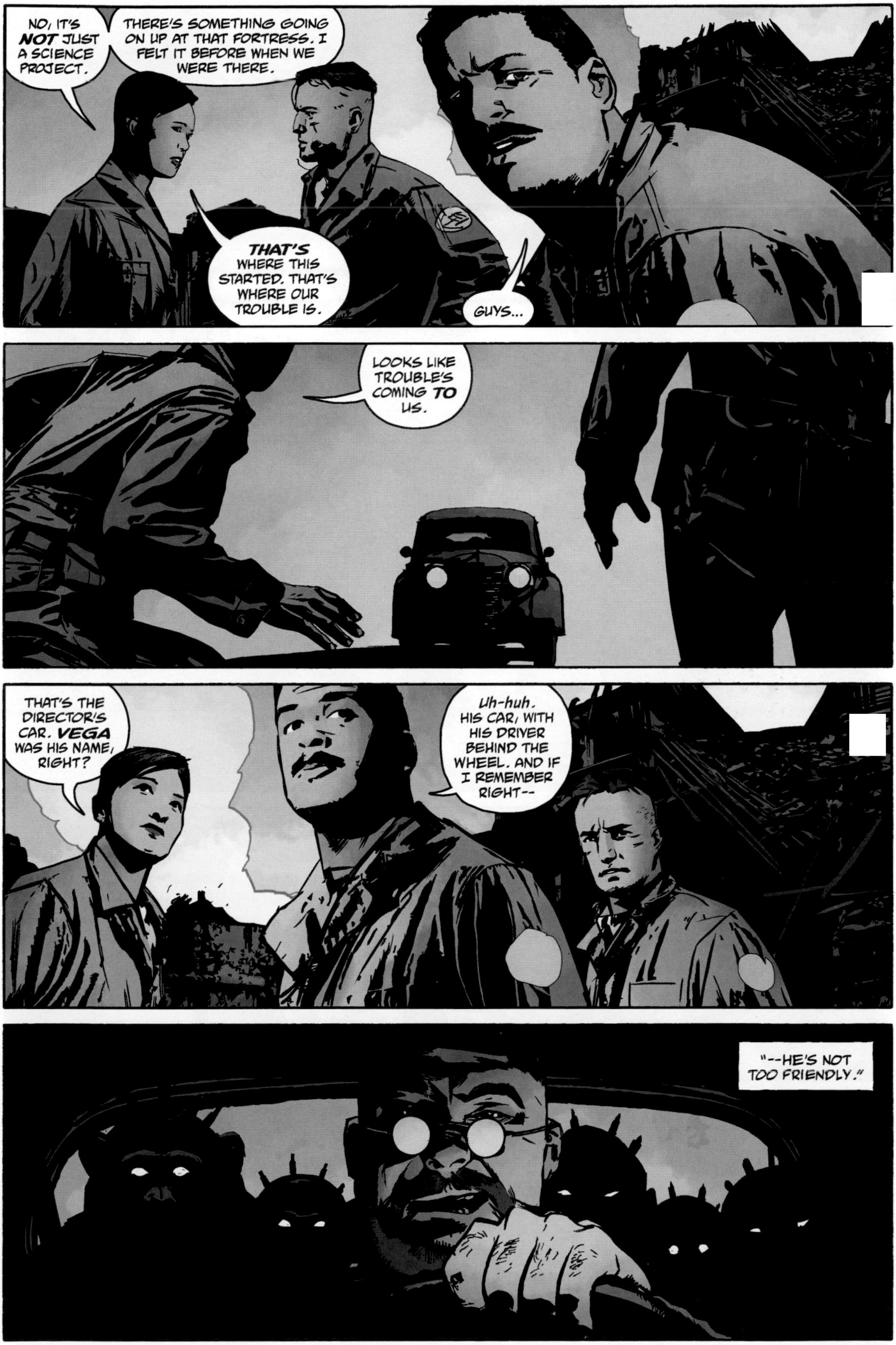
NO, IT'S NOT JUST A SCIENCE PROJECT.
THERE'S SOMETHING GOING ON UP AT THAT FORTRESS. I FELT IT BEFORE WHEN WE WERE THERE.
THAT'S WHERE THIS STARTED. THAT'S WHERE OUR TROUBLE IS.
GUYS...
LOOKS LIKE TROUBLE'S COMING TO US.
THAT'S THE DIRECTOR'S CAR. VEGA WAS HIS NAME, RIGHT?
Uh-huh. HIS CAR, WITH HIS DRIVER BEHIND THE WHEEL. AND IF I REMEMBER RIGHT--
"--HE'S NOT TOO FRIENDLY."

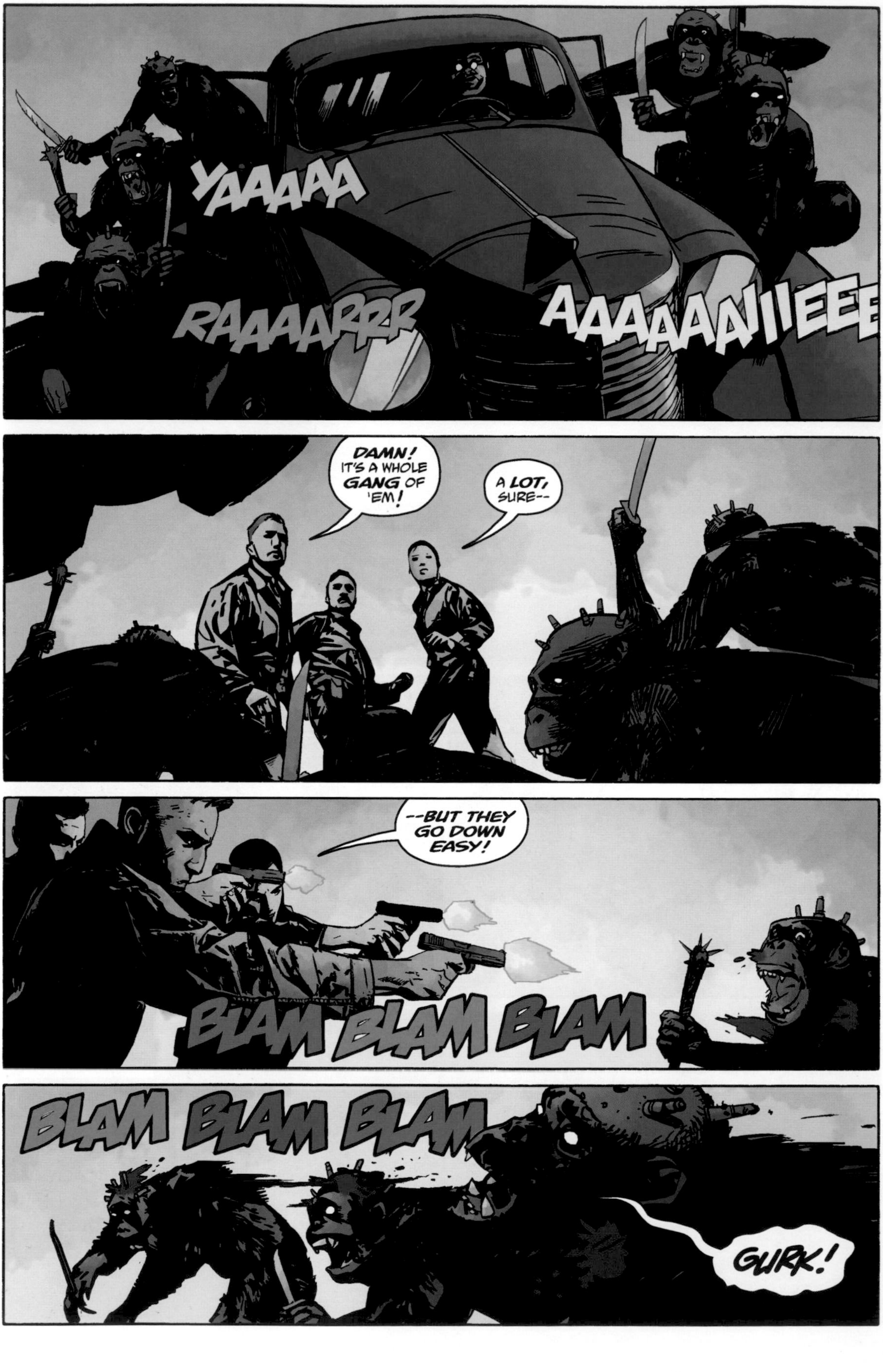
YAAAAA
RAAAARRR
AAAAAAIIIEEE
DAMN! IT'S A WHOLE GANG OF 'EM!
A LOT, SURE--
--BUT THEY GO DOWN EASY!
BLAM BLAM BLAM
BLAM BLAM BLAM
GURK!

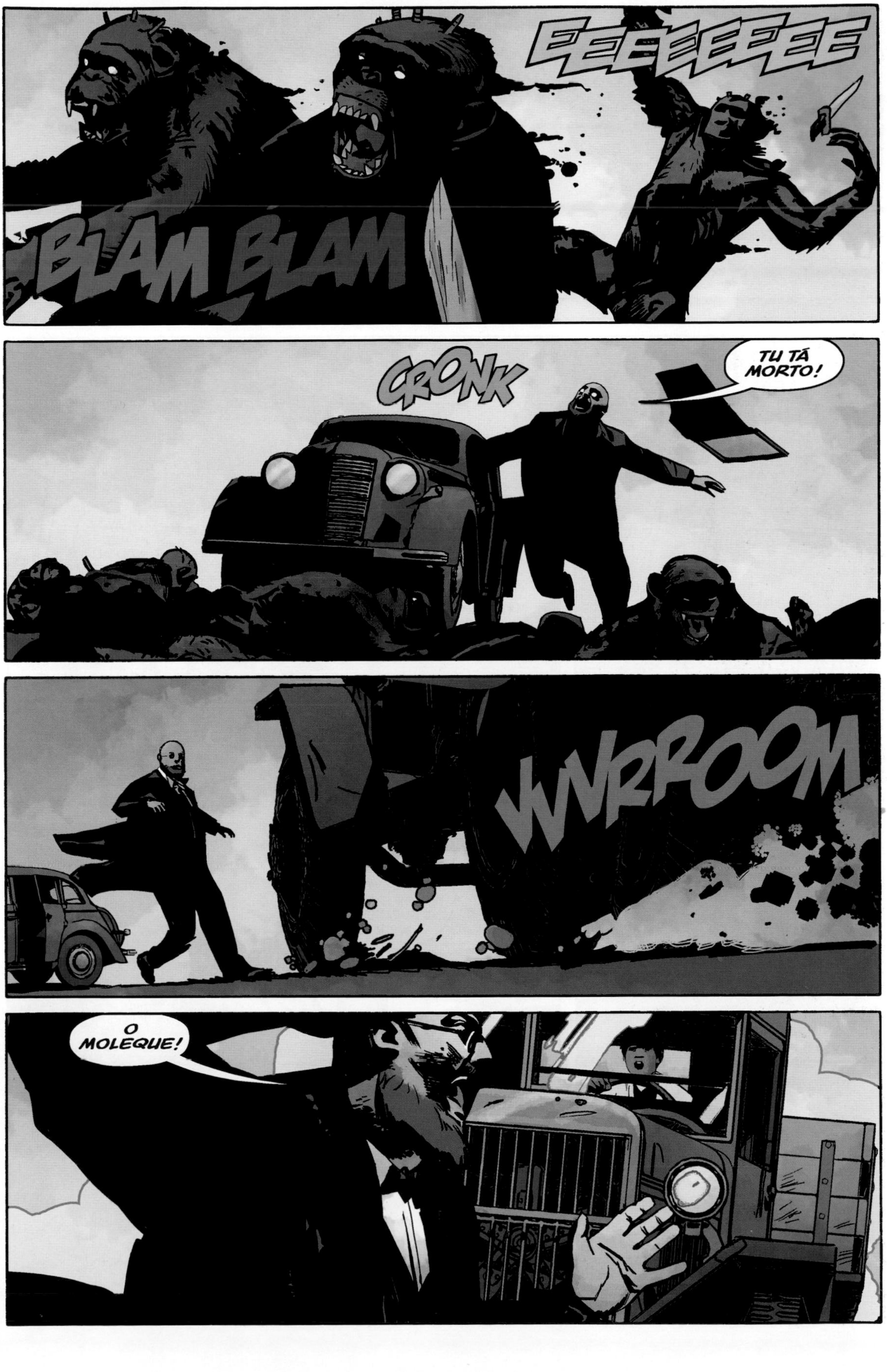
EEEEEEEEE
BLAM BLAM
CRONK
TU TÁ MORTO!
WRROOM
O MOLEQUE!

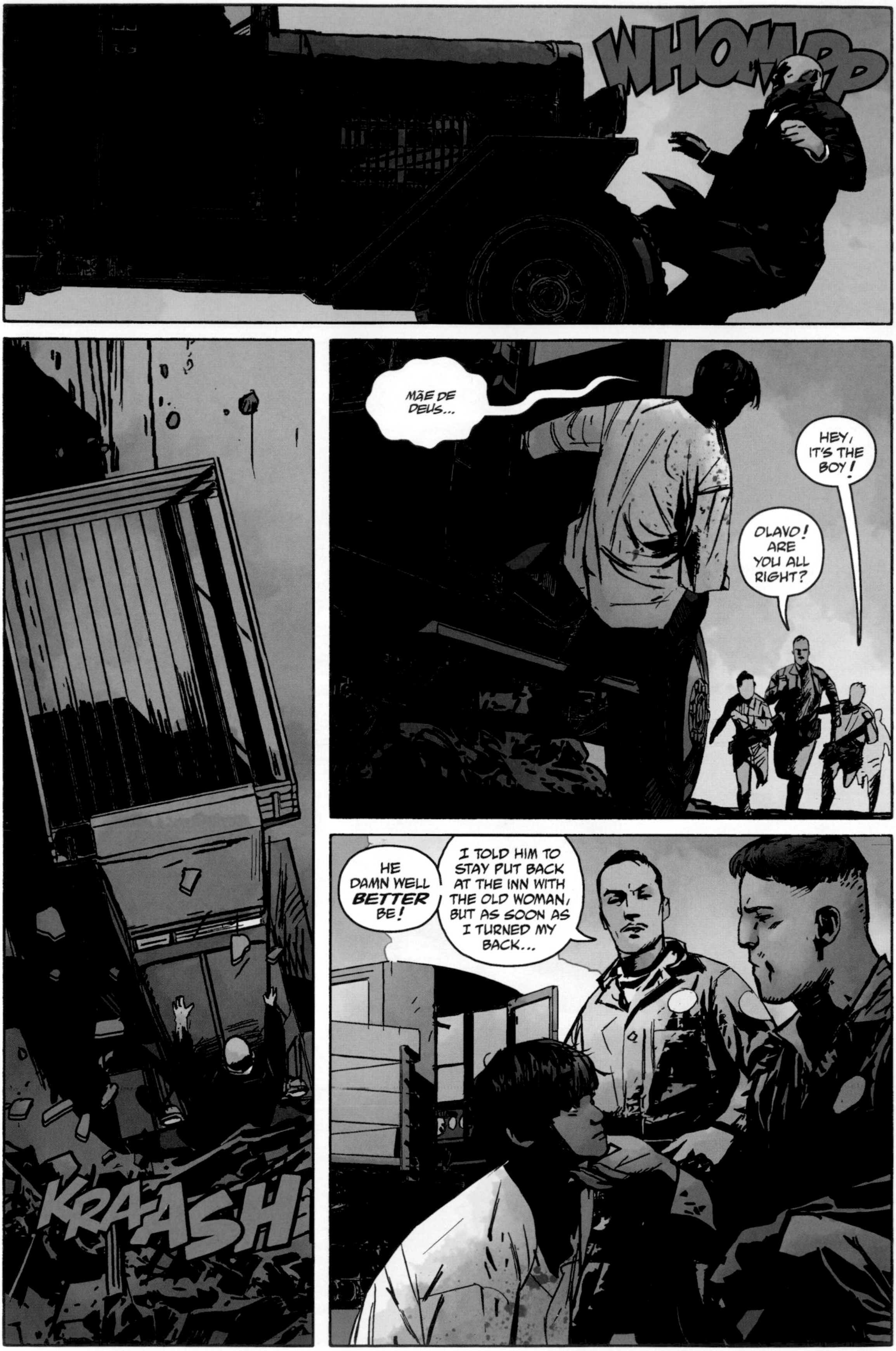
WHOMPP
KRAASH
MÃE DE DEUS...
HEY, IT'S THE BOY!
OLAVO! ARE YOU ALL RIGHT?
HE DAMN WELL BETTER BE!
I TOLD HIM TO STAY PUT BACK AT THE INN WITH THE OLD WOMAN, BUT AS SOON AS I TURNED MY BACK...

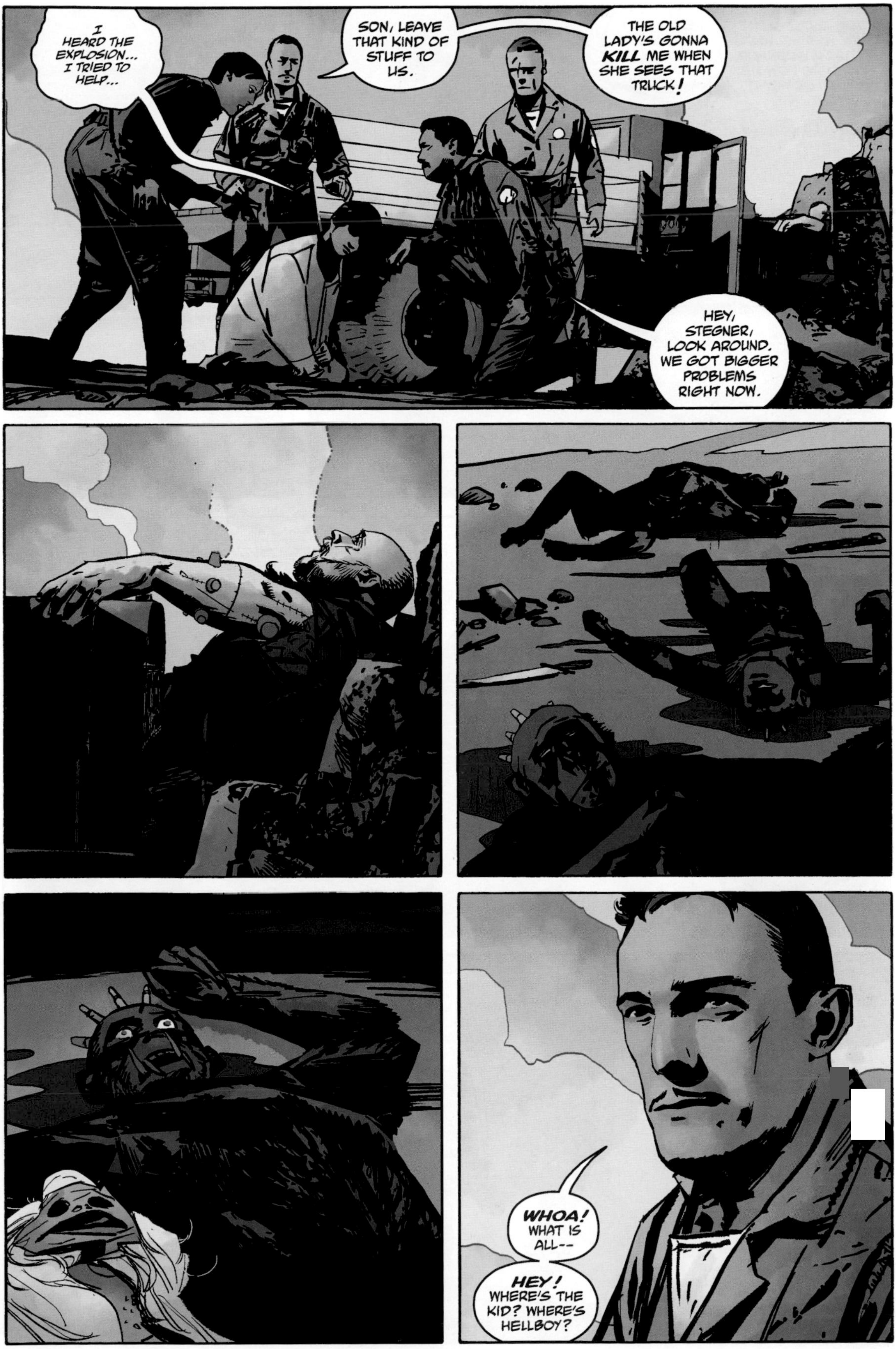
I HEARD THE EXPLOSION... I TRIED TO HELP...
SON, LEAVE THAT KIND OF STUFF TO US.
THE OLD LADY'S GONNA KILL ME WHEN SHE SEES THAT TRUCK!
HEY, STEGNER, LOOK AROUND. WE GOT BIGGER PROBLEMS RIGHT NOW.
WHOA! WHAT IS ALL--
HEY! WHERE'S THE KID? WHERE'S HELLBOY?

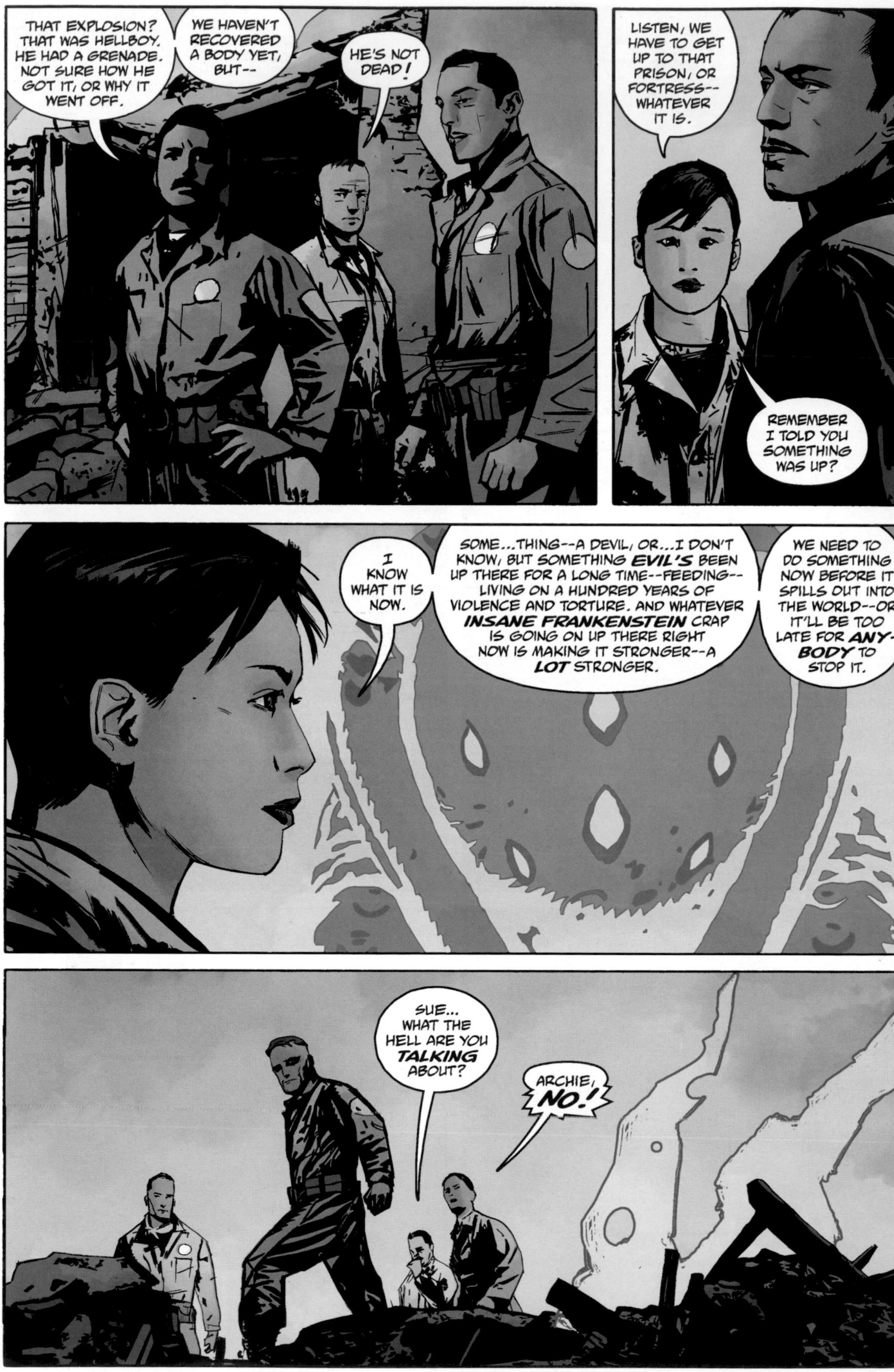
THAT EXPLOSION? THAT WAS HELLBOY. HE HAD A GRENADE. NOT SURE HOW HE GOT IT, OR WHY IT WENT OFF.
WE HAVEN'T RECOVERED A BODY YET, BUT--
HE'S NOT DEAD!
LISTEN, WE HAVE TO GET UP TO THAT PRISON, OR FORTRESS--WHATEVER IT IS.
REMEMBER I TOLD YOU SOMETHING WAS UP?
I KNOW WHAT IT IS NOW.
SOME...THING--A DEVIL, OR...I DON'T KNOW, BUT SOMETHING EVIL'S BEEN UP THERE FOR A LONG TIME--FEEDING--LIVING ON A HUNDRED YEARS OF VIOLENCE AND TORTURE. AND WHATEVER INSANE FRANKENSTEIN CRAP IS GOING ON UP THERE RIGHT NOW IS MAKING IT STRONGER--A LOT STRONGER.
WE NEED TO DO SOMETHING NOW BEFORE IT SPILLS OUT INTO THE WORLD--OR IT'LL BE TOO LATE FOR ANYBODY TO STOP IT.
SUE... WHAT THE HELL ARE YOU TALKING ABOUT?
ARCHIE, NO!

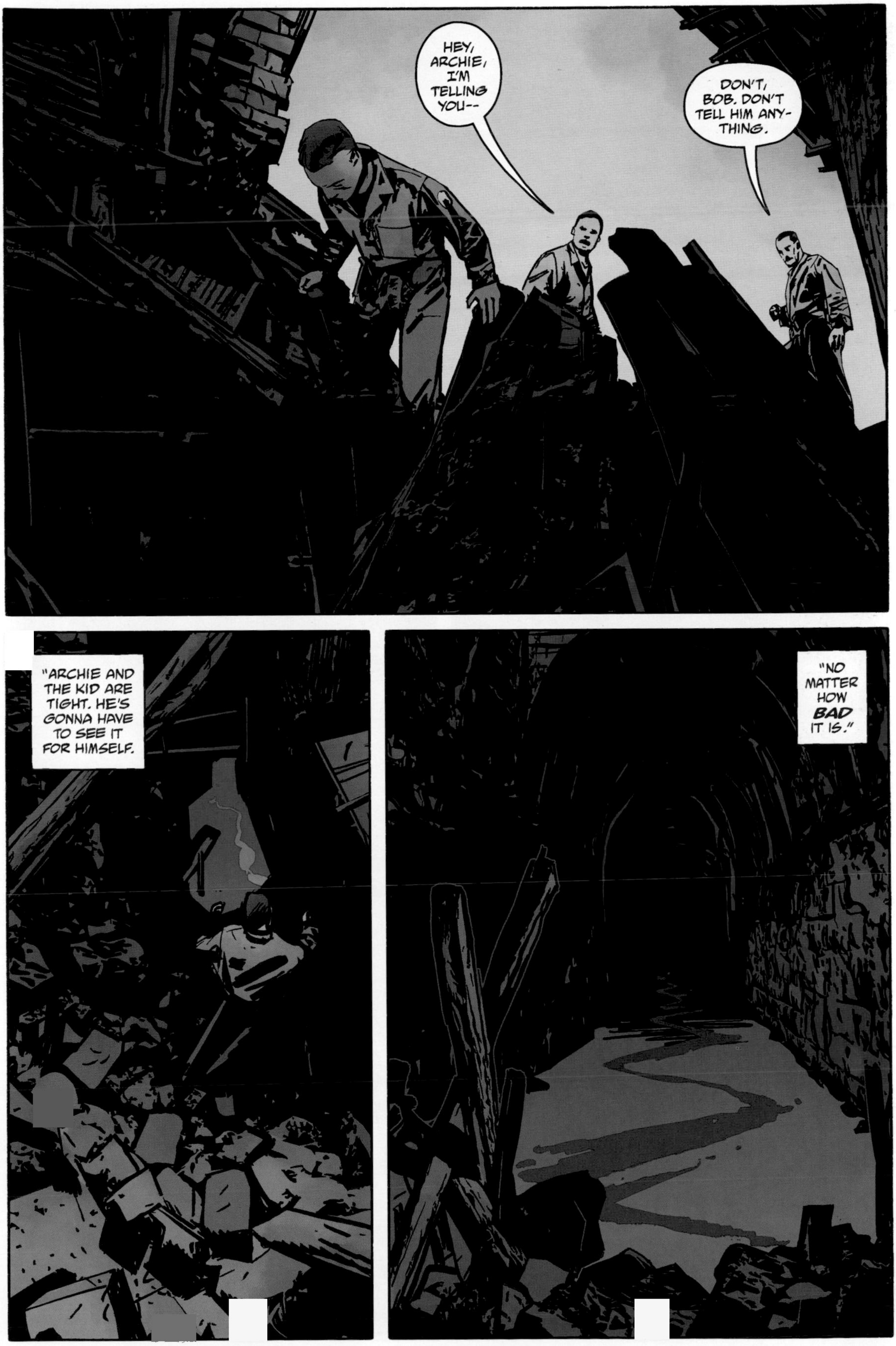
HEY, ARCHIE, I'M TELLING YOU--
DON'T, BOB. DON'T TELL HIM ANY-THING.
"ARCHIE AND THE KID ARE TIGHT. HE'S GONNA HAVE TO SEE IT FOR HIMSELF.
"NO MATTER HOW **BAD** IT IS."

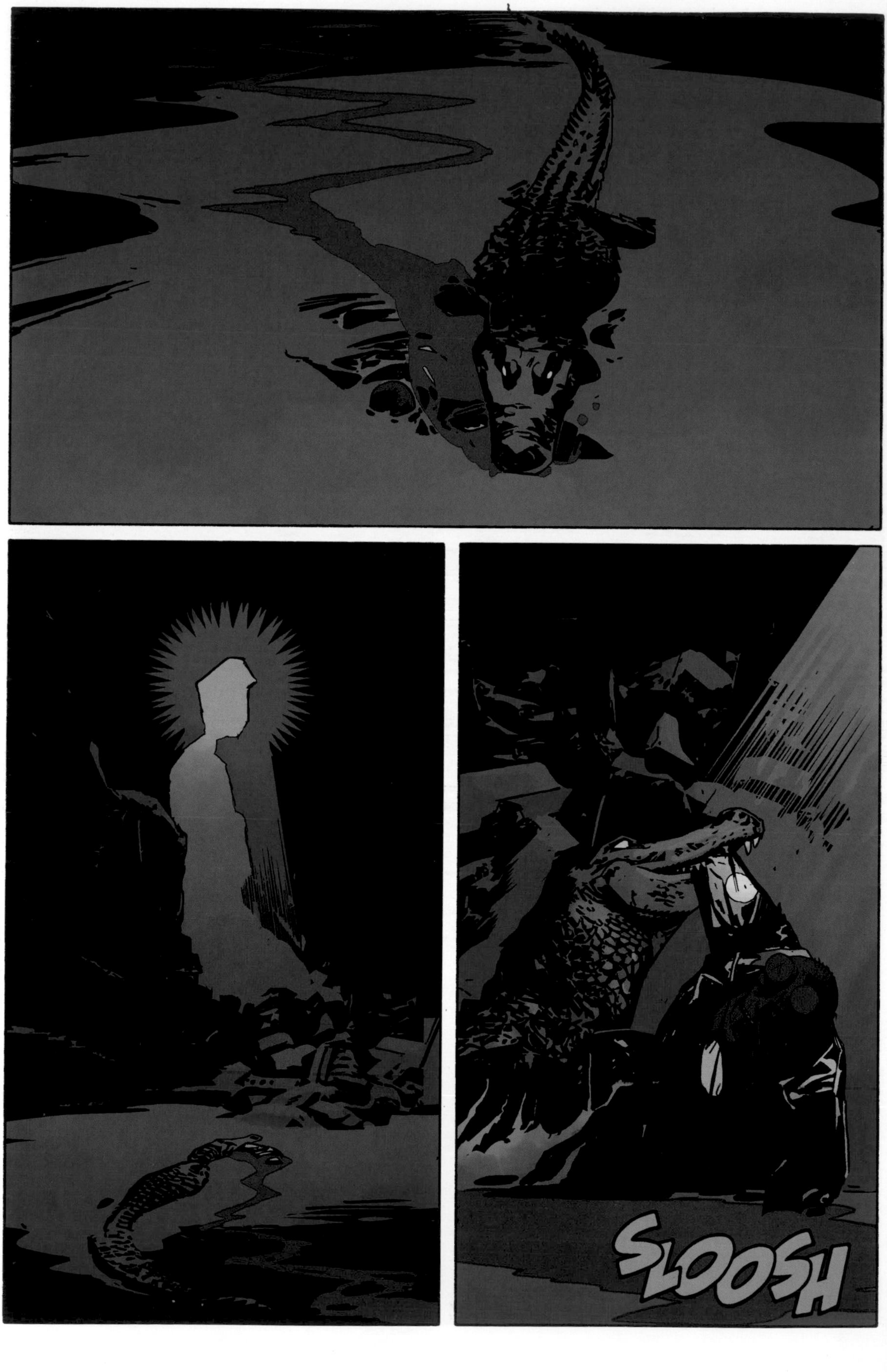
SLOOSH

JAPETEQUARA, WHAT IS THAT YOU HAVE THERE, AND WHAT ARE YOU GOING TO DO WITH IT?

NO, NO, I DON'T THINK YOU SHOULD.

I WILL EAT PART OF IT. THE REST I THINK I MIGHT BURY IN A HOLE WHERE IT CANNOT CAUSE ANY TROUBLE.

YOU KNOW WHAT HE IS?

I DO.

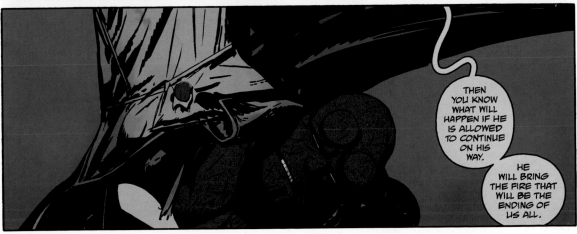

THEN YOU KNOW WHAT WILL HAPPEN IF HE IS ALLOWED TO CONTINUE ON HIS WAY.

HE WILL BRING THE FIRE THAT WILL BE THE ENDING OF US ALL.

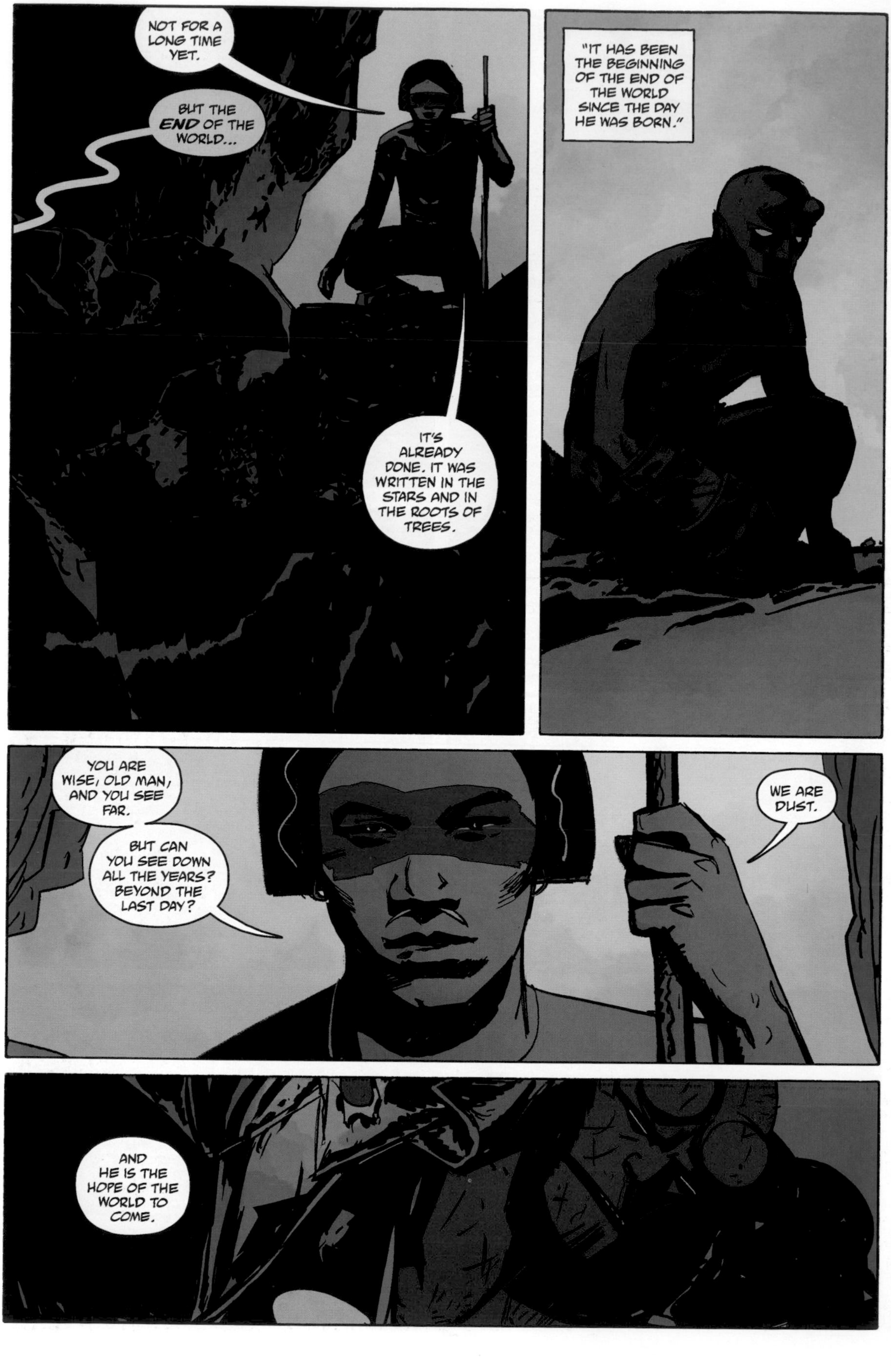
NOT FOR A LONG TIME YET.
BUT THE **END** OF THE WORLD...
IT'S ALREADY DONE. IT WAS WRITTEN IN THE STARS AND IN THE ROOTS OF TREES.
"IT HAS BEEN THE BEGINNING OF THE END OF THE WORLD SINCE THE DAY HE WAS BORN."
YOU ARE WISE, OLD MAN, AND YOU SEE FAR.
BUT CAN YOU SEE DOWN ALL THE YEARS? BEYOND THE LAST DAY?
WE ARE DUST.
AND HE IS THE HOPE OF THE WORLD TO COME.

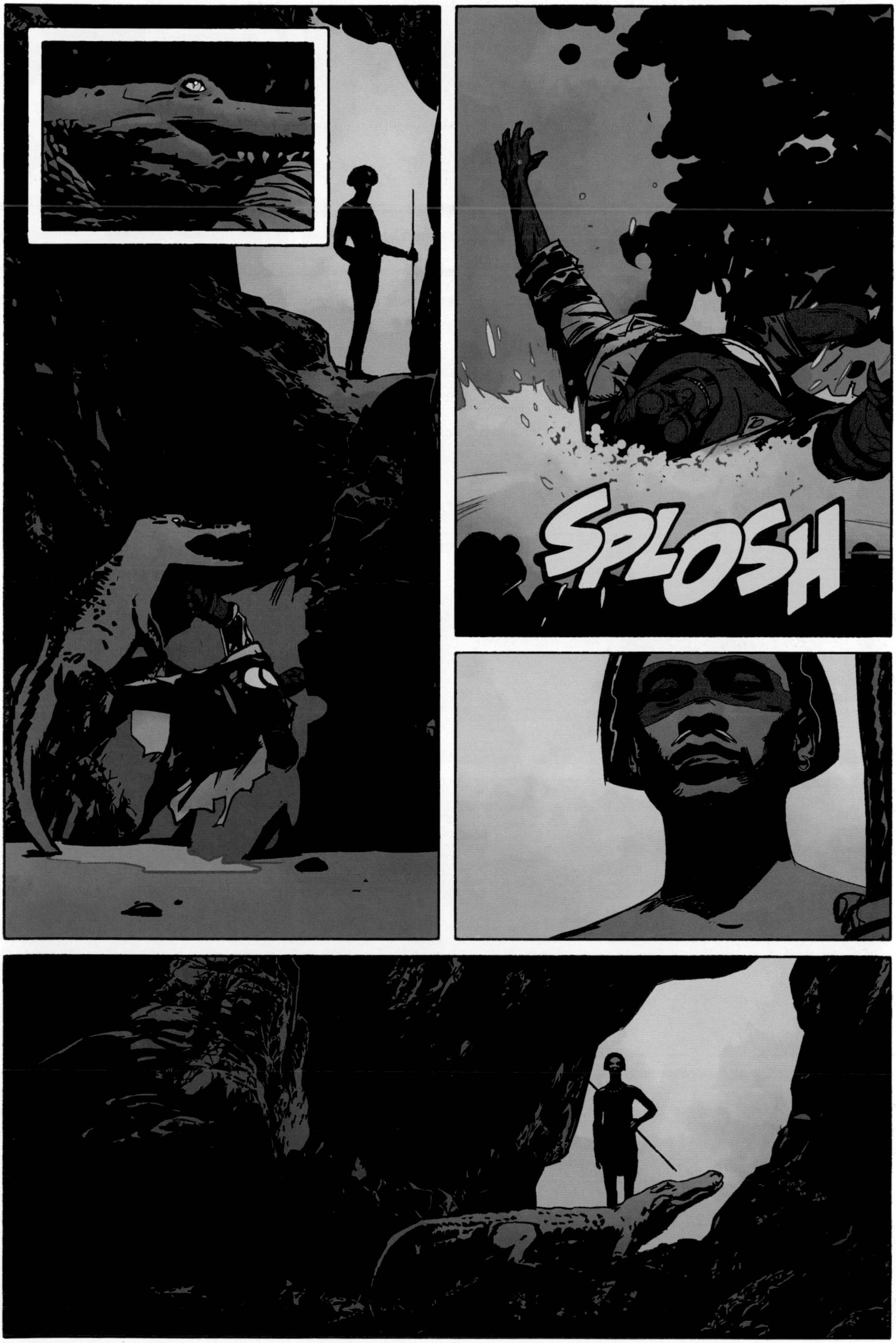
SPLOSH

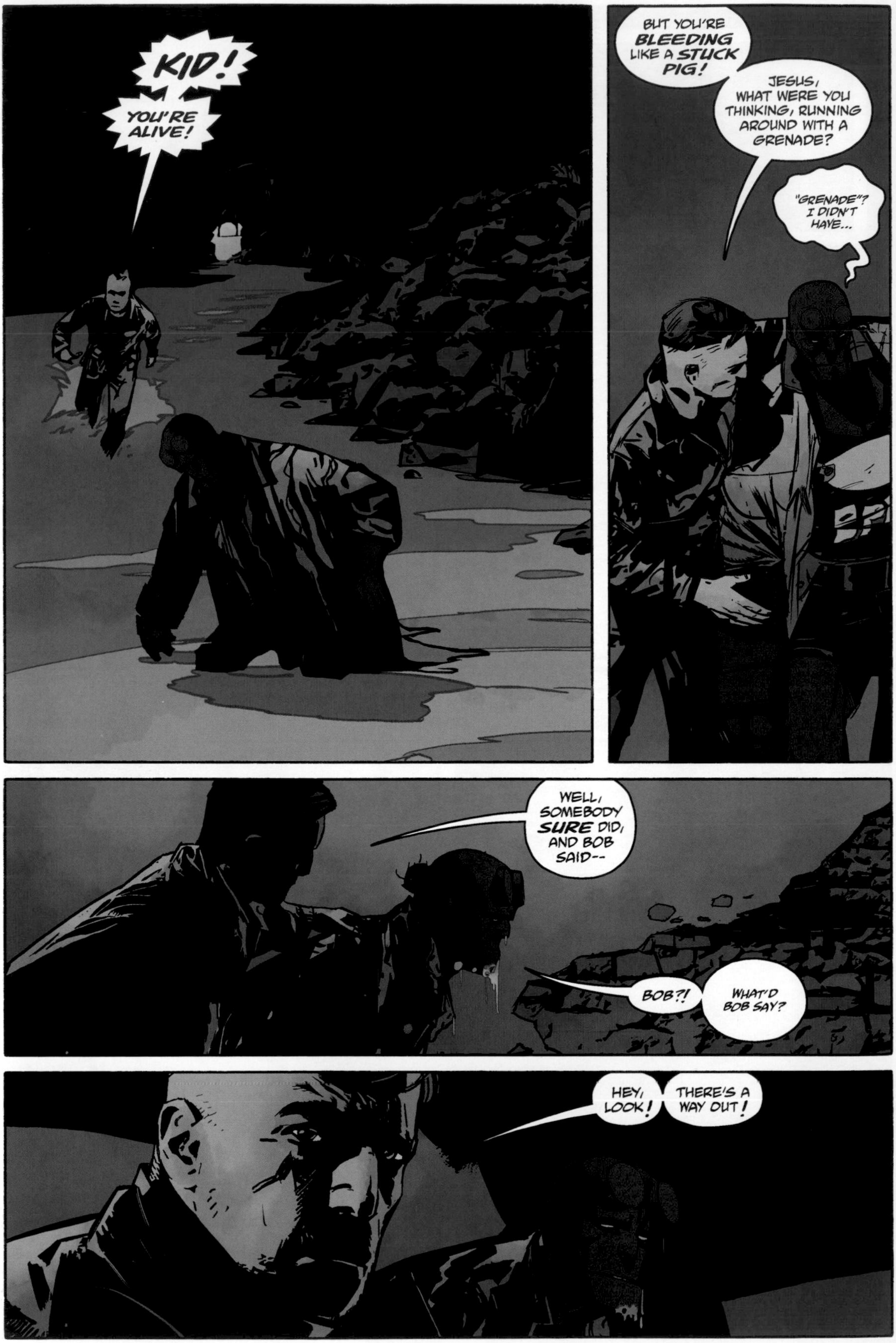
KID!
YOU'RE ALIVE!
BUT YOU'RE BLEEDING LIKE A STUCK PIG!
JESUS, WHAT WERE YOU THINKING, RUNNING AROUND WITH A GRENADE?
"GRENADE"? I DIDN'T HAVE...
WELL, SOMEBODY SURE DID, AND BOB SAID--
BOB?!
WHAT'D BOB SAY?
HEY, LOOK!
THERE'S A WAY OUT!

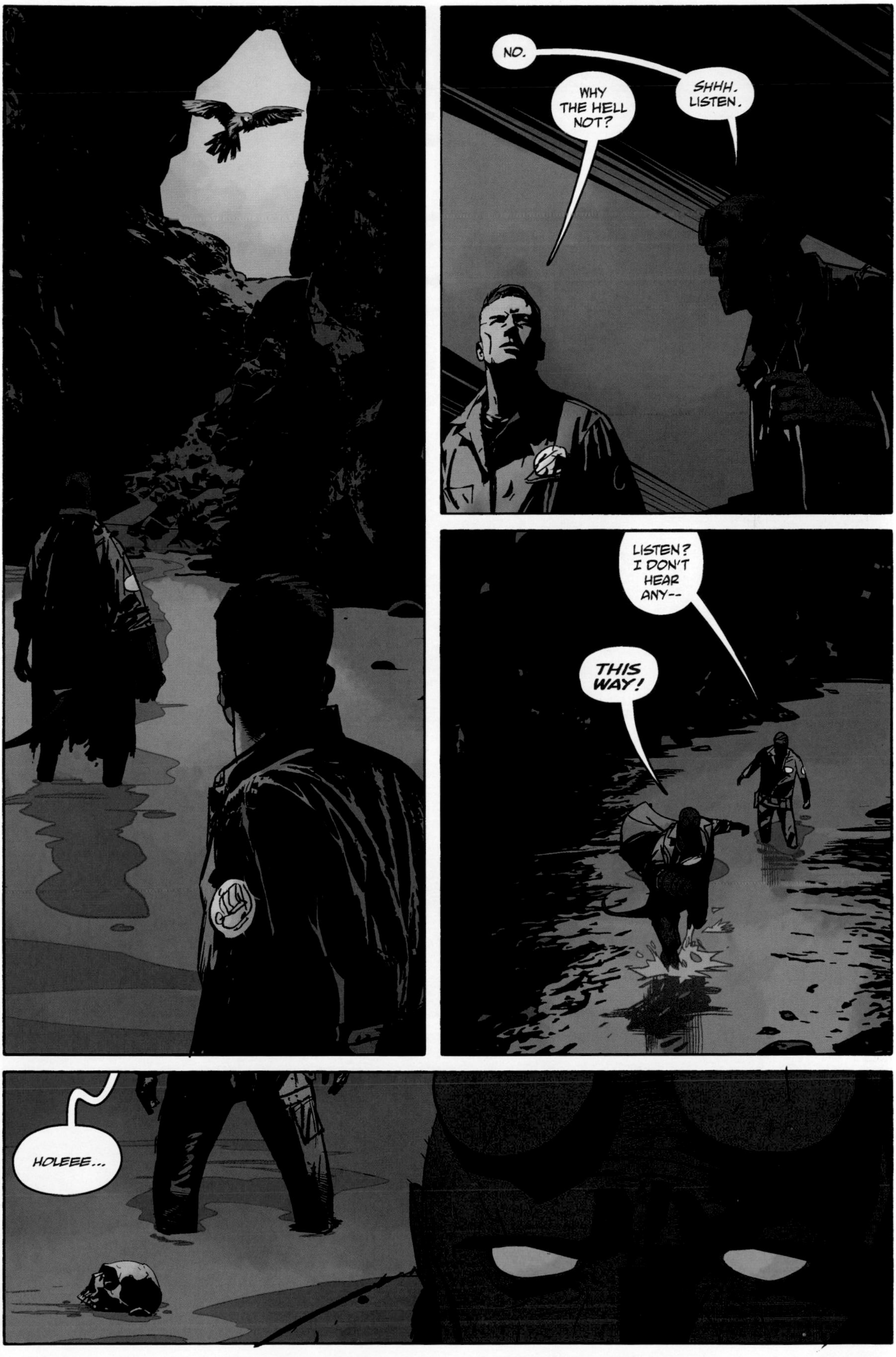
NO.
WHY THE HELL NOT?
SHHH. LISTEN.
LISTEN? I DON'T HEAR ANY--
THIS WAY!
HOLEEE...

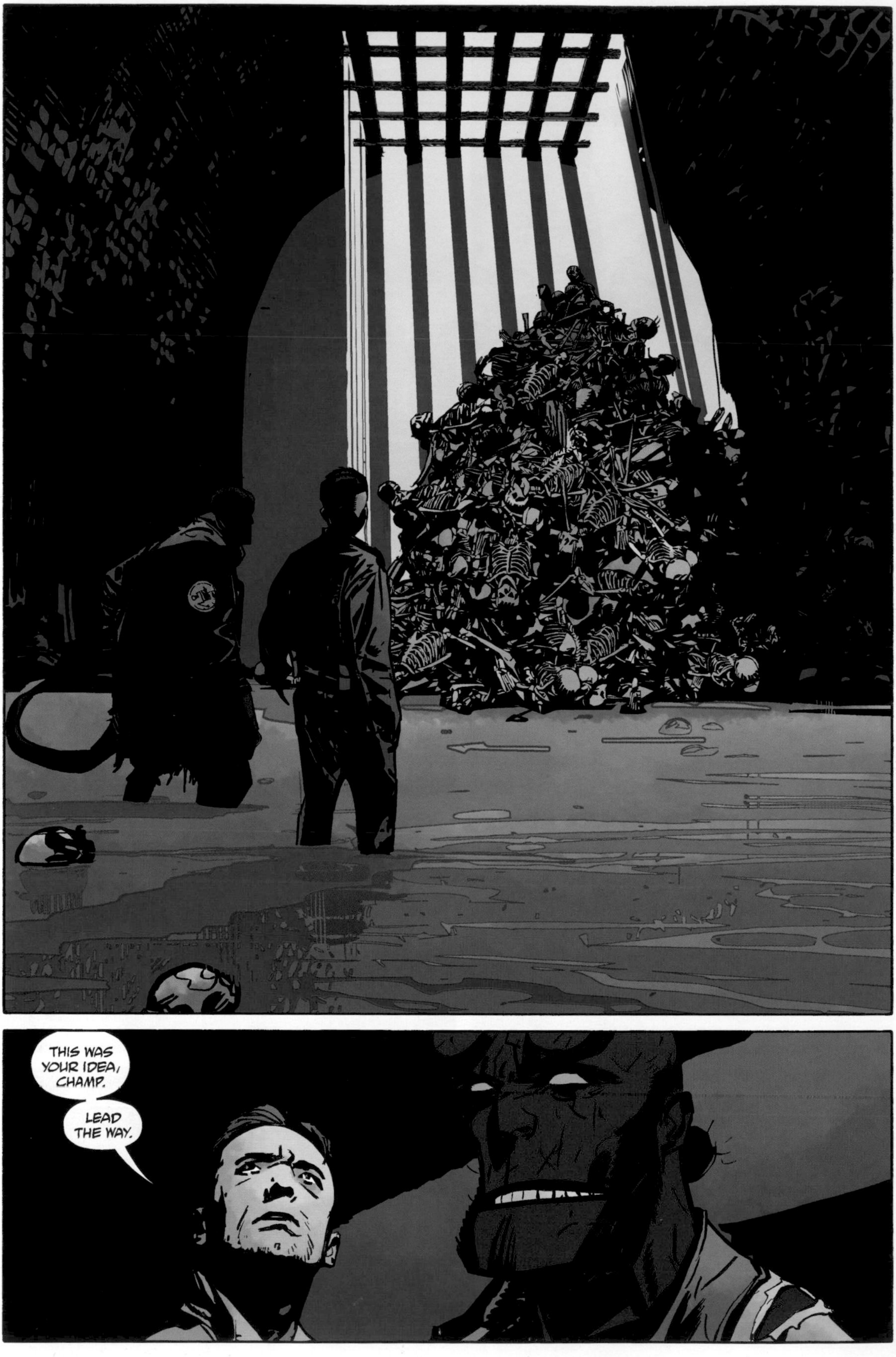
THIS WAS YOUR IDEA, CHAMP.
LEAD THE WAY.

Chapter Four

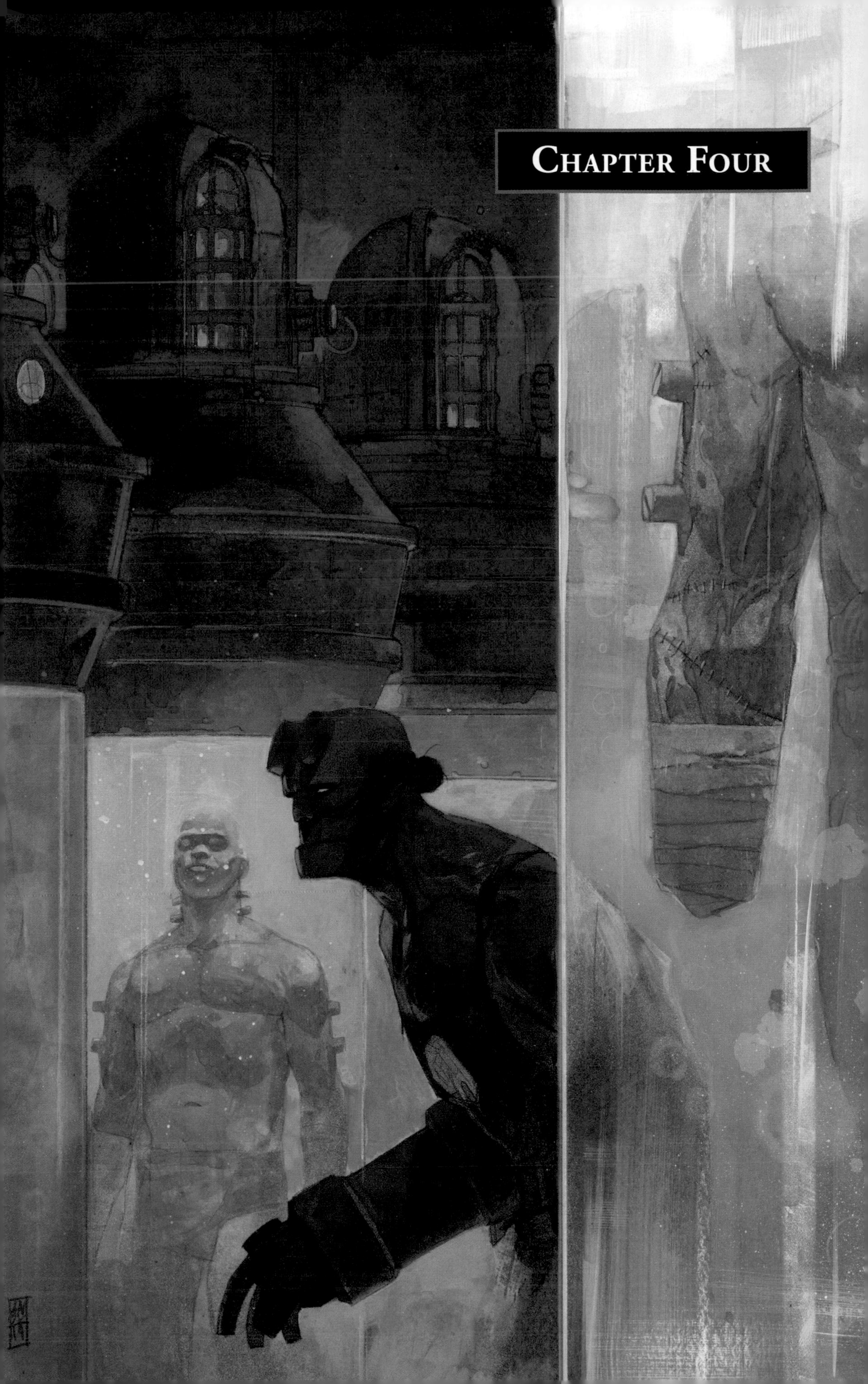

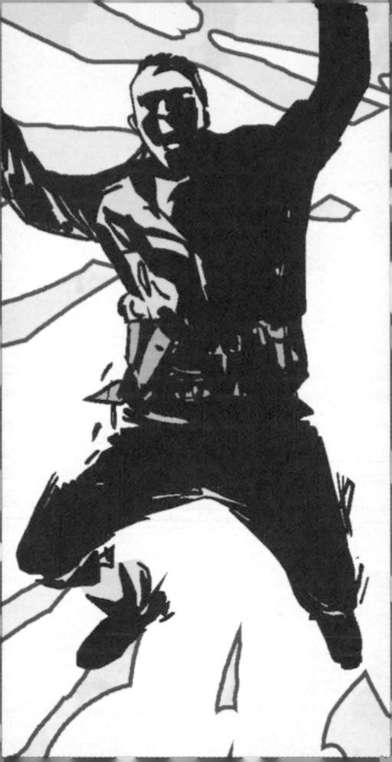

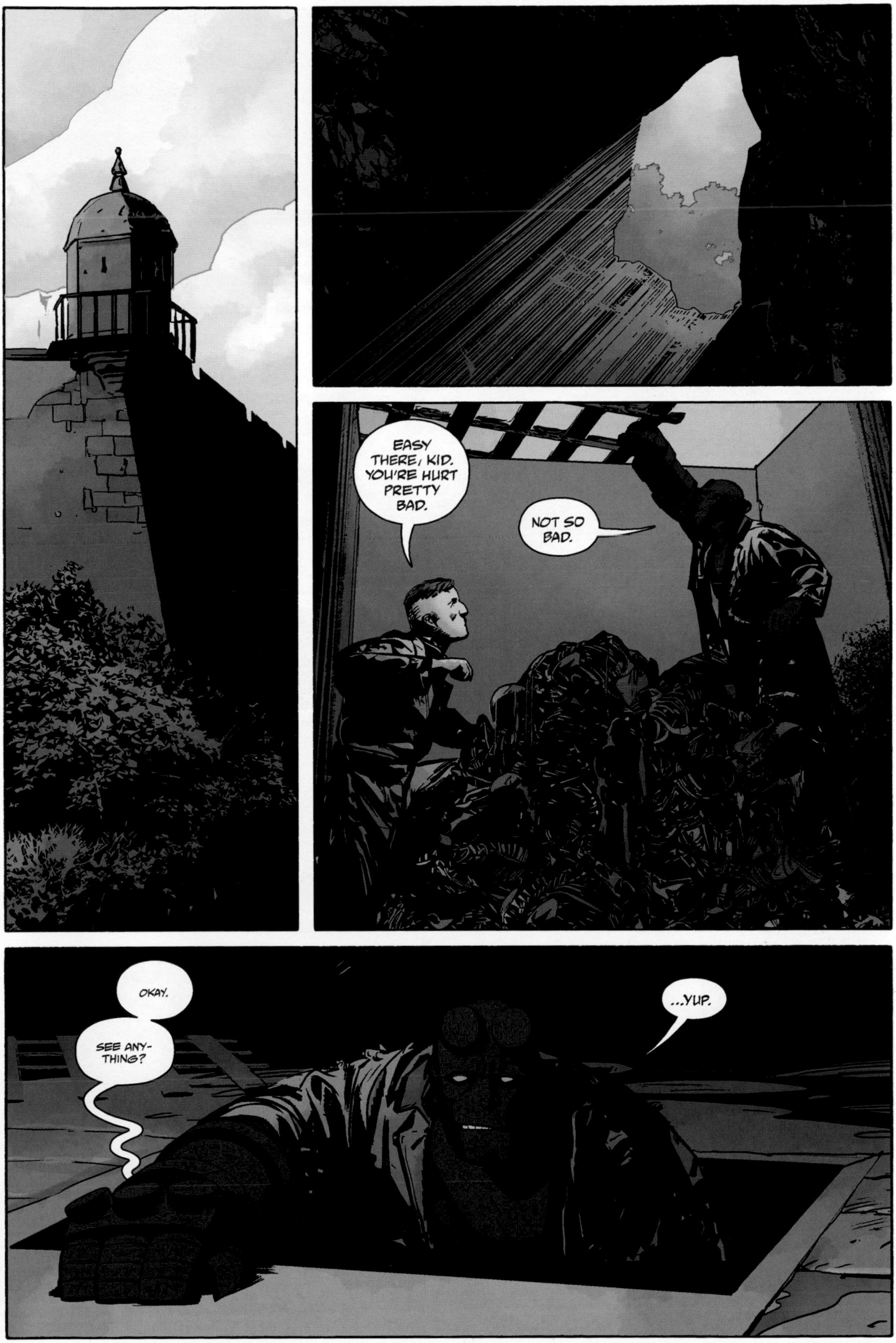
EASY THERE, KID. YOU'RE HURT PRETTY BAD.
NOT SO BAD.
OKAY.
SEE ANY-THING?
...YUP.

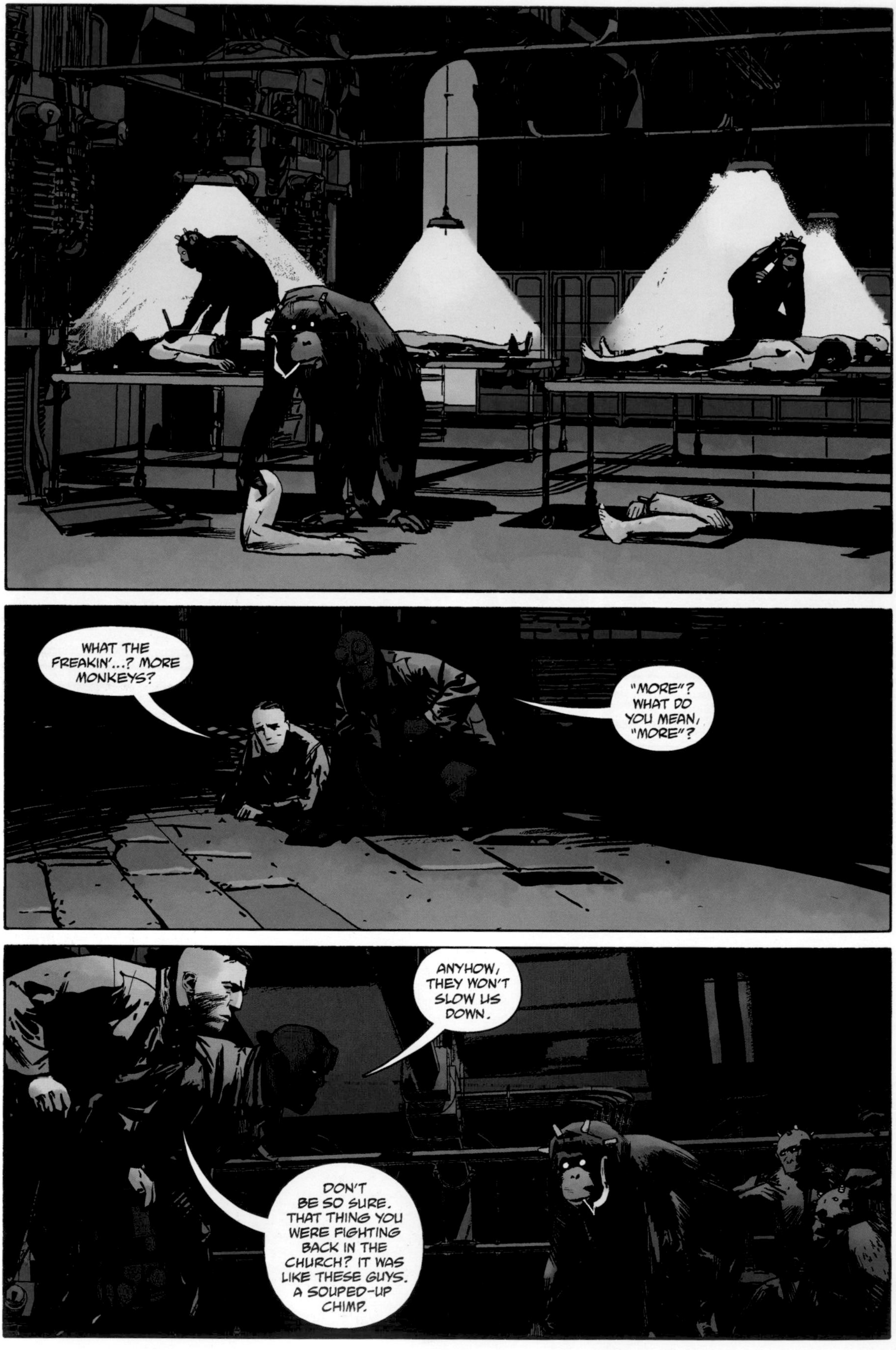
WHAT THE FREAKIN'...? MORE MONKEYS?
"MORE"? WHAT DO YOU MEAN, "MORE"?
ANYHOW, THEY WON'T SLOW US DOWN.
DON'T BE SO SURE. THAT THING YOU WERE FIGHTING BACK IN THE CHURCH? IT WAS LIKE THESE GUYS. A SOUPED-UP CHIMP.

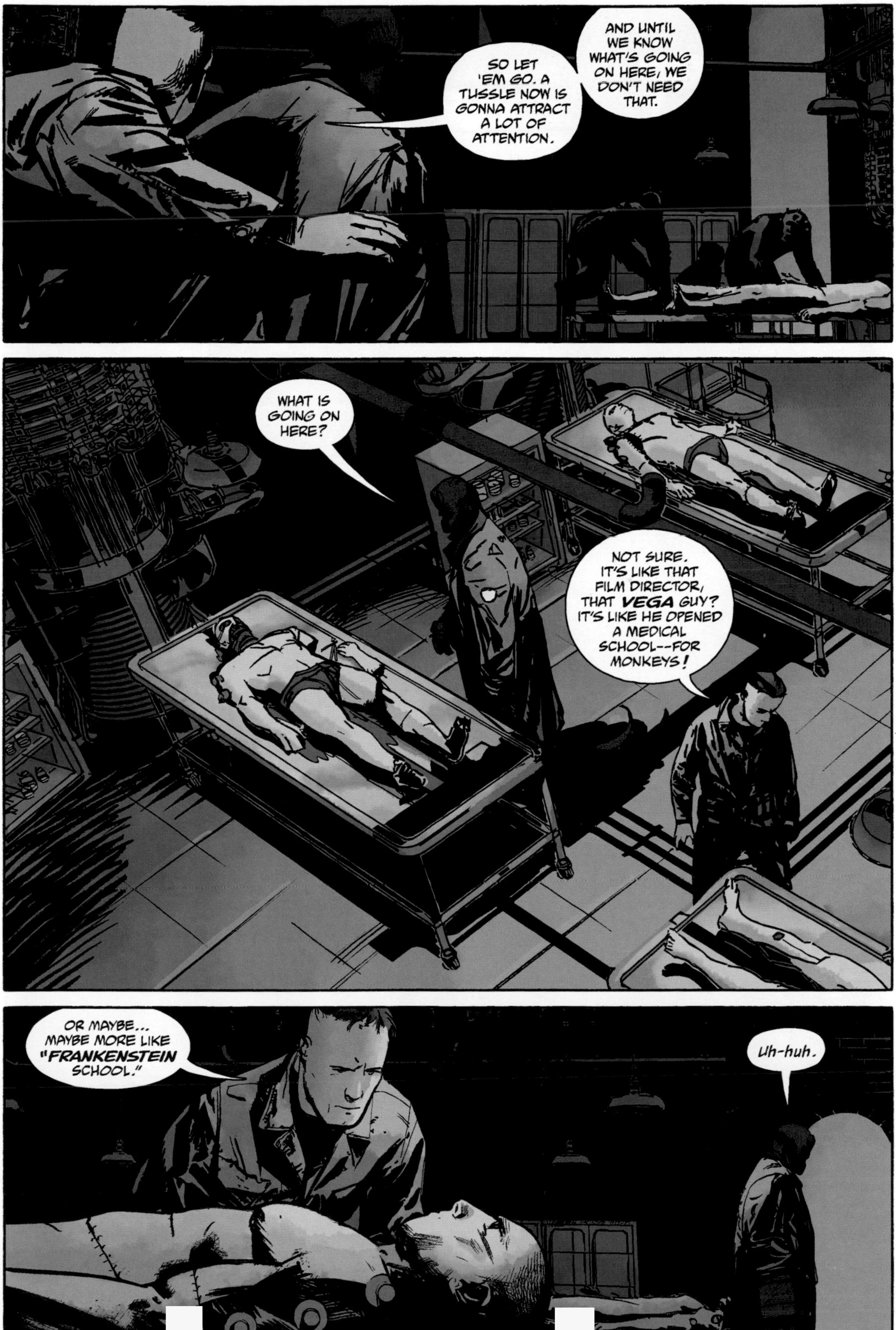
SO LET 'EM GO. A TUSSLE NOW IS GONNA ATTRACT A LOT OF ATTENTION.
AND UNTIL WE KNOW WHAT'S GOING ON HERE, WE DON'T NEED THAT.
WHAT IS GOING ON HERE?
NOT SURE. IT'S LIKE THAT FILM DIRECTOR, THAT VEGA GUY? IT'S LIKE HE OPENED A MEDICAL SCHOOL--FOR MONKEYS!
OR MAYBE... MAYBE MORE LIKE "FRANKENSTEIN SCHOOL."
Uh-huh.

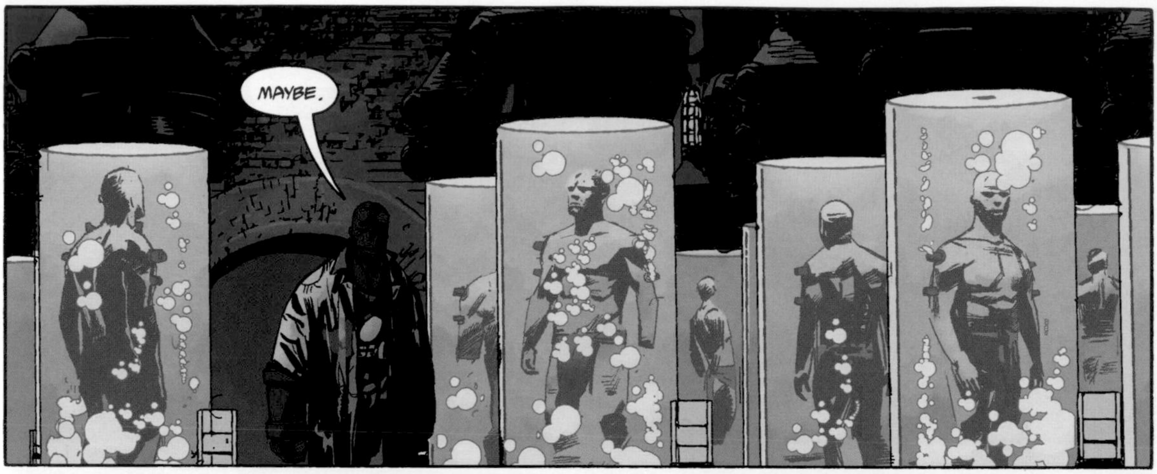
MAYBE.

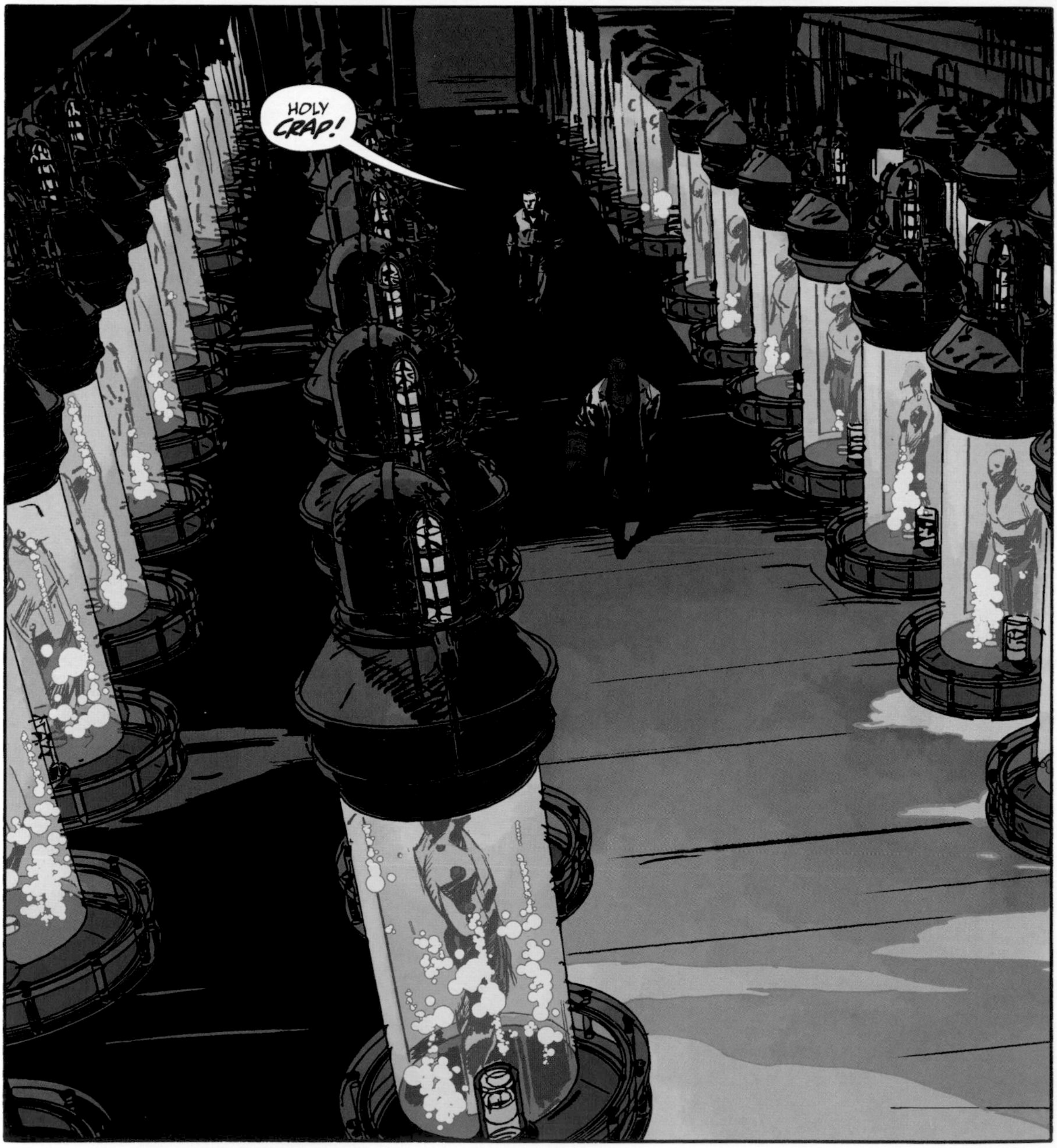
HOLY CRAP!

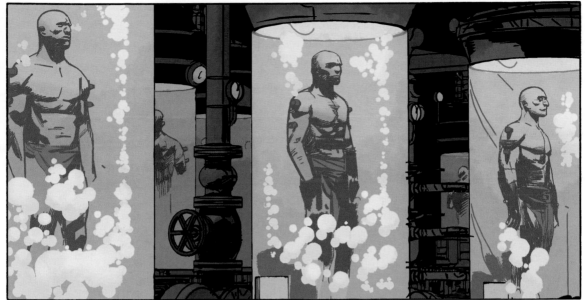

THERE MUST BE A **HUNDRED** OF THEM IN HERE!

MAYBE MORE.

BUT THAT'S A LOT OF BODY PARTS. WHERE ARE THEY GETTING THEM? I MEAN, THEY ALL LOOK SO... **FRESH.**

NO. THESE ARE ALL MEN. **HEALTHY** MEN.

FROM THE PEOPLE KILLED IN THE VILLAGE, Y'THINK?

MY GUESS IS, THAT CHIMP WAS KILLING FOLKS ONLY TO SCARE 'EM AWAY, SO VEGA COULD BE LEFT ALONE TO DO...WELL, WHATEVER **THIS** IS.

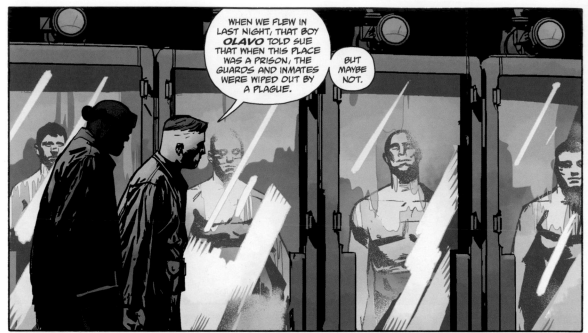

WHEN WE FLEW IN LAST NIGHT, THAT BOY *OLAVO* TOLD SUE THAT WHEN THIS PLACE WAS A PRISON, THE GUARDS AND INMATES WERE WIPED OUT BY A PLAGUE.

BUT MAYBE NOT.

AND MAYBE ALL THOSE *GRAVES* OUT THERE ARE EMPTY.

ARCHIE, YOU'VE BEEN DOING THIS A WHILE. IS THIS... NORMAL? I MEAN FOR WHAT YOU GUYS DO.

I'VE NEVER SEEN ANYTHING LIKE IT--BUT THE PROFESSOR, HE MENTIONED SOMETHING TO ME ONCE.

"HE SAW IT RIGHT AFTER THE WAR, IN BERLIN. MEN--OR *THINGS,* ANYWAY--IN BIG TUBES."

REALLY? I NEVER HEARD HIM TALK ABOUT THAT.

NO SURPRISE THERE. I THINK HE REGRETTED TELLING *ME.*

I THINK SOMETHING HAPPENED TO HIM THERE, OR HE *SAW* SOMETHING...

I DON'T KNOW. WHAT-EVER IT IS, HE JUST DOESN'T LIKE TO TALK--

SSHHK

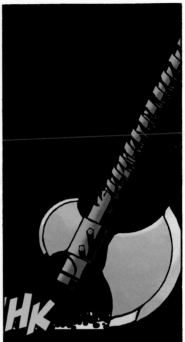

WHOA... *THAT'S* NOT A MONKEY.

NO.

RRRRRRRRRR

IT SURE AIN'T.

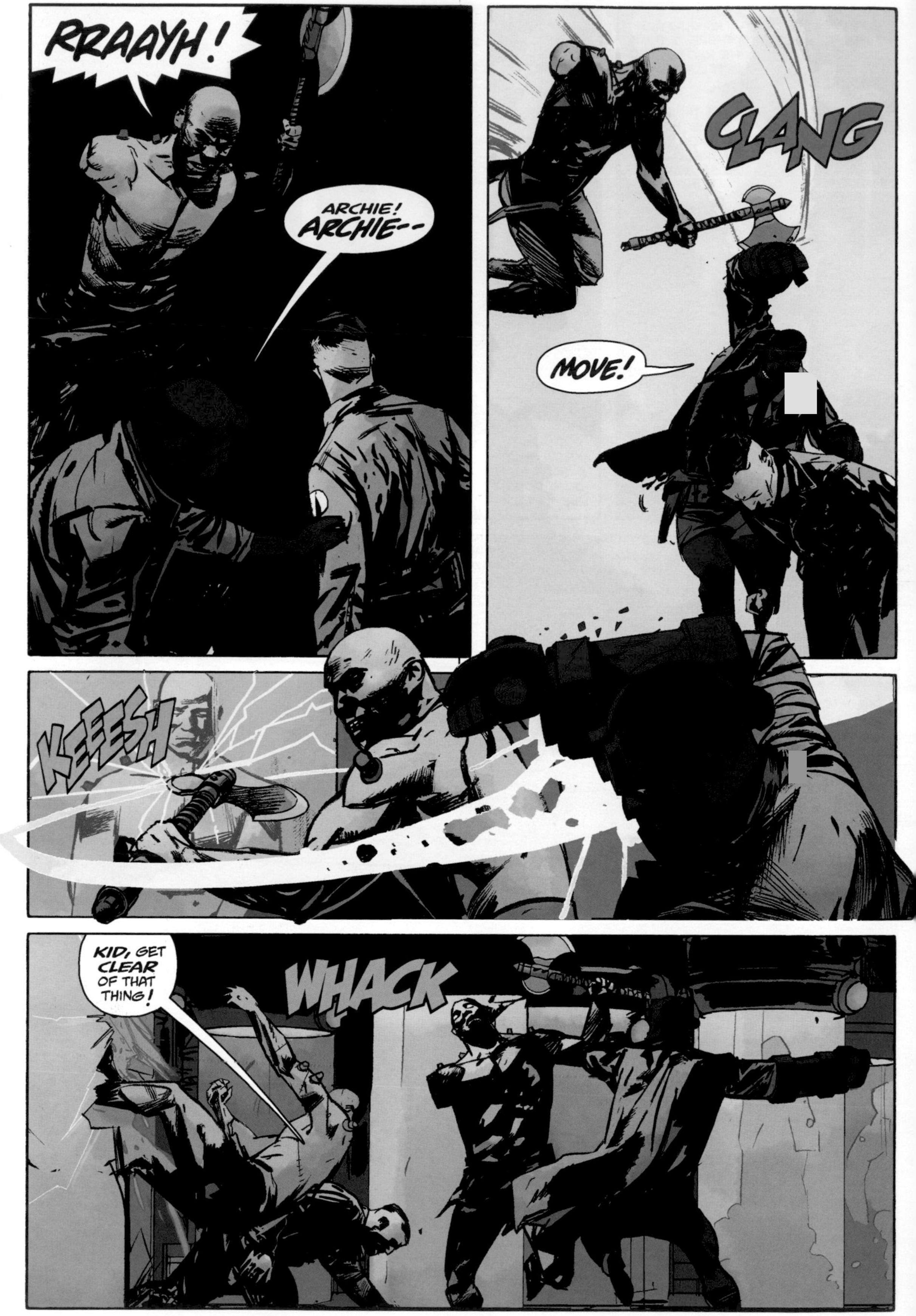
RRAAYH!
ARCHIE! ARCHIE--
CLANG
MOVE!
KEEESH
KID, GET CLEAR OF THAT THING!
WHACK

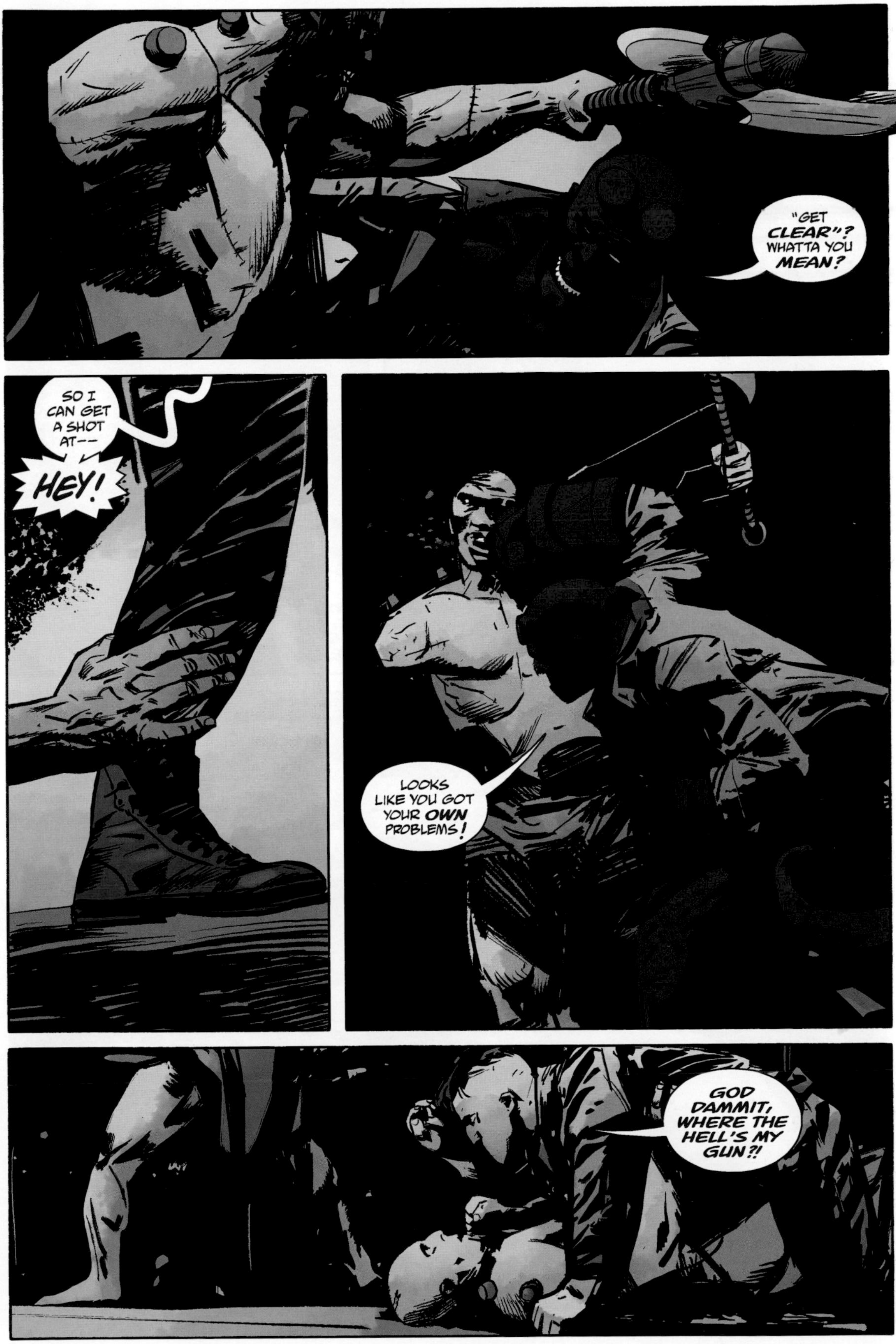
"GET CLEAR"? WHATTA YOU MEAN?
SO I CAN GET A SHOT AT--
HEY!
LOOKS LIKE YOU GOT YOUR OWN PROBLEMS!
GOD DAMMIT, WHERE THE HELL'S MY GUN?!

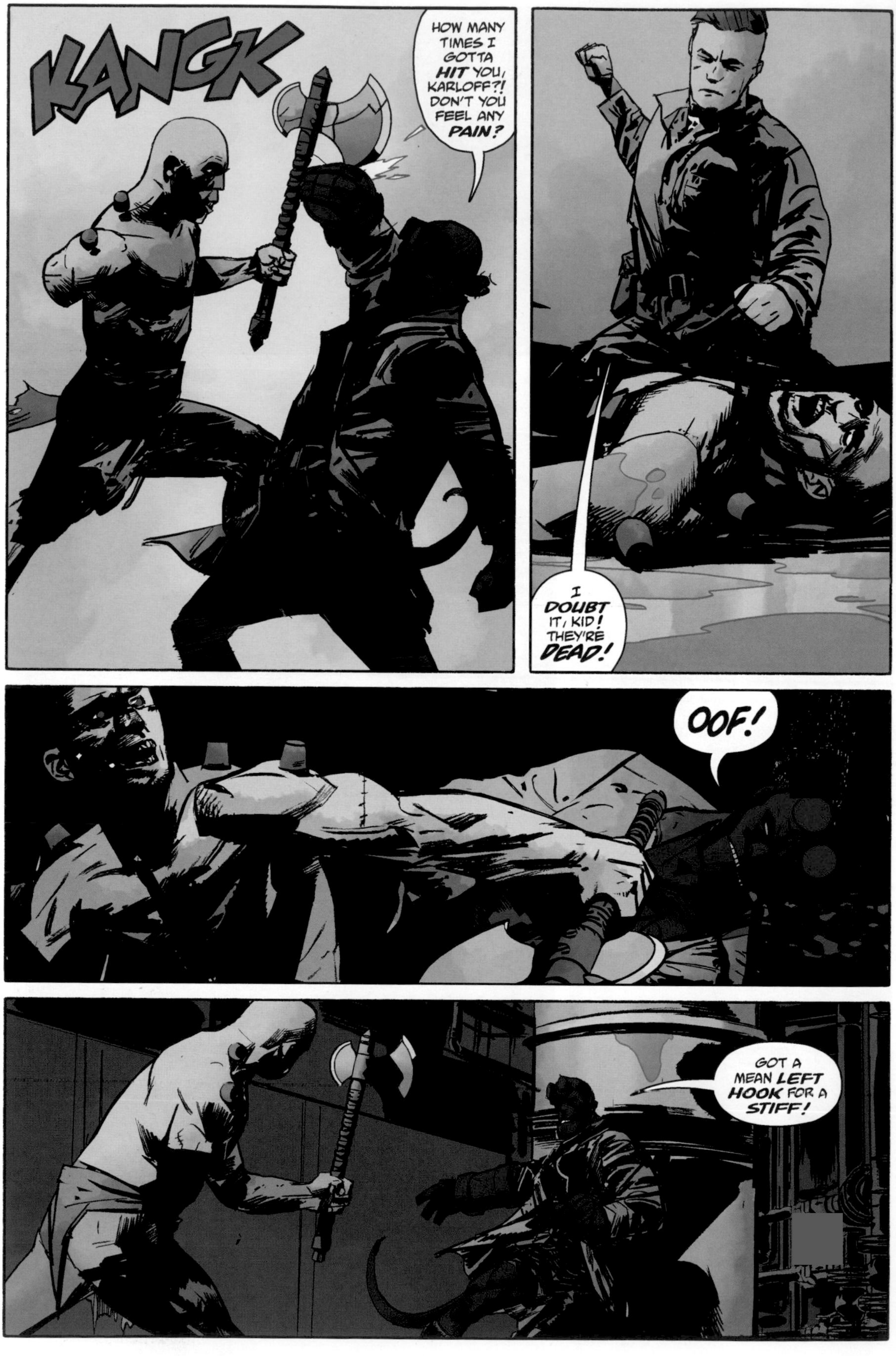
KANGK
HOW MANY TIMES I GOTTA HIT YOU, KARLOFF?! DON'T YOU FEEL ANY PAIN?
I DOUBT IT, KID! THEY'RE DEAD!
OOF!
GOT A MEAN LEFT HOOK FOR A STIFF!

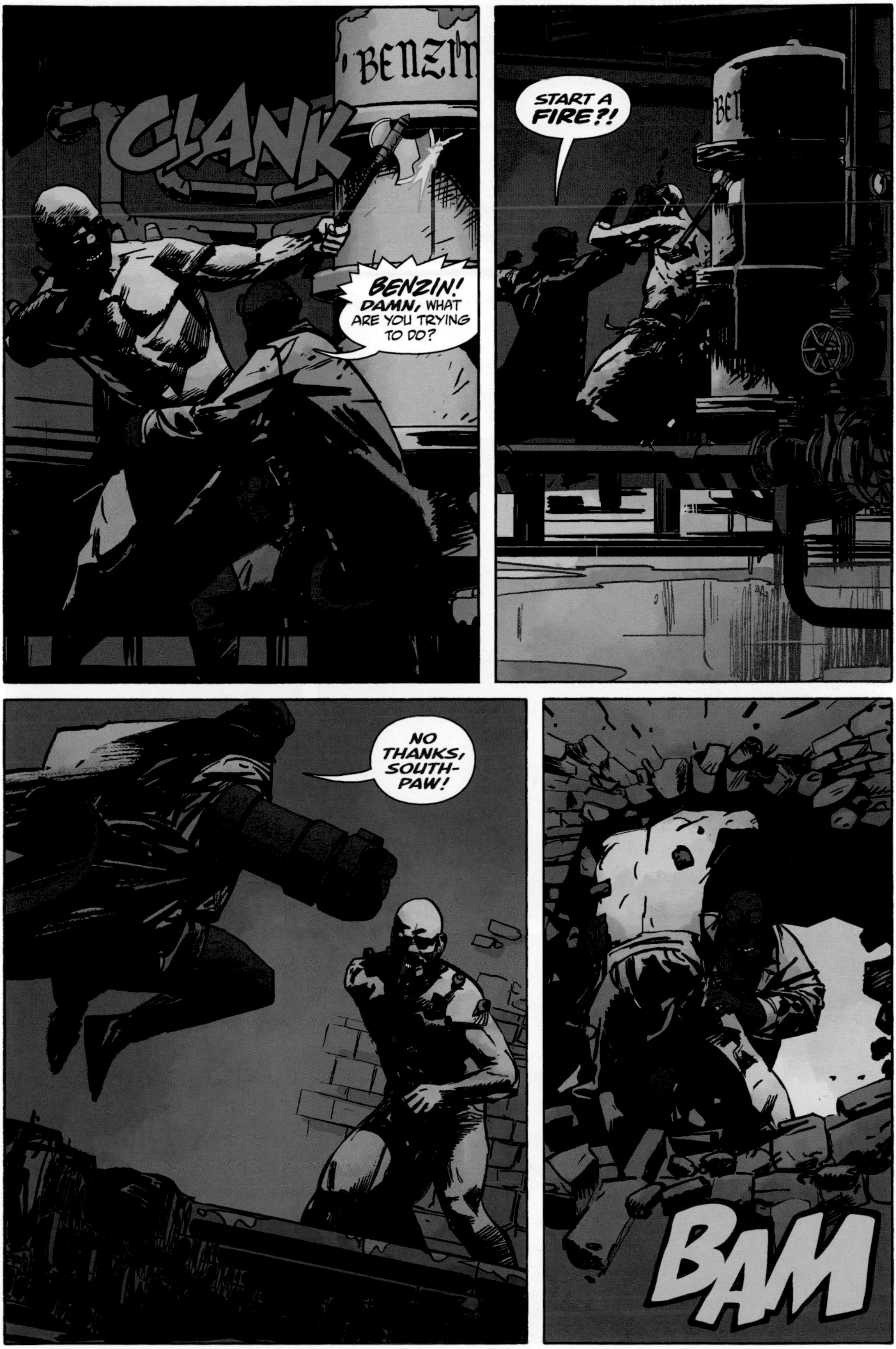
CLANK
BENZIN! DAMN, WHAT ARE YOU TRYING TO DO?
START A FIRE?!
NO THANKS, SOUTH-PAW!
BAM

WAIT—— WHERE...?

THIS JUST GETS WEIRDER AND WEIRDER.

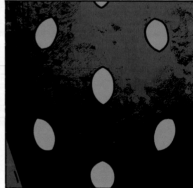

GUH!

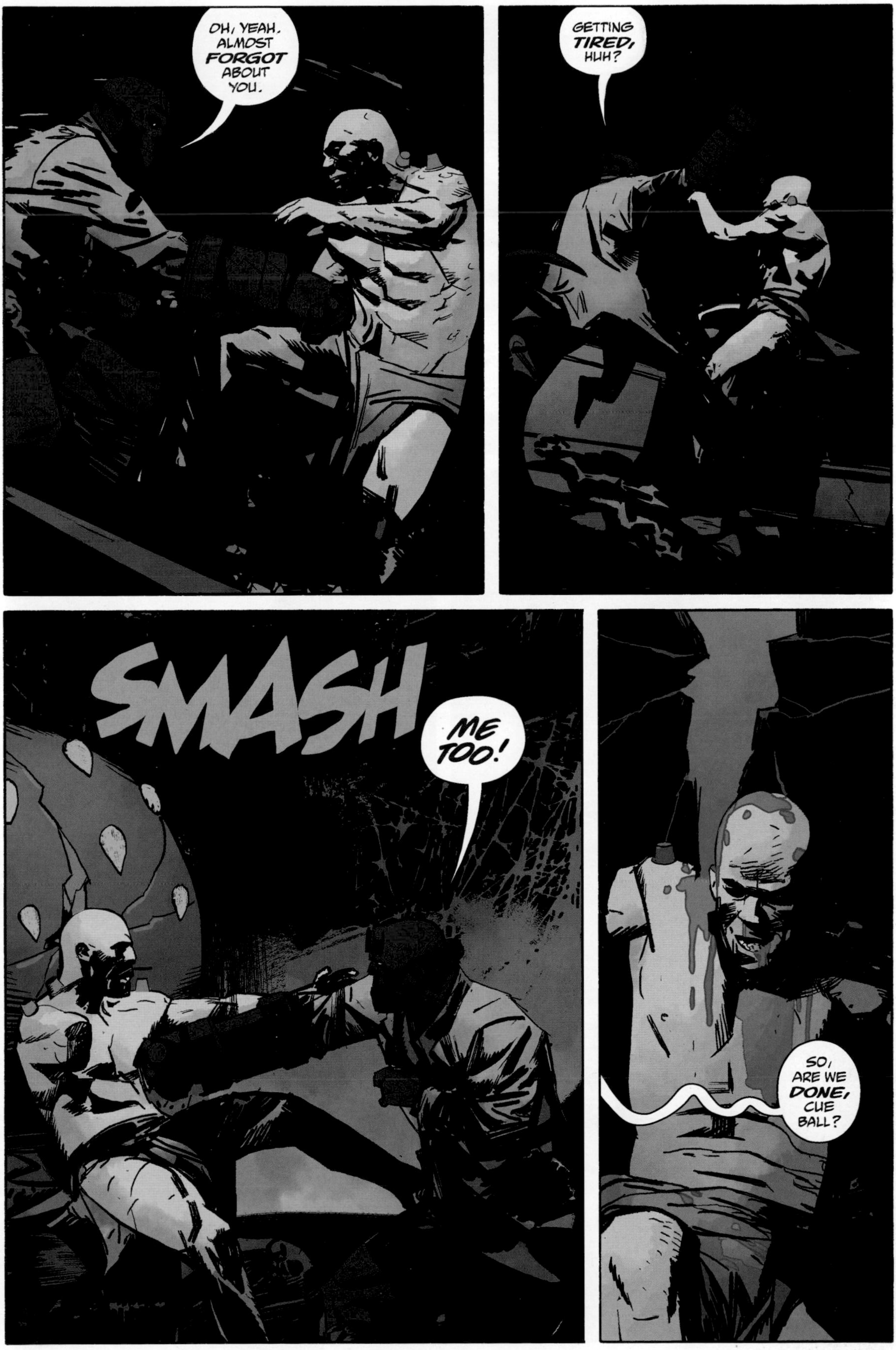
OH, YEAH. ALMOST FORGOT ABOUT YOU.
GETTING TIRED, HUH?
SMASH
ME TOO!
SO, ARE WE DONE, CUE BALL?

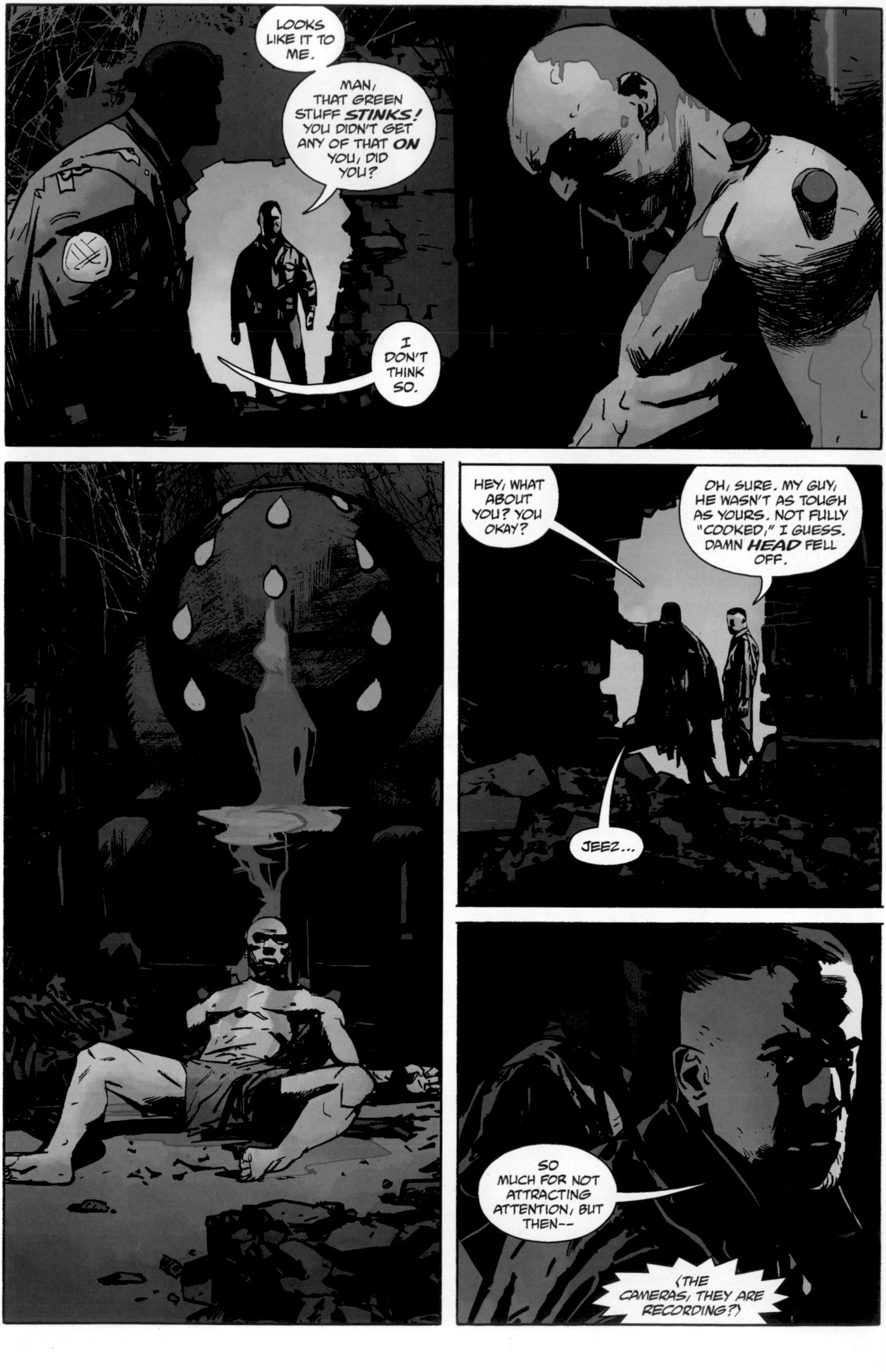
LOOKS LIKE IT TO ME.
MAN, THAT GREEN STUFF STINKS! YOU DIDN'T GET ANY OF THAT ON YOU, DID YOU?
I DON'T THINK SO.
HEY, WHAT ABOUT YOU? YOU OKAY?
OH, SURE. MY GUY, HE WASN'T AS TOUGH AS YOURS. NOT FULLY "COOKED," I GUESS. DAMN HEAD FELL OFF.
JEEZ...
SO MUCH FOR NOT ATTRACTING ATTENTION, BUT THEN--
<THE CAMERAS, THEY ARE RECORDING?>

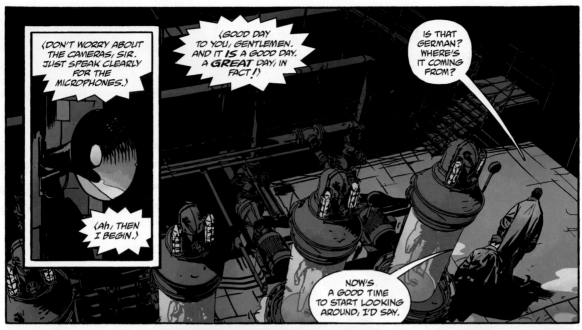

⟨DON'T WORRY ABOUT THE CAMERAS, SIR. JUST SPEAK CLEARLY FOR THE MICROPHONES.⟩

⟨GOOD DAY TO YOU, GENTLEMEN. AND IT *IS* A GOOD DAY. A *GREAT* DAY, IN FACT!⟩

IS THAT GERMAN? WHERE'S IT COMING FROM?

⟨AH, THEN I BEGIN.⟩

NOW'S A GOOD TIME TO START LOOKING AROUND, I'D SAY.

⟨FOR THIS IS THE FIRST DAY THAT OUR RENDEZVOUS WITH DESTINY BECOMES CLEAR. IT IS THE DAY THAT WE MUST ASK OURSELVES, WHAT WILL WE DO?⟩

⟨WILL WE PRESERVE FOR THE FUTURE THIS, THE LAST BEST HOPE OF MAN ON EARTH? OR WILL WE TAKE THE FIRST STEP INTO A THOUSAND YEARS OF A BLACK AND DEADLY NIGHT?⟩

⟨NOT WORK WITH US, BUT WORK *FOR* US!⟩

⟨NO, IT IS NOT OUR INTENTION TO DO AWAY WITH THE WORLD ORDER. RATHER WE SHALL MAKE IT FINALLY WORK!⟩

⟨TRANSLATED FROM GERMAN⟩

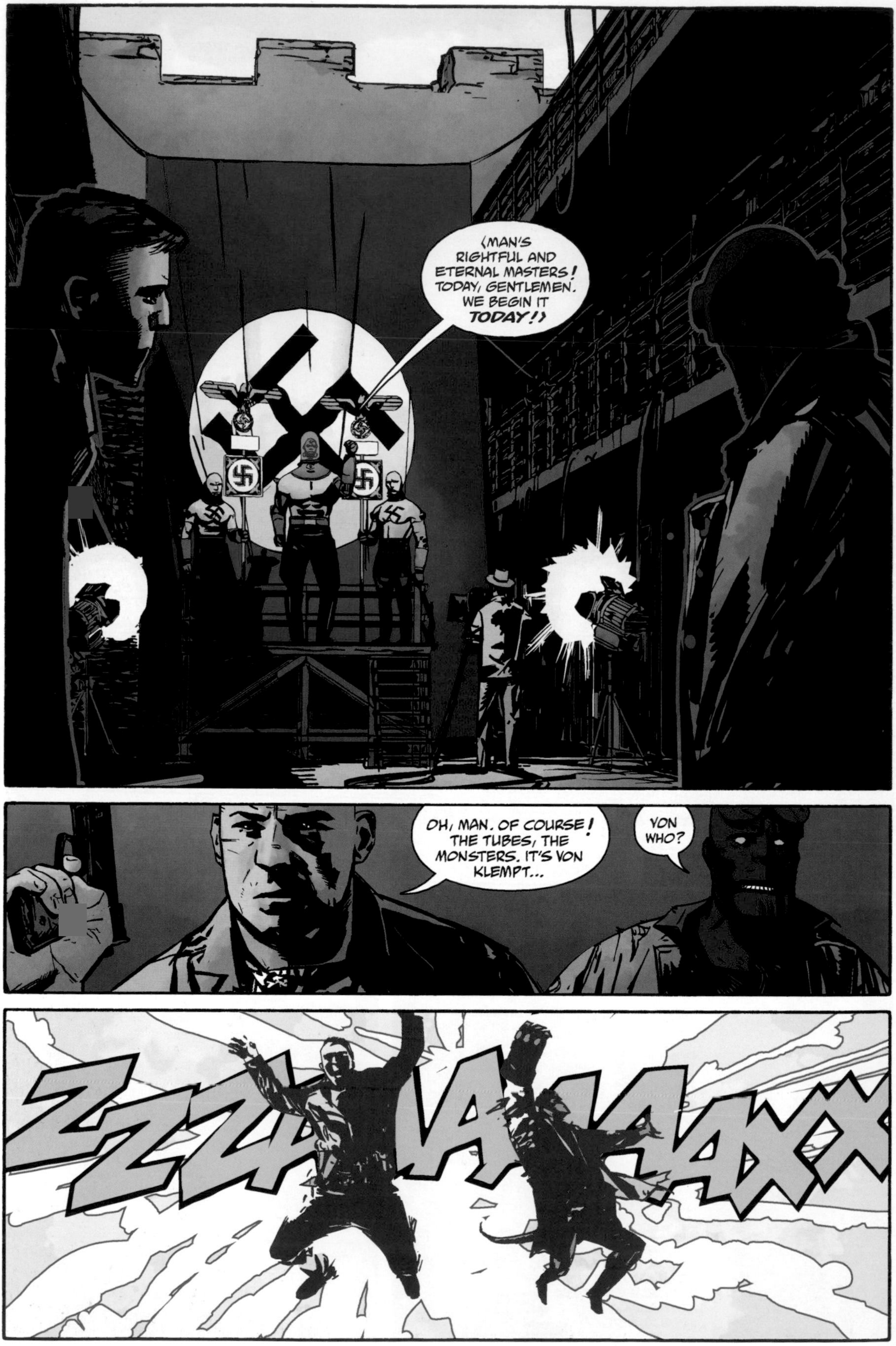
‹MAN'S RIGHTFUL AND ETERNAL MASTERS! TODAY, GENTLEMEN. WE BEGIN IT TODAY!›
OH, MAN. OF COURSE! THE TUBES, THE MONSTERS. IT'S VON KLEMPT...
VON WHO?
ZZZAAAAAXX

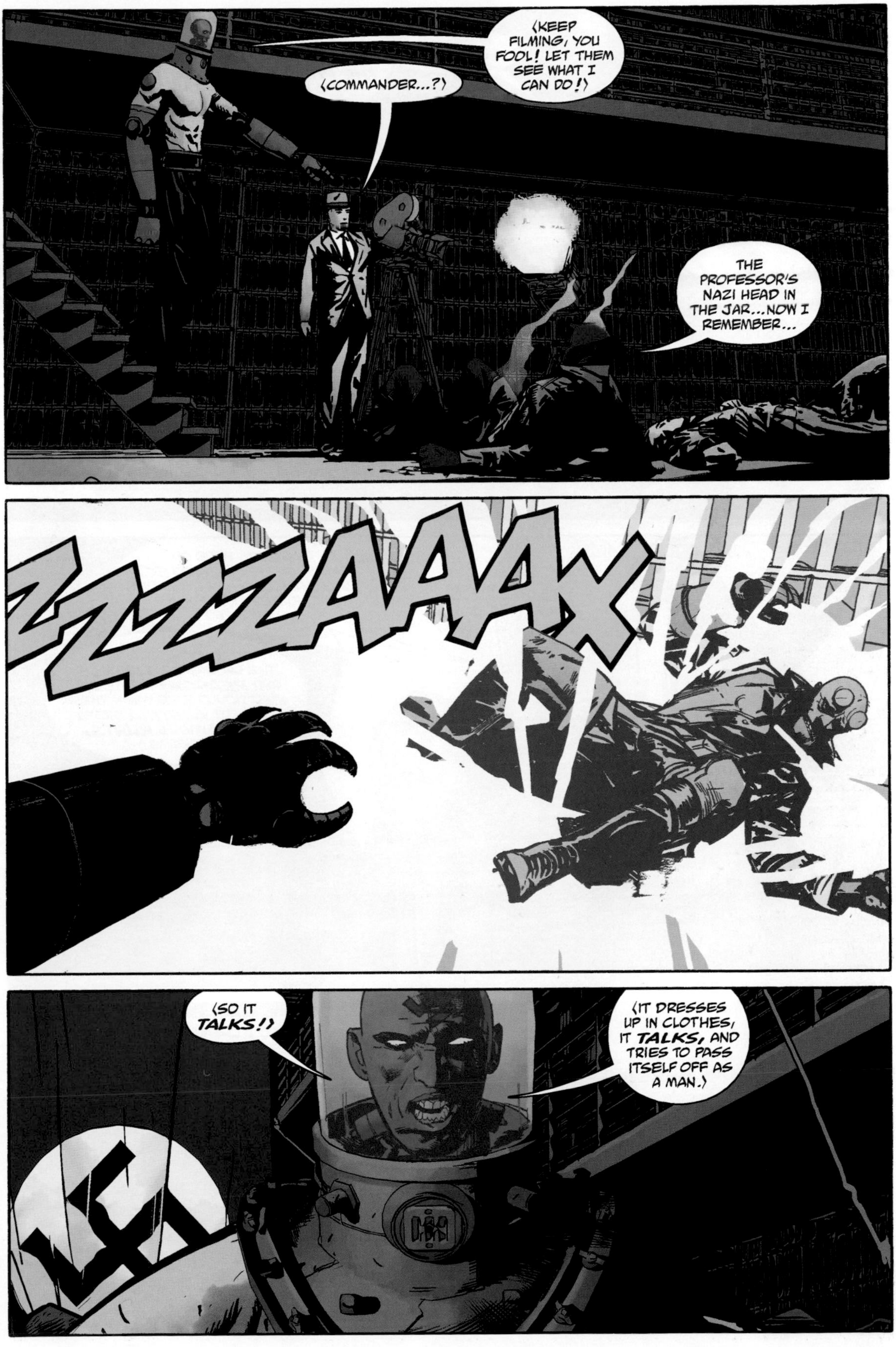

‹COMMANDER...?›
‹KEEP FILMING, YOU FOOL! LET THEM SEE WHAT I CAN DO!›
THE PROFESSOR'S NAZI HEAD IN THE JAR...NOW I REMEMBER...
ZZZZAAAX
‹SO IT TALKS!›
‹IT DRESSES UP IN CLOTHES, IT TALKS, AND TRIES TO PASS ITSELF OFF AS A MAN.›

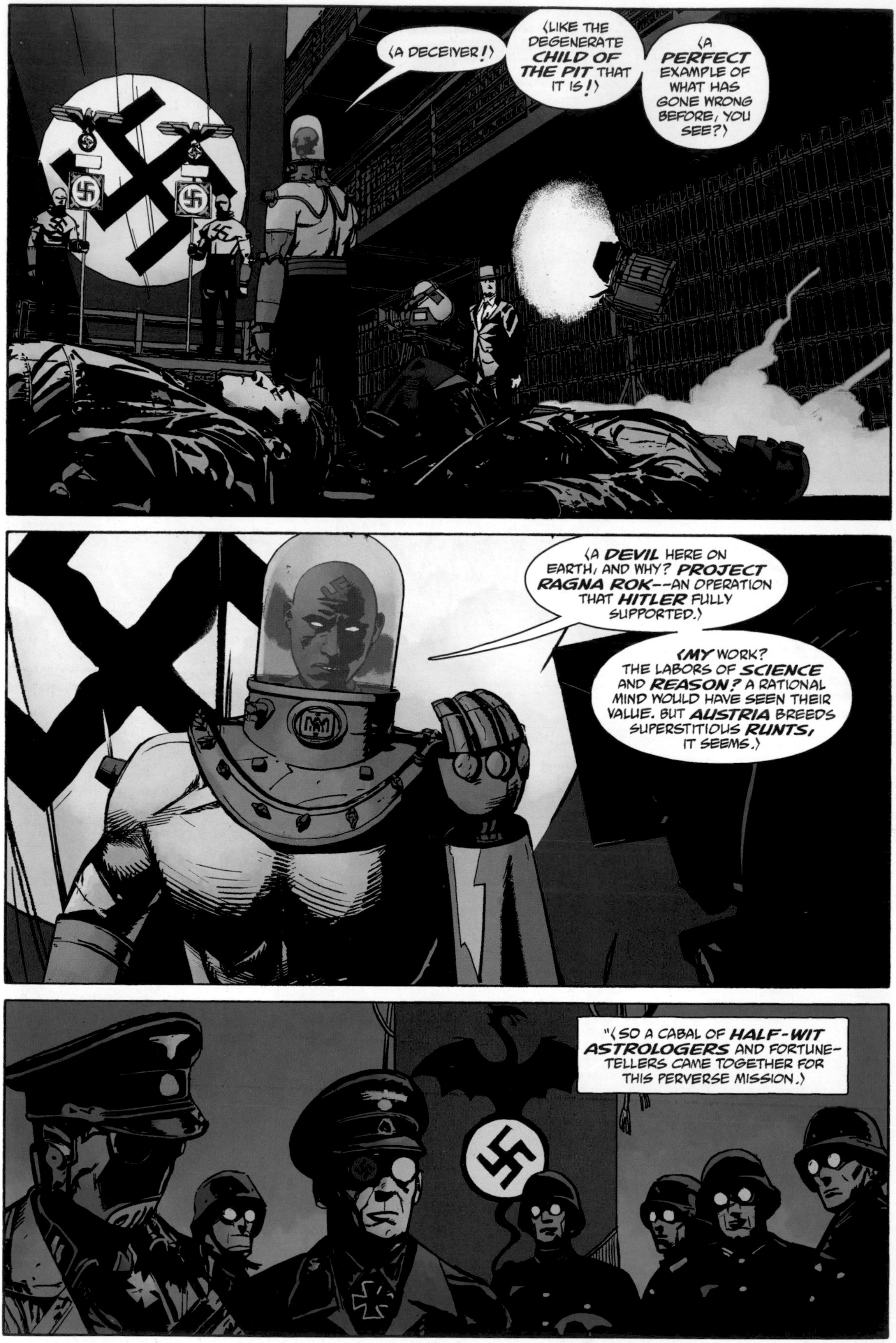

⟨A DECEIVER!⟩
⟨LIKE THE DEGENERATE CHILD OF THE PIT THAT IT IS!⟩
⟨A PERFECT EXAMPLE OF WHAT HAS GONE WRONG BEFORE, YOU SEE?⟩
⟨A DEVIL HERE ON EARTH, AND WHY? PROJECT RAGNA ROK--AN OPERATION THAT HITLER FULLY SUPPORTED.⟩
⟨MY WORK? THE LABORS OF SCIENCE AND REASON? A RATIONAL MIND WOULD HAVE SEEN THEIR VALUE. BUT AUSTRIA BREEDS SUPERSTITIOUS RUNTS, IT SEEMS.⟩
"⟨SO A CABAL OF HALF-WIT ASTROLOGERS AND FORTUNE-TELLERS CAME TOGETHER FOR THIS PERVERSE MISSION.⟩

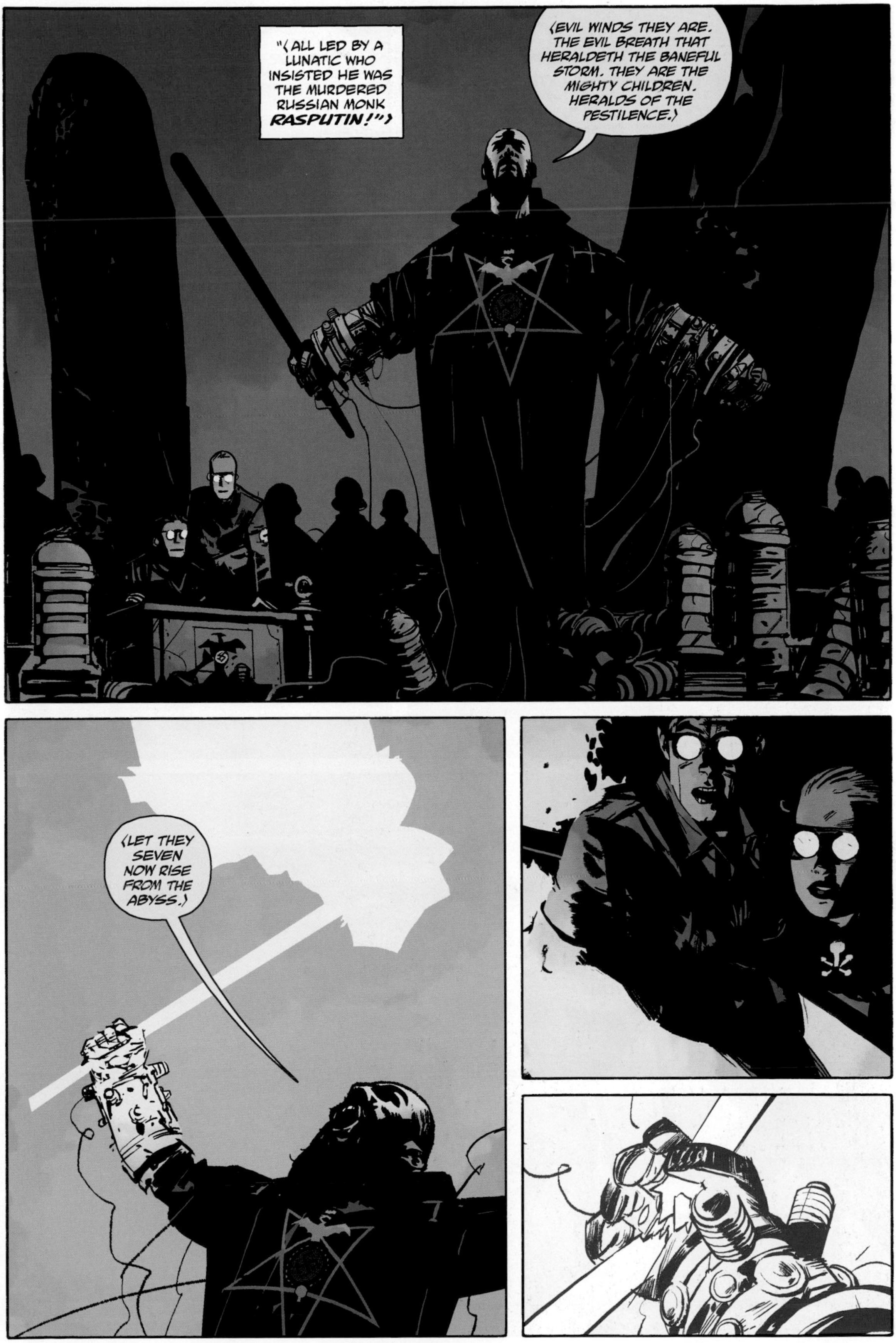
"⟨ALL LED BY A LUNATIC WHO INSISTED HE WAS THE MURDERED RUSSIAN MONK **RASPUTIN!**"⟩
⟨EVIL WINDS THEY ARE. THE EVIL BREATH THAT HERALDETH THE BANEFUL STORM. THEY ARE THE MIGHTY CHILDREN. HERALDS OF THE PESTILENCE.⟩
⟨LET THEY SEVEN NOW RISE FROM THE ABYSS.⟩

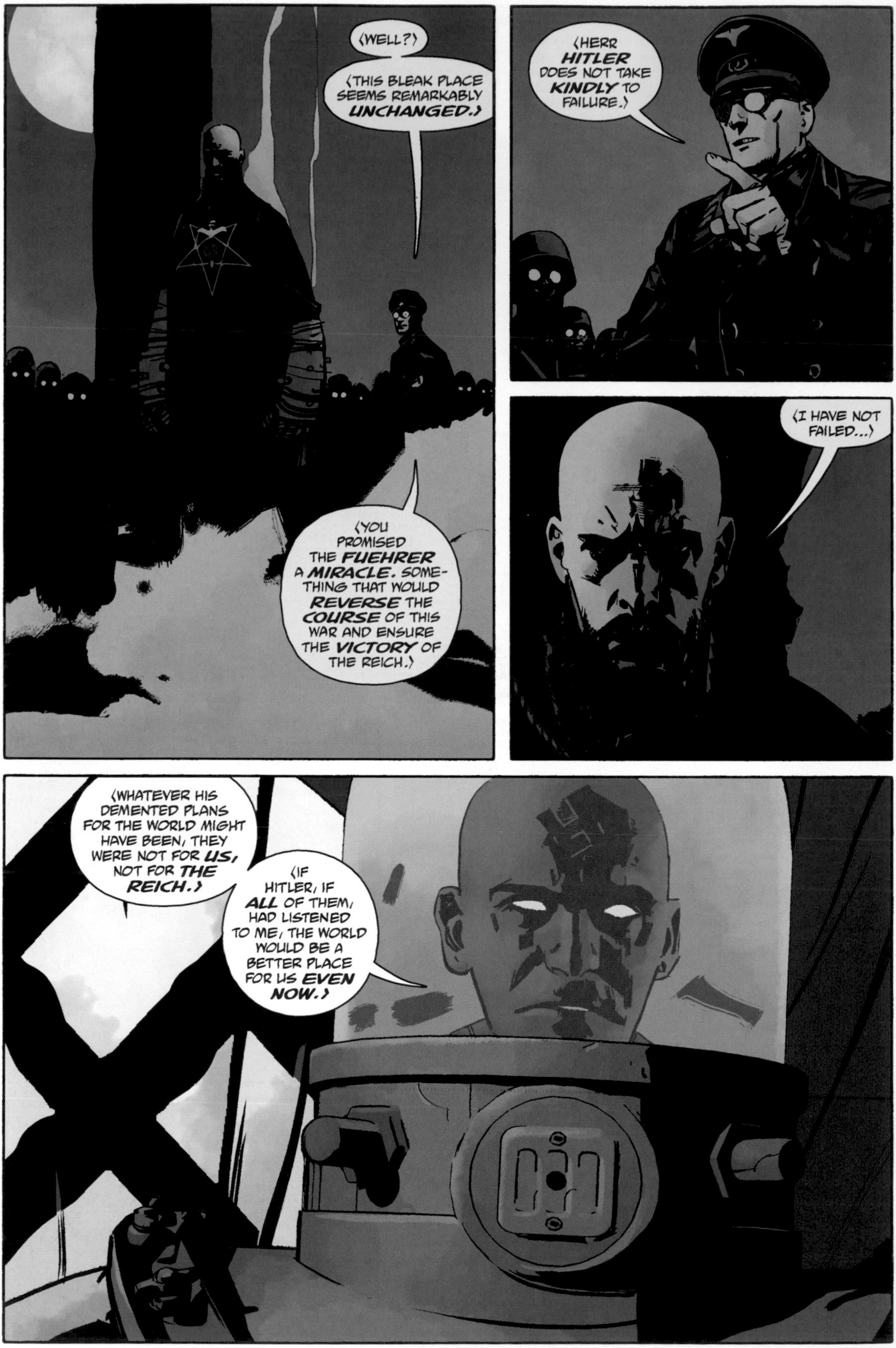
‹WELL?›
‹THIS BLEAK PLACE SEEMS REMARKABLY UNCHANGED.›
‹YOU PROMISED THE FUEHRER A MIRACLE. SOME-THING THAT WOULD REVERSE THE COURSE OF THIS WAR AND ENSURE THE VICTORY OF THE REICH.›
‹HERR HITLER DOES NOT TAKE KINDLY TO FAILURE.›
‹I HAVE NOT FAILED...›
‹WHATEVER HIS DEMENTED PLANS FOR THE WORLD MIGHT HAVE BEEN, THEY WERE NOT FOR US, NOT FOR THE REICH.›
‹IF HITLER, IF ALL OF THEM, HAD LISTENED TO ME, THE WORLD WOULD BE A BETTER PLACE FOR US EVEN NOW.›

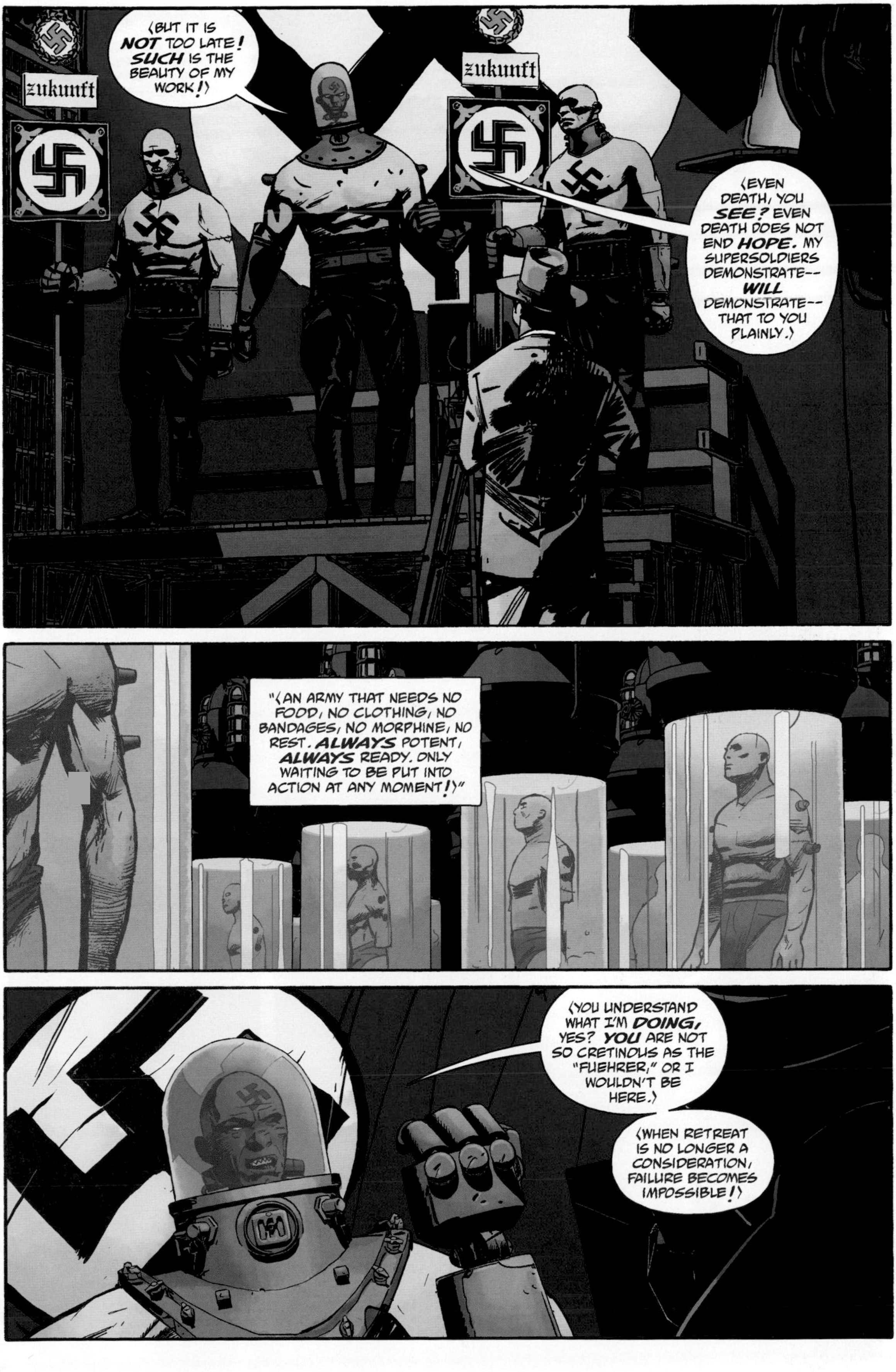
zukunft
zukunft
⟨BUT IT IS NOT TOO LATE! SUCH IS THE BEAUTY OF MY WORK!⟩
⟨EVEN DEATH, YOU SEE? EVEN DEATH DOES NOT END HOPE. MY SUPERSOLDIERS DEMONSTRATE-- WILL DEMONSTRATE-- THAT TO YOU PLAINLY.⟩
"⟨AN ARMY THAT NEEDS NO FOOD, NO CLOTHING, NO BANDAGES, NO MORPHINE, NO REST. ALWAYS POTENT, ALWAYS READY. ONLY WAITING TO BE PUT INTO ACTION AT ANY MOMENT!⟩"
⟨YOU UNDERSTAND WHAT I'M DOING, YES? YOU ARE NOT SO CRETINOUS AS THE "FUEHRER," OR I WOULDN'T BE HERE.⟩
⟨WHEN RETREAT IS NO LONGER A CONSIDERATION, FAILURE BECOMES IMPOSSIBLE!⟩

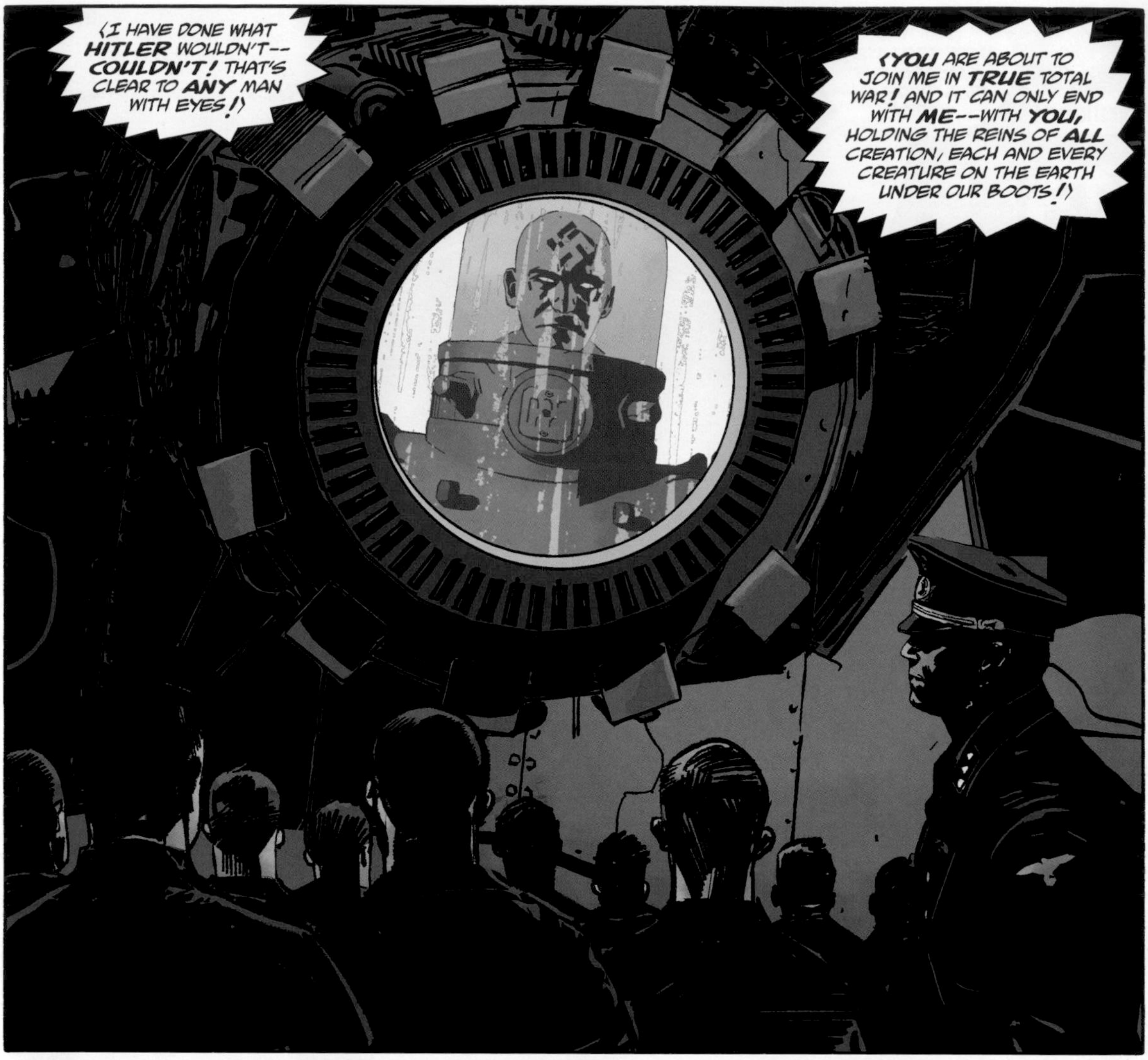
⟨I HAVE DONE WHAT HITLER WOULDN'T-- COULDN'T! THAT'S CLEAR TO ANY MAN WITH EYES!⟩
⟨YOU ARE ABOUT TO JOIN ME IN TRUE TOTAL WAR! AND IT CAN ONLY END WITH ME--WITH YOU, HOLDING THE REINS OF ALL CREATION, EACH AND EVERY CREATURE ON THE EARTH UNDER OUR BOOTS!⟩
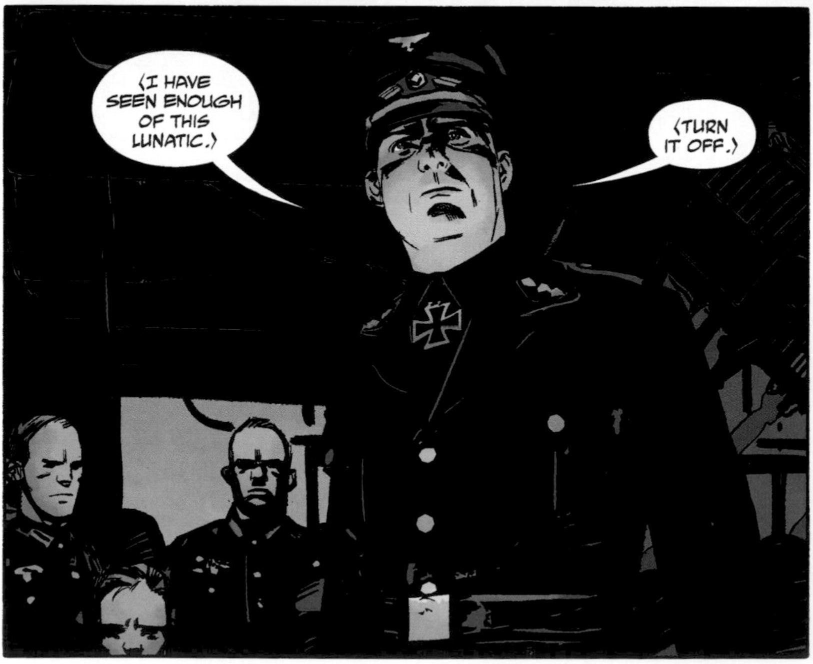
⟨I HAVE SEEN ENOUGH OF THIS LUNATIC.⟩
⟨TURN IT OFF.⟩
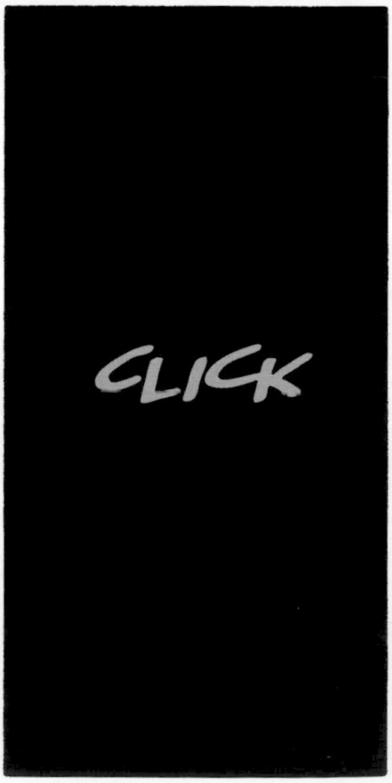
CLICK

Chapter Five

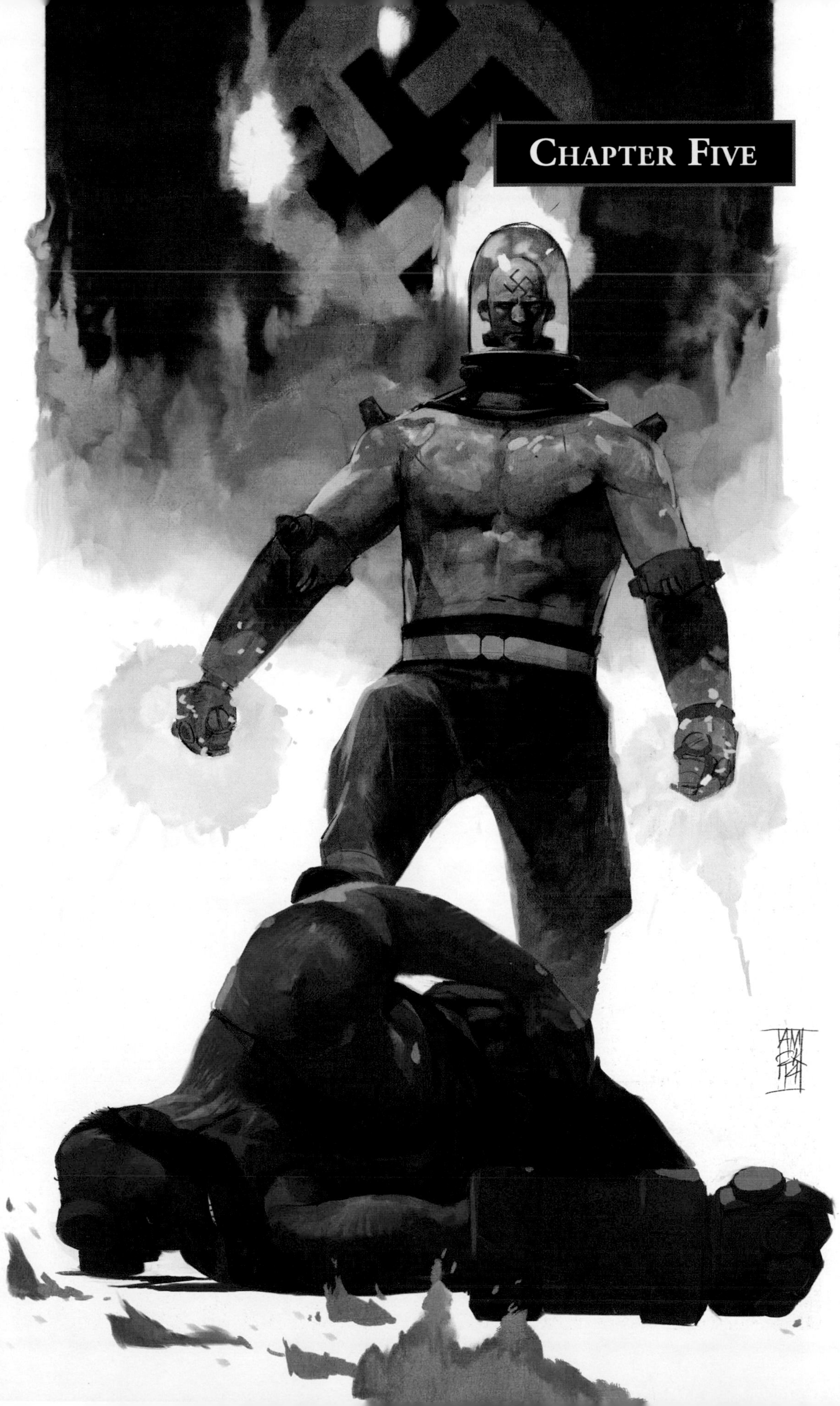

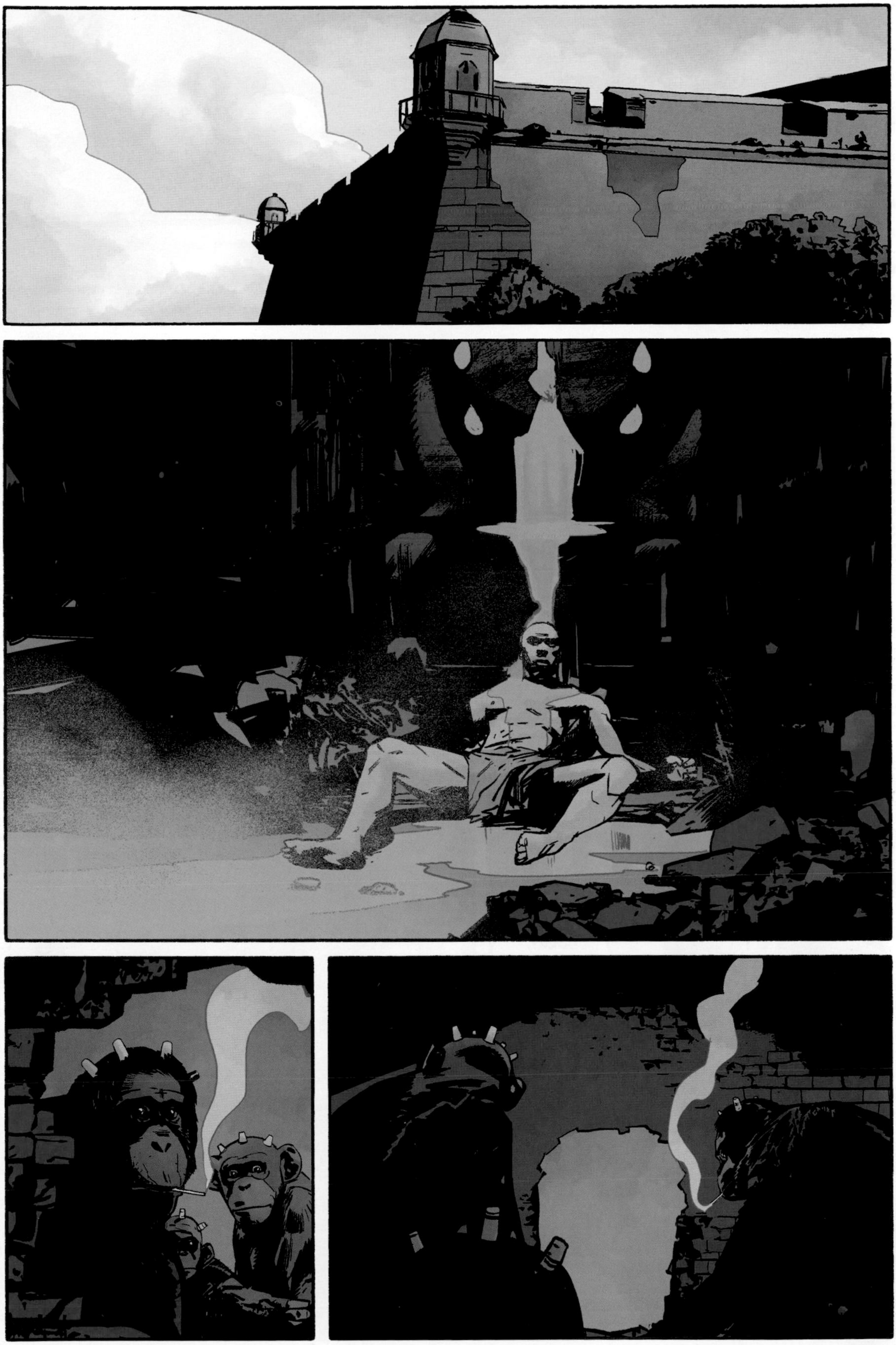

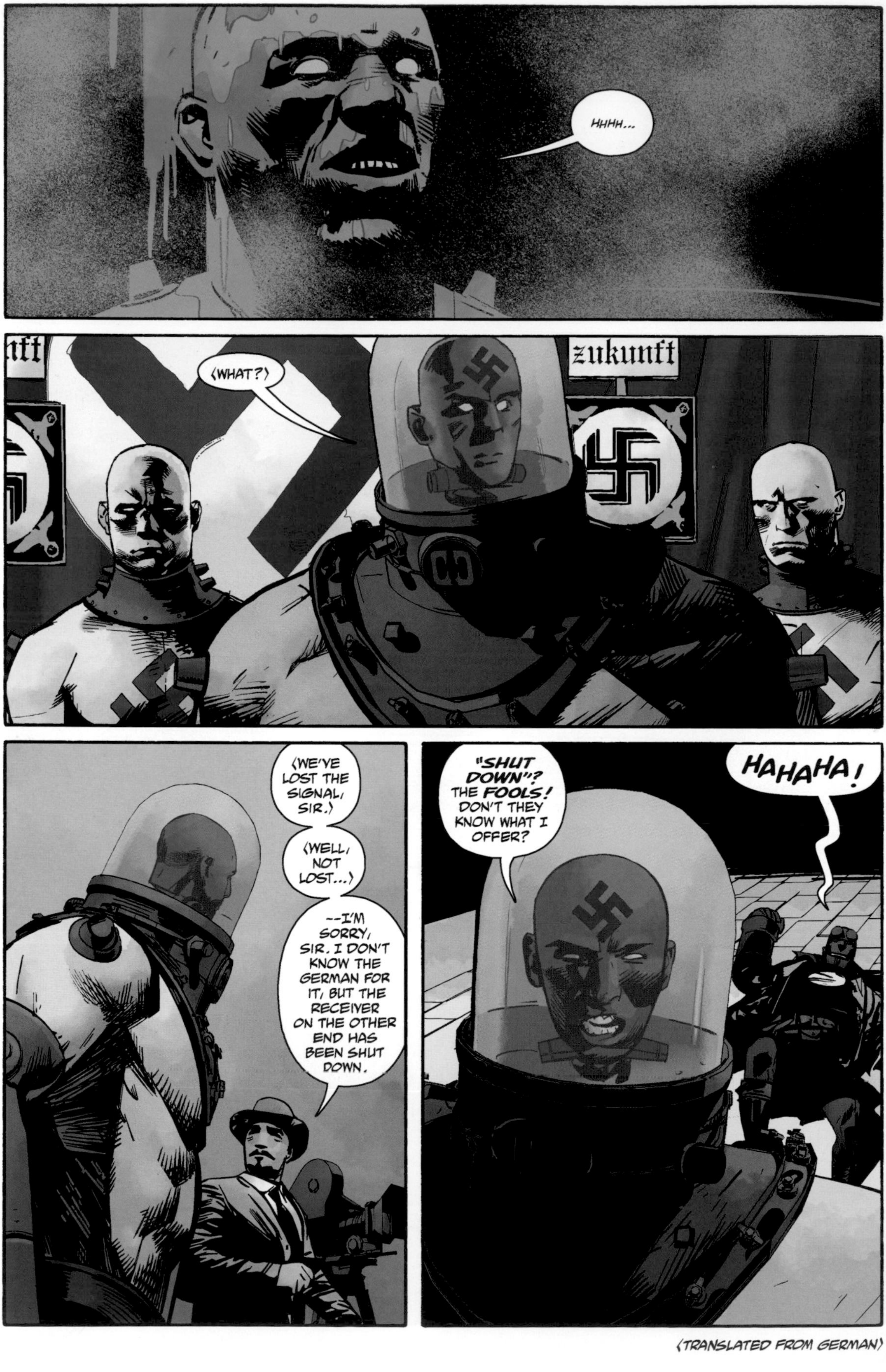
HHHH...
⟨WHAT?⟩
zukunft
⟨WE'VE LOST THE SIGNAL, SIR.⟩
⟨WELL, NOT LOST...⟩
--I'M SORRY, SIR. I DON'T KNOW THE GERMAN FOR IT, BUT THE RECEIVER ON THE OTHER END HAS BEEN SHUT DOWN.
"SHUT DOWN"? THE FOOLS! DON'T THEY KNOW WHAT I OFFER?
HAHAHA!
⟨TRANSLATED FROM GERMAN⟩

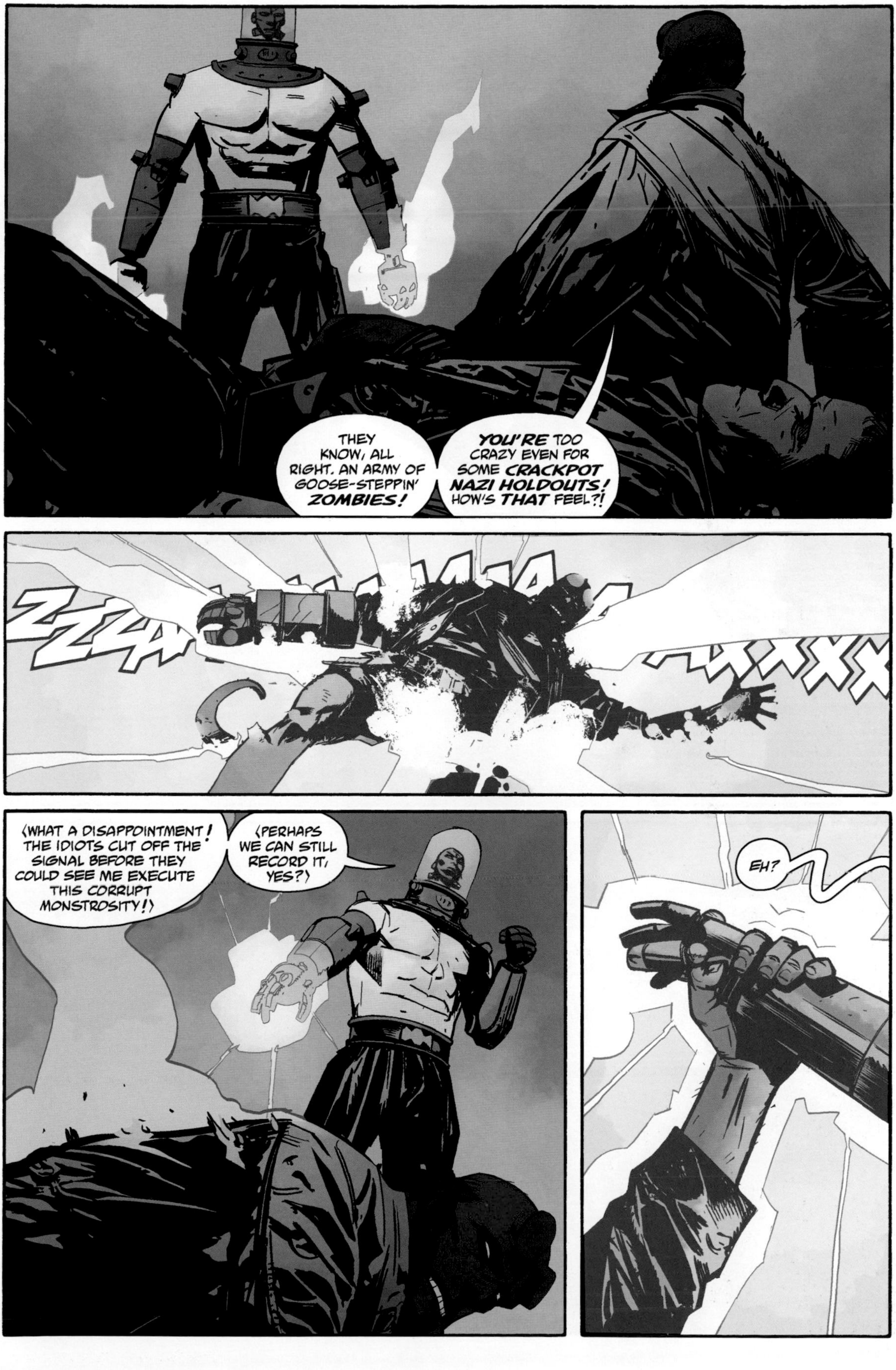
THEY KNOW, ALL RIGHT. AN ARMY OF GOOSE-STEPPIN' ZOMBIES!
YOU'RE TOO CRAZY EVEN FOR SOME CRACKPOT NAZI HOLDOUTS! HOW'S THAT FEEL?!
ZZZAAAAAAAAAAAAAXXXXX
‹WHAT A DISAPPOINTMENT! THE IDIOTS CUT OFF THE SIGNAL BEFORE THEY COULD SEE ME EXECUTE THIS CORRUPT MONSTROSITY!›
‹PERHAPS WE CAN STILL RECORD IT, YES?›
EH?

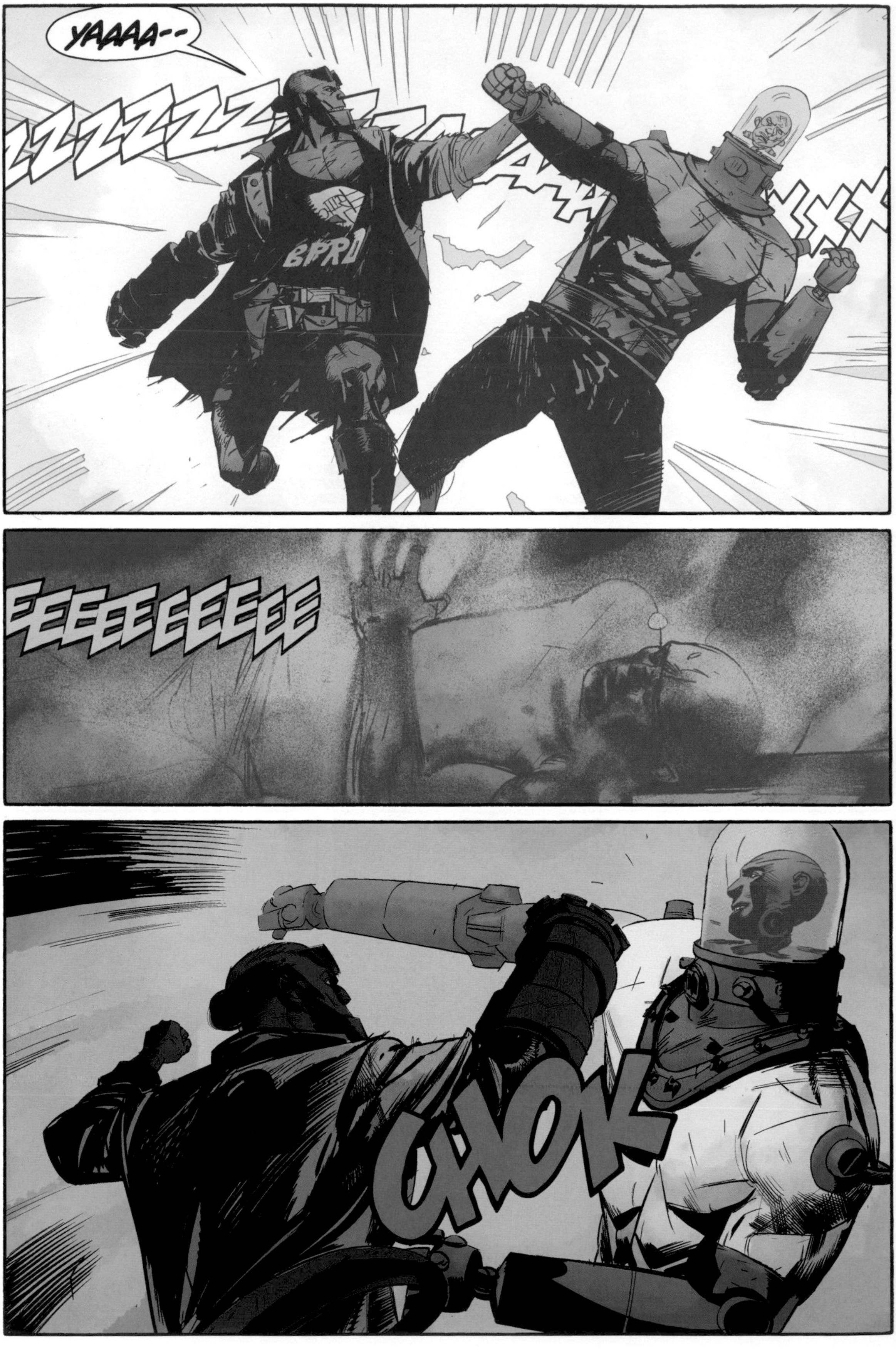
YAAAA--
EEEEEEEEEEE
CHOK

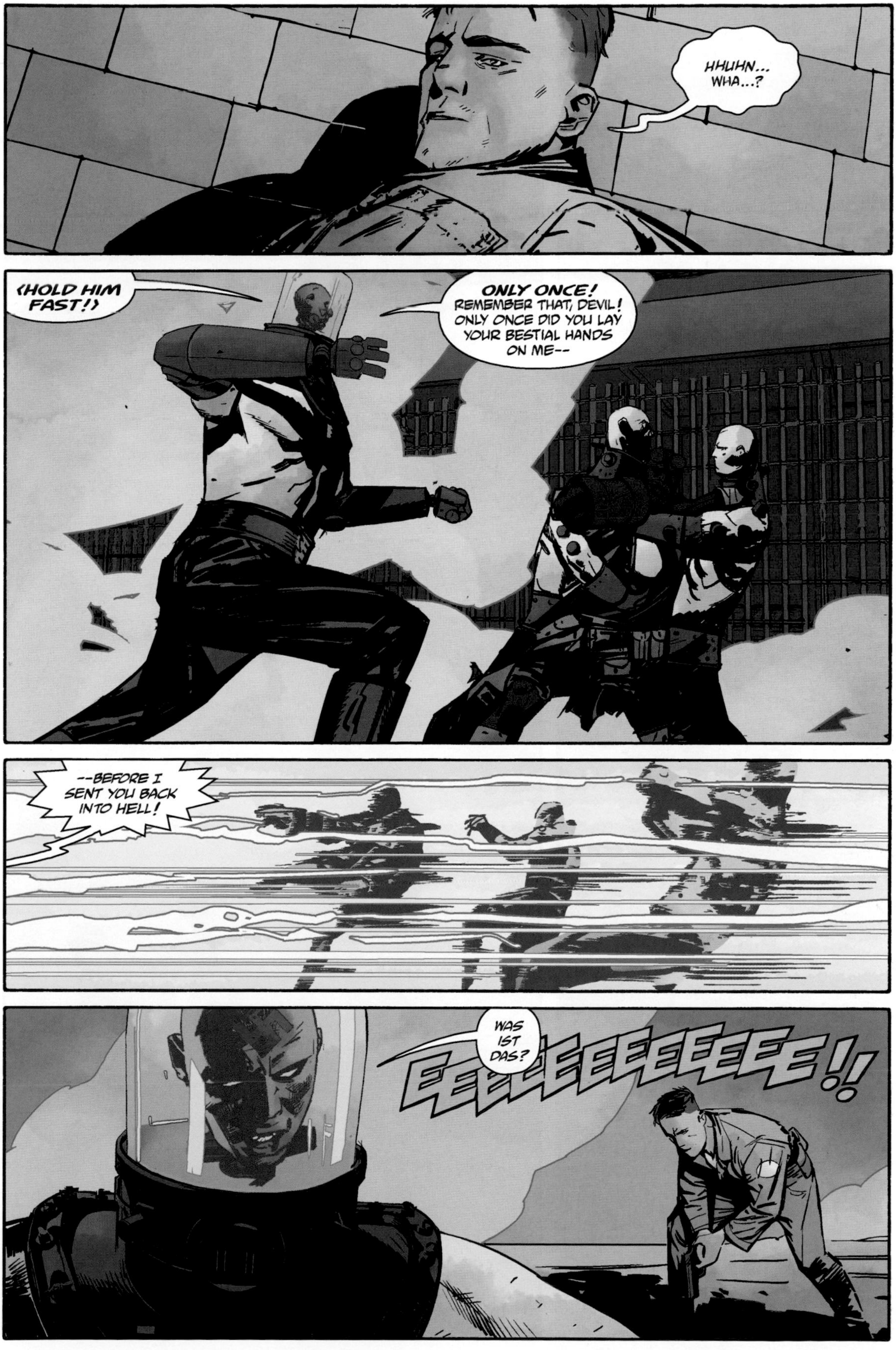
HHUHN... WHA...?
‹HOLD HIM FAST!›
ONLY ONCE! REMEMBER THAT, DEVIL! ONLY ONCE DID YOU LAY YOUR BESTIAL HANDS ON ME--
--BEFORE I SENT YOU BACK INTO HELL!
WAS IST DAS?
EEEEEEEEEEEEEE!!

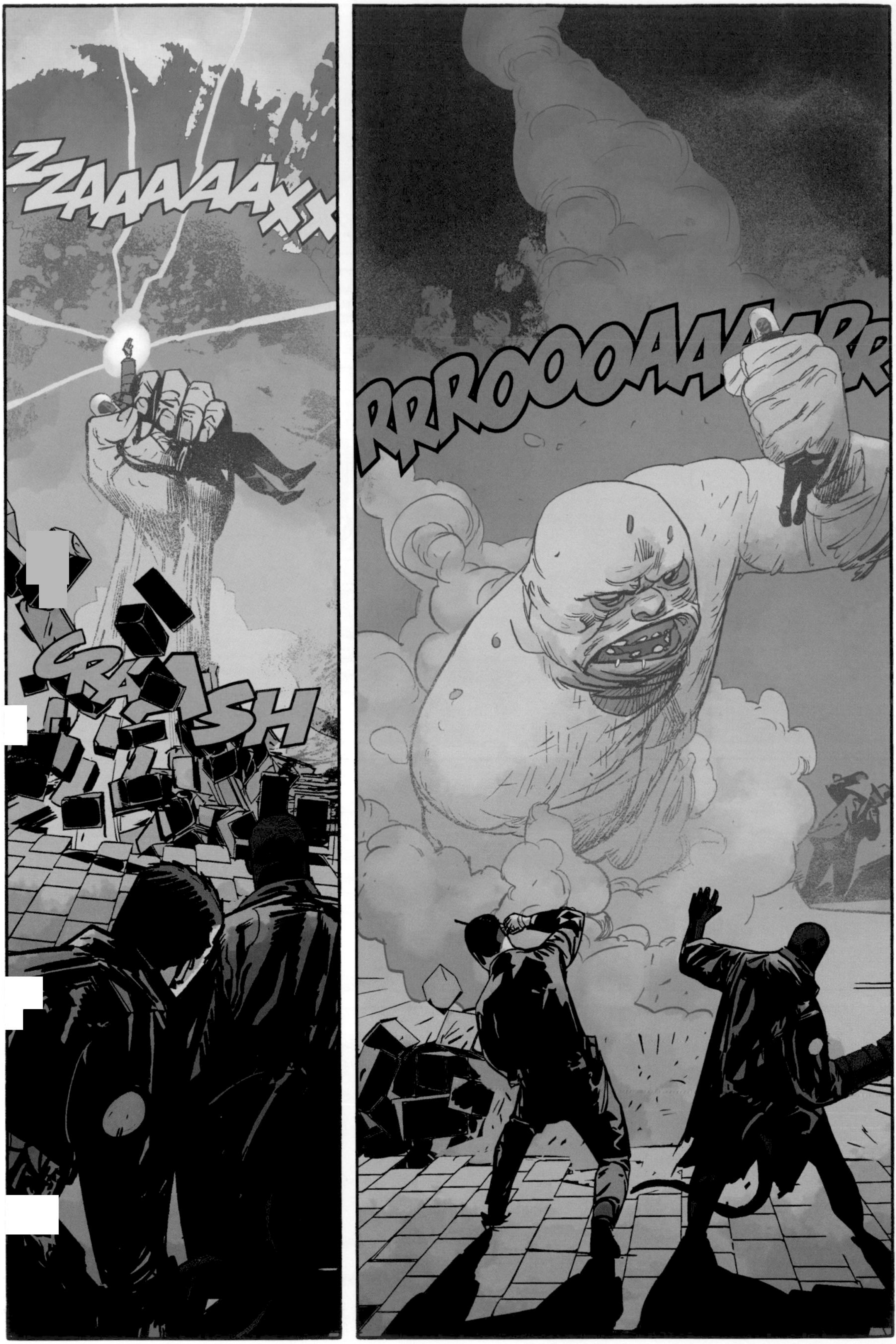
ZZAAAAAXX
CRASH
RRROOOAARR

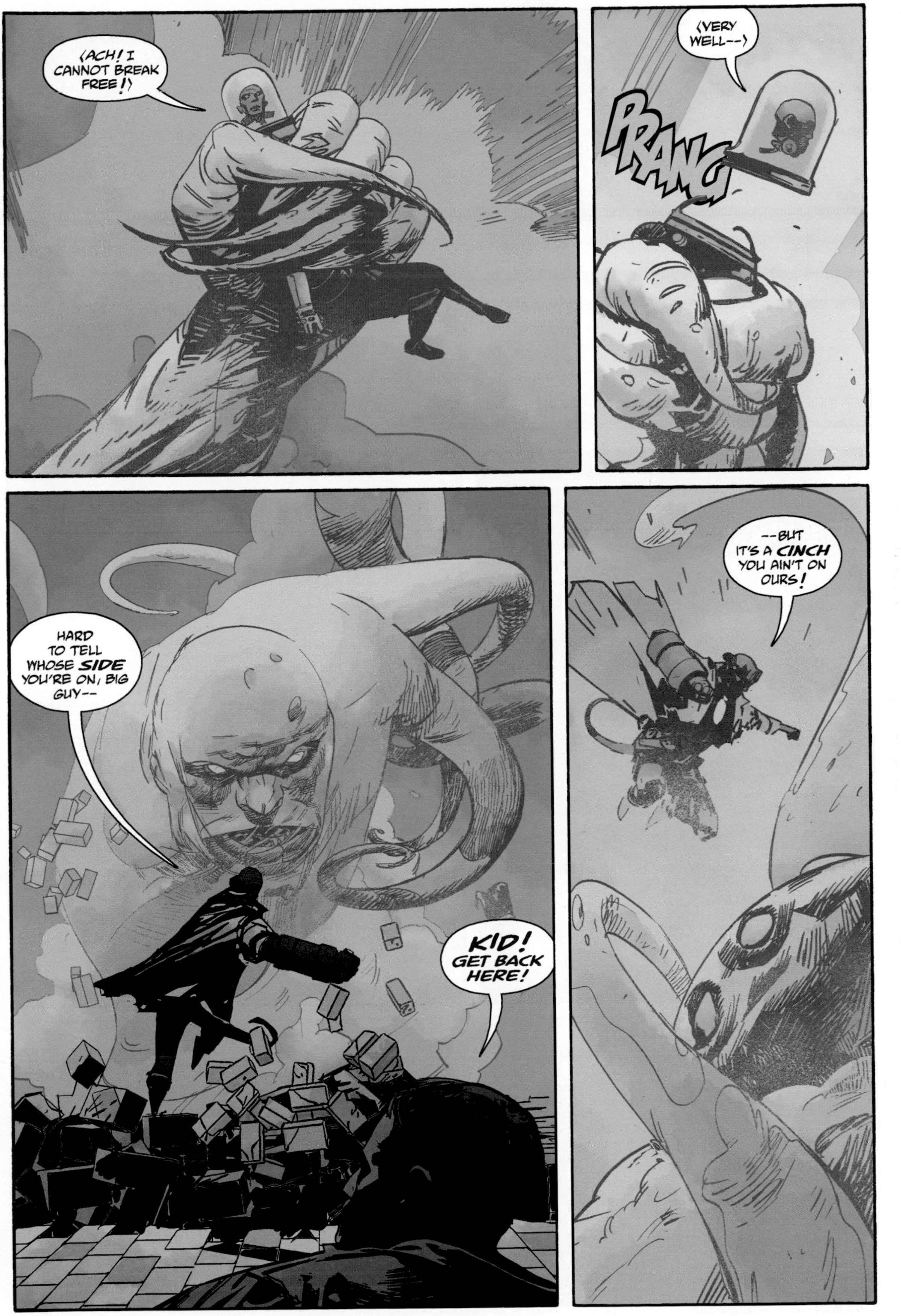
‹ACH! I CANNOT BREAK FREE!›
‹VERY WELL--›
PRANG
HARD TO TELL WHOSE SIDE YOU'RE ON, BIG GUY--
KID! GET BACK HERE!
--BUT IT'S A CINCH YOU AIN'T ON OURS!

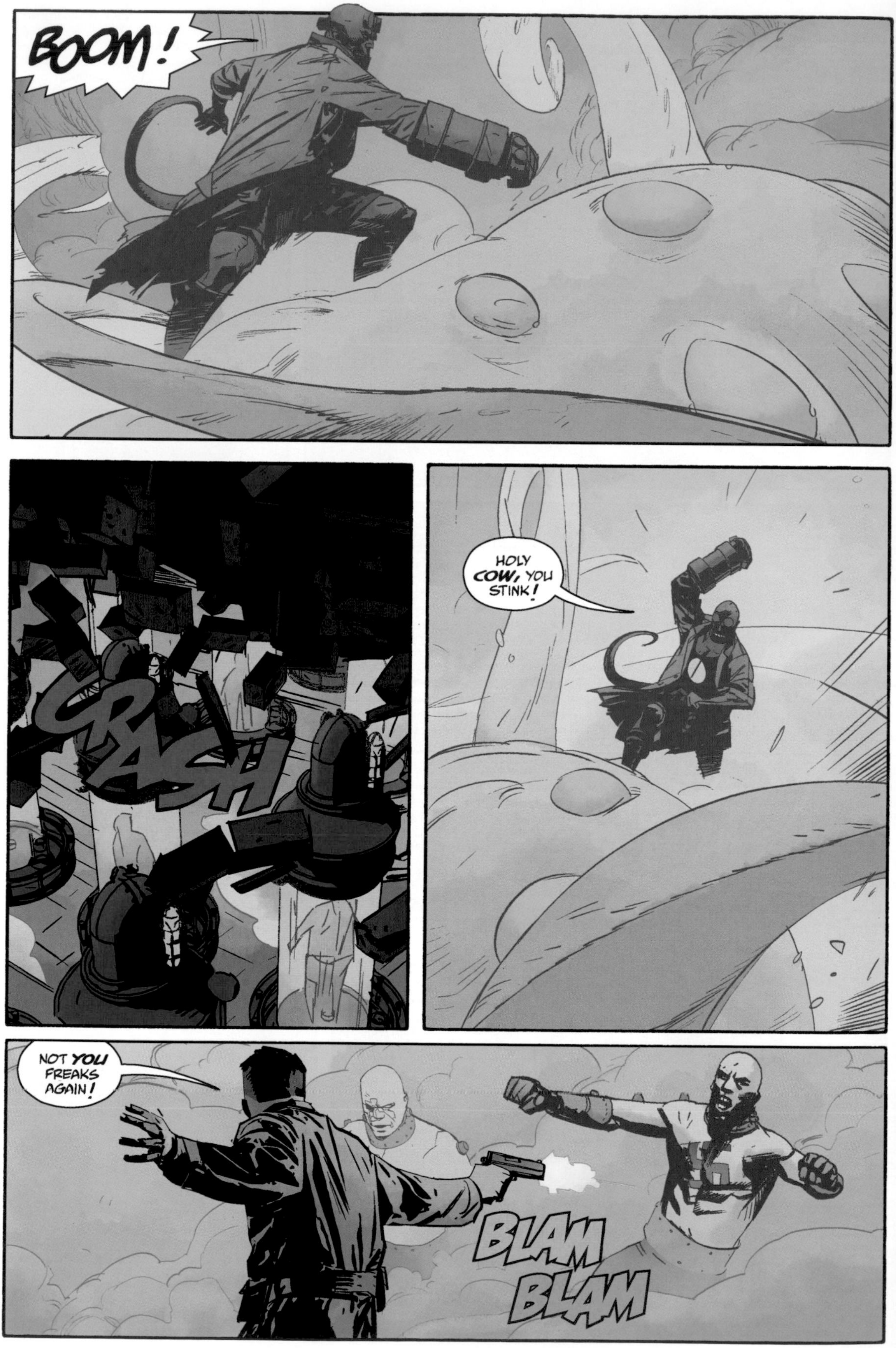
BOOM!
CRASH
HOLY COW, YOU STINK!
NOT YOU FREAKS AGAIN!
BLAM BLAM

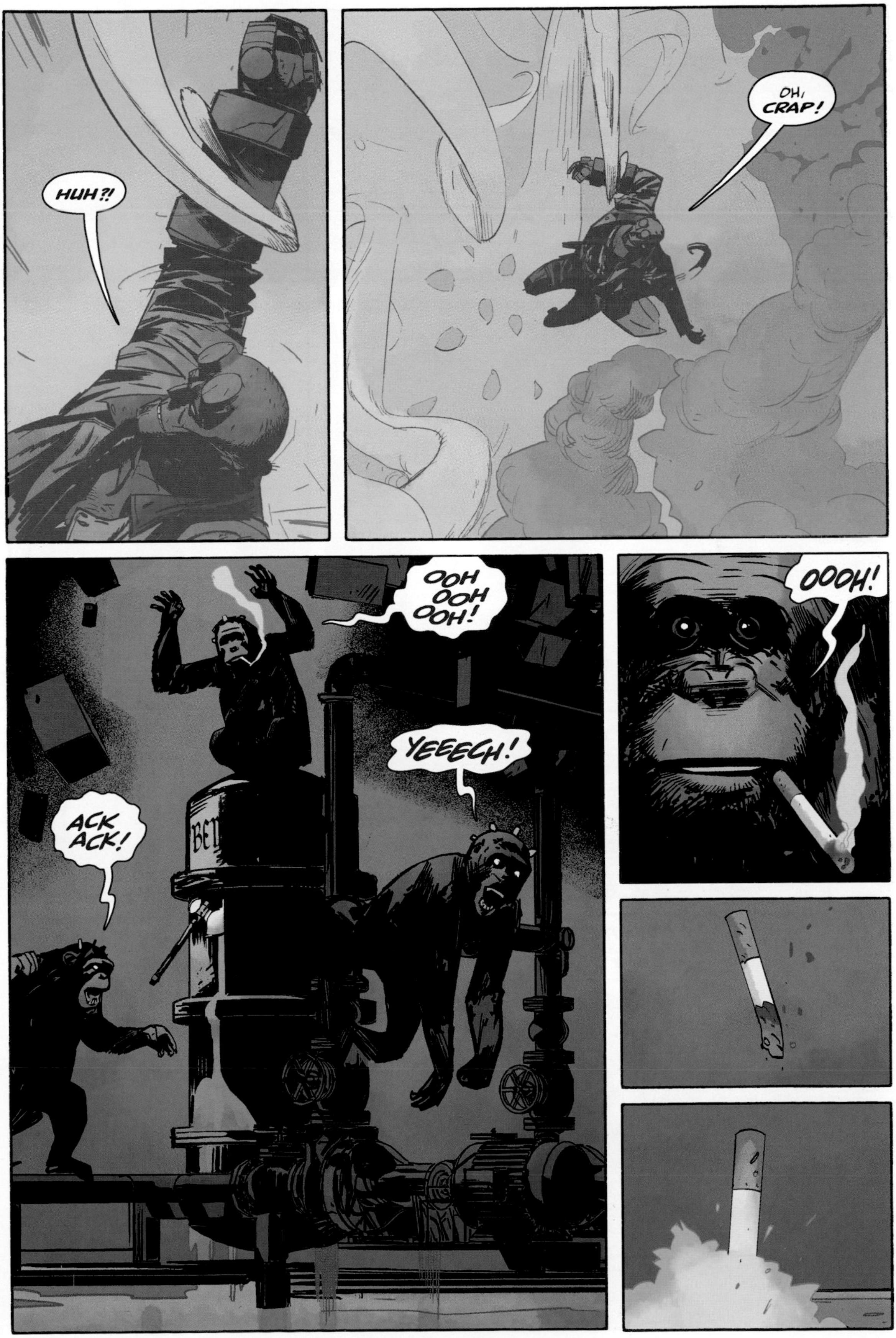
HUH?!
OH, CRAP!
OOH OOH OOH!
YEEECH!
ACK ACK!
OOOH!

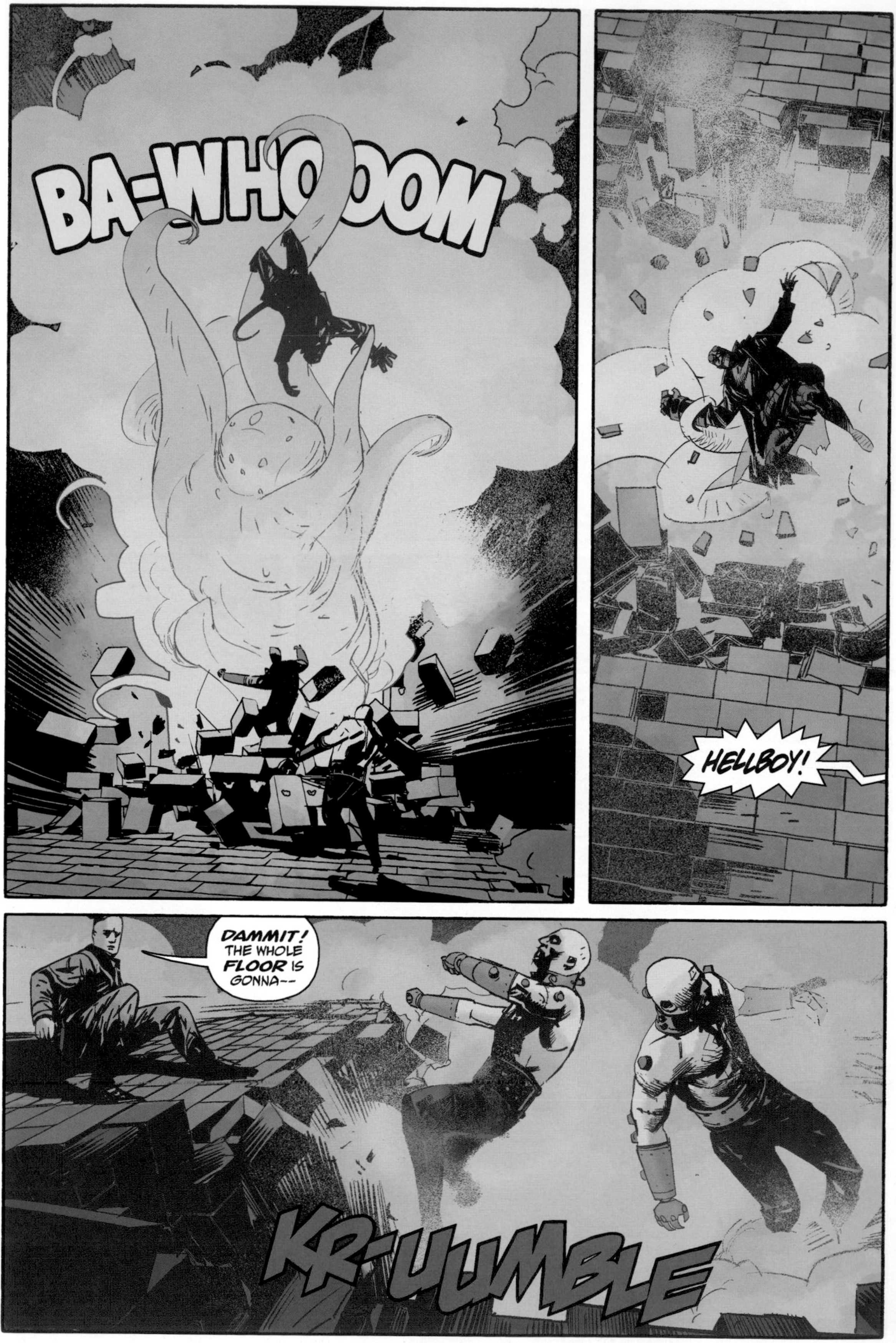
BA-WHOOOM
HELLBOY!
DAMMIT! THE WHOLE FLOOR IS GONNA--
KR-UUMBLE

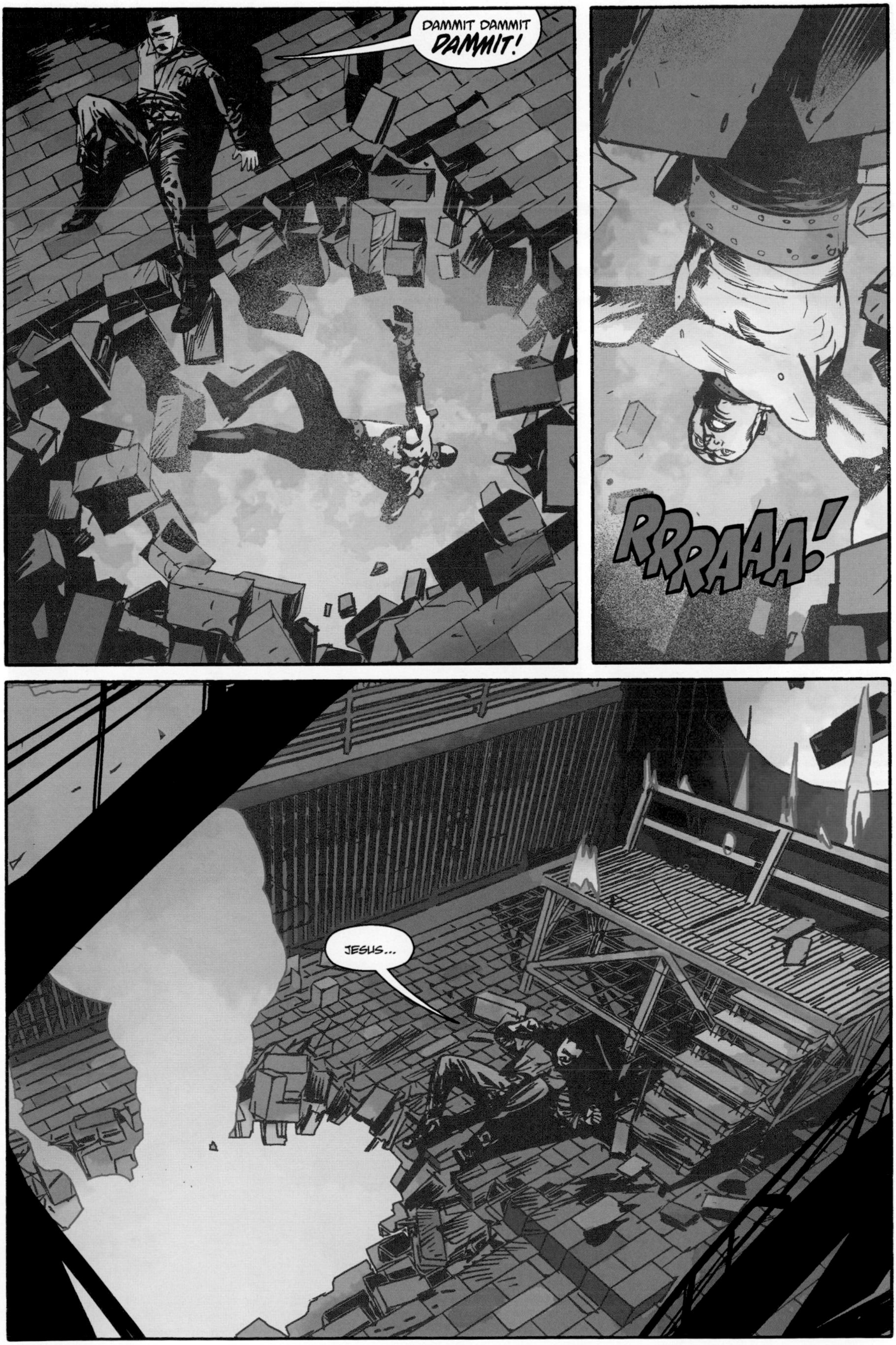
DAMMIT DAMMIT DAMMIT!
RRRAAA!
JESUS...

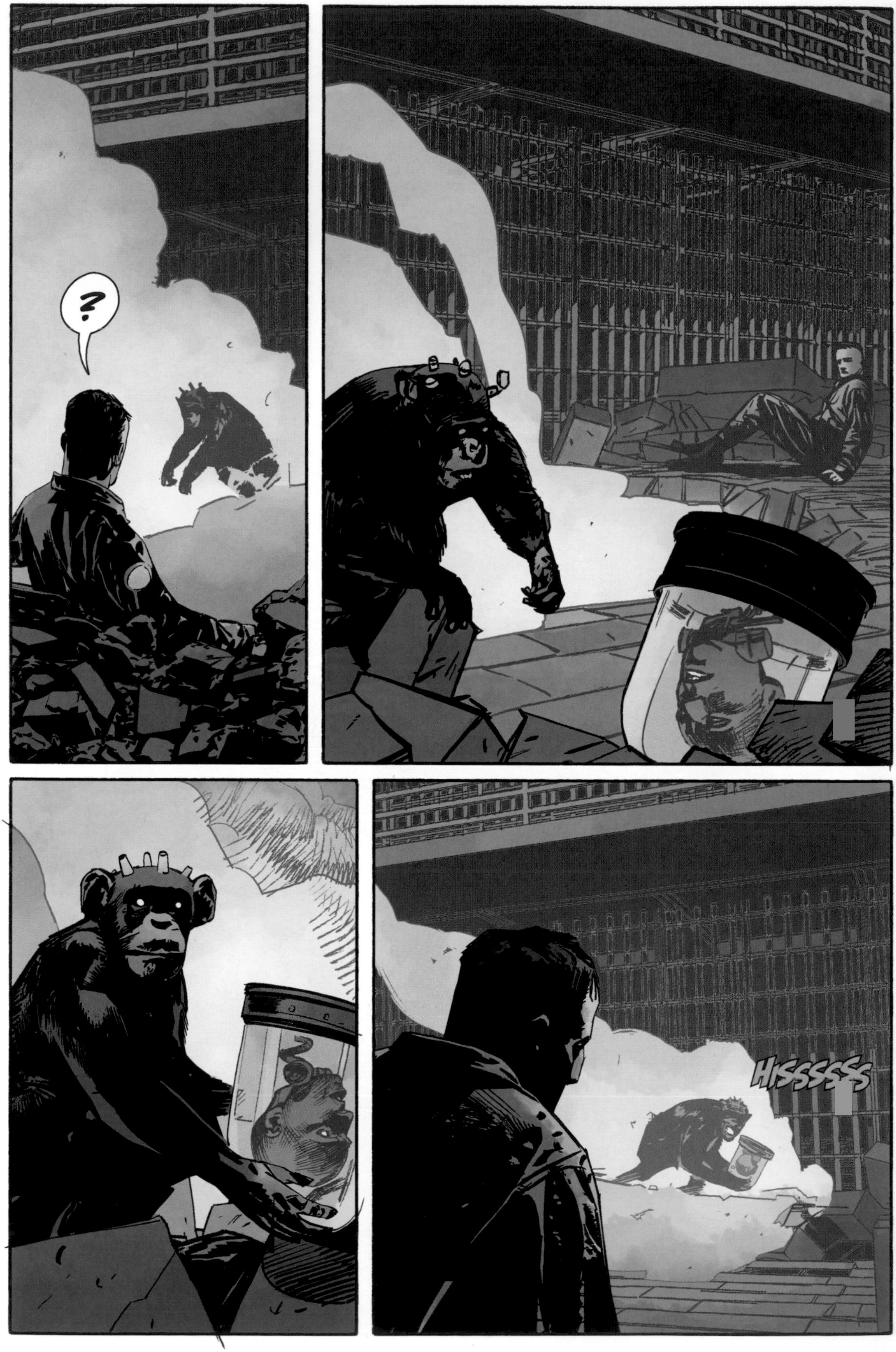
?
HISSSSSS

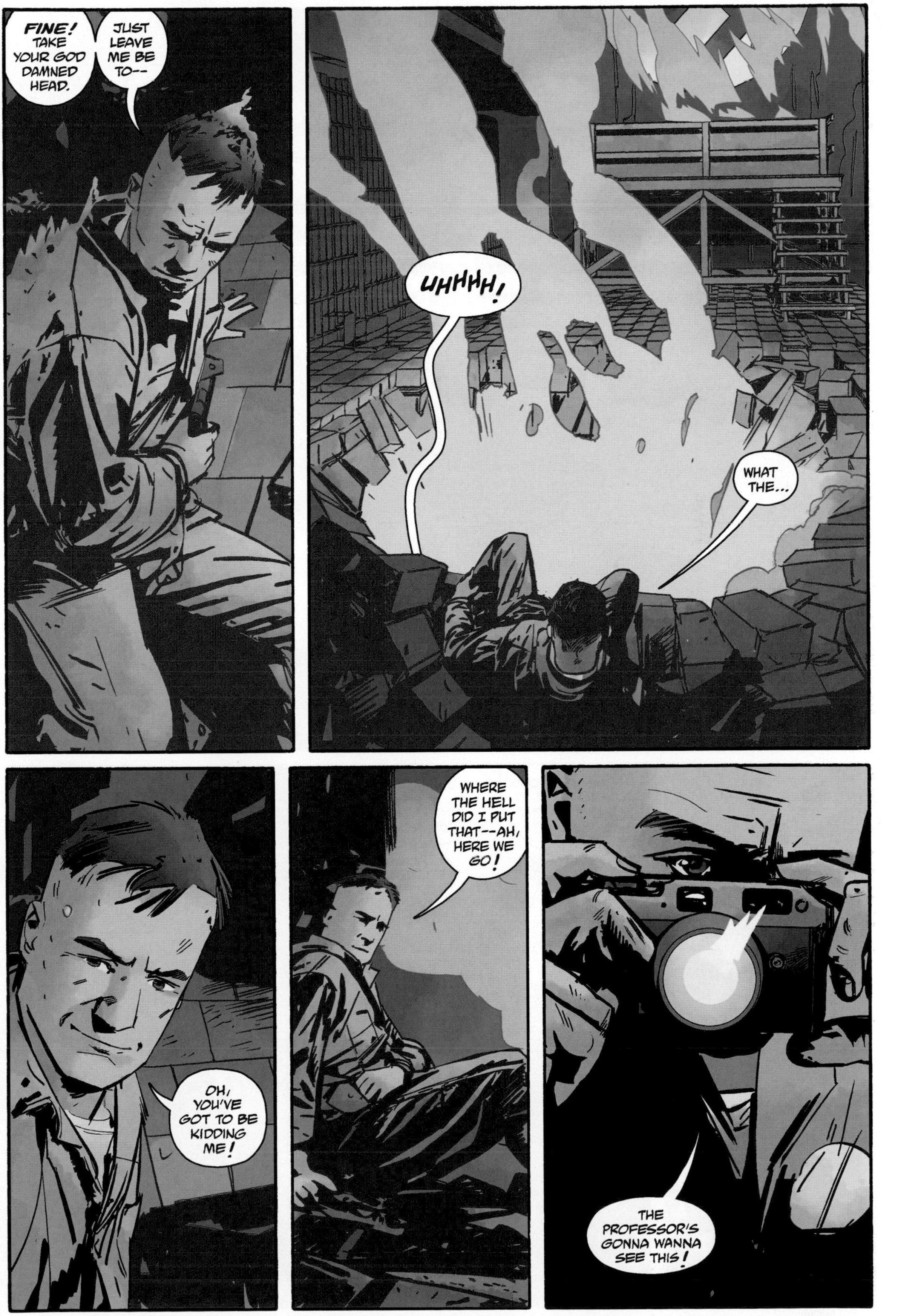
FINE! TAKE YOUR GOD DAMNED HEAD.
JUST LEAVE ME BE TO--
UHHHH!
WHAT THE...
OH, YOU'VE GOT TO BE KIDDING ME!
WHERE THE HELL DID I PUT THAT--AH, HERE WE GO!
THE PROFESSOR'S GONNA WANNA SEE THIS!

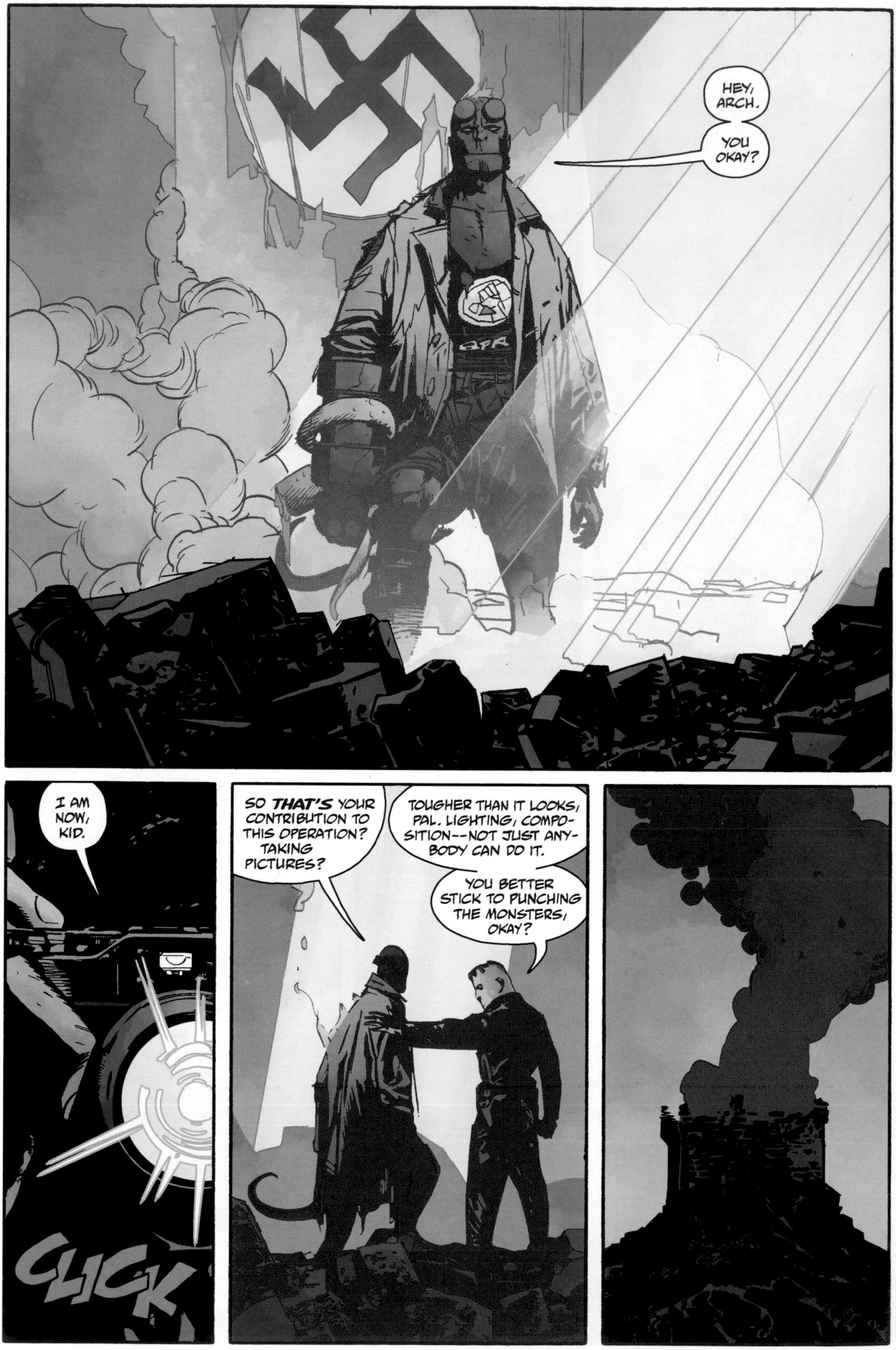
HEY, ARCH.
YOU OKAY?
I AM NOW, KID.
CLICK
SO THAT'S YOUR CONTRIBUTION TO THIS OPERATION? TAKING PICTURES?
TOUGHER THAN IT LOOKS, PAL. LIGHTING, COMPOSITION--NOT JUST ANYBODY CAN DO IT.
YOU BETTER STICK TO PUNCHING THE MONSTERS, OKAY?

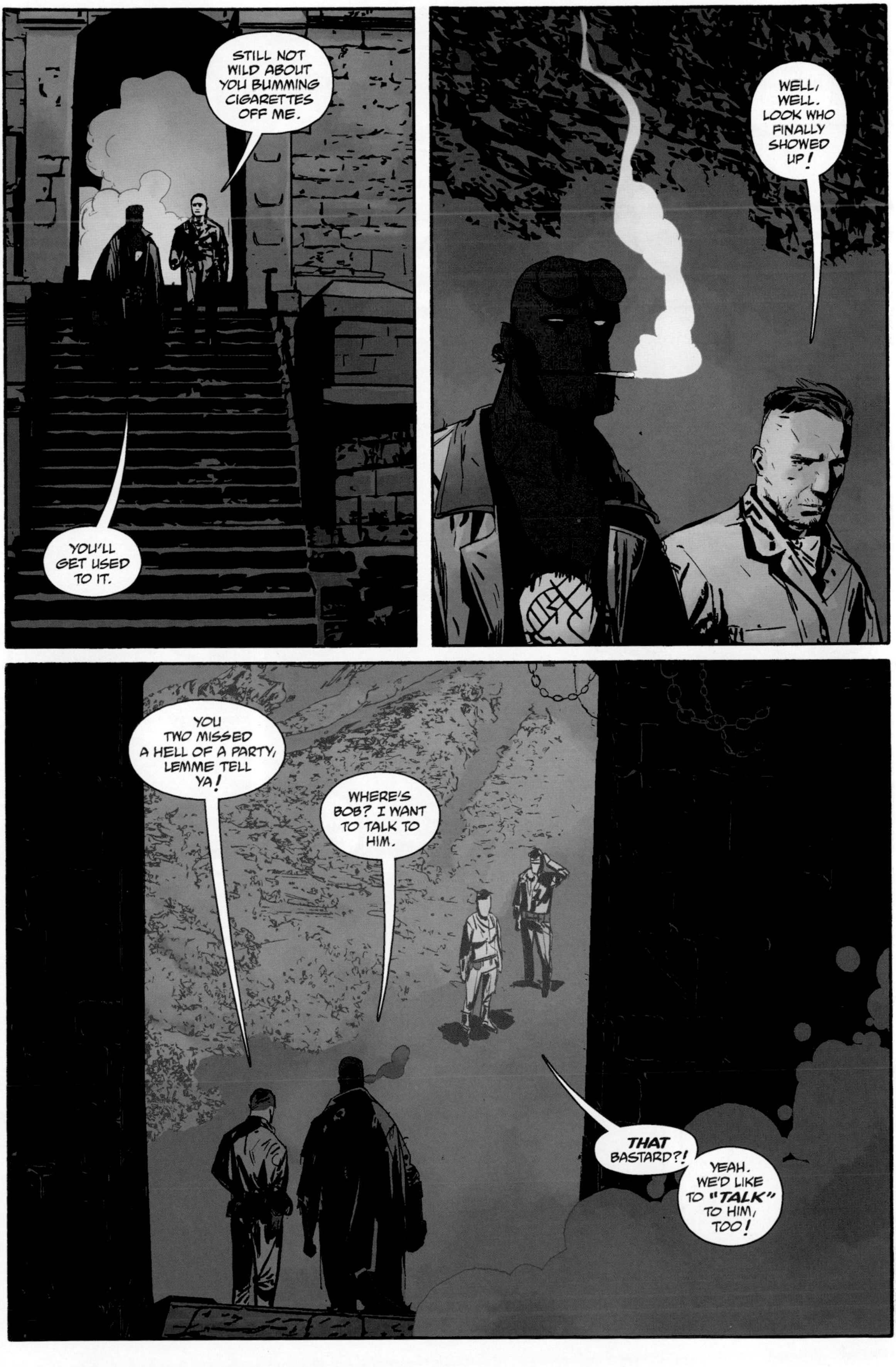
STILL NOT WILD ABOUT YOU BUMMING CIGARETTES OFF ME.
YOU'LL GET USED TO IT.
WELL, WELL. LOOK WHO FINALLY SHOWED UP!
YOU TWO MISSED A HELL OF A PARTY, LEMME TELL YA!
WHERE'S BOB? I WANT TO TALK TO HIM.
THAT BASTARD?!
YEAH. WE'D LIKE TO "TALK" TO HIM, TOO!

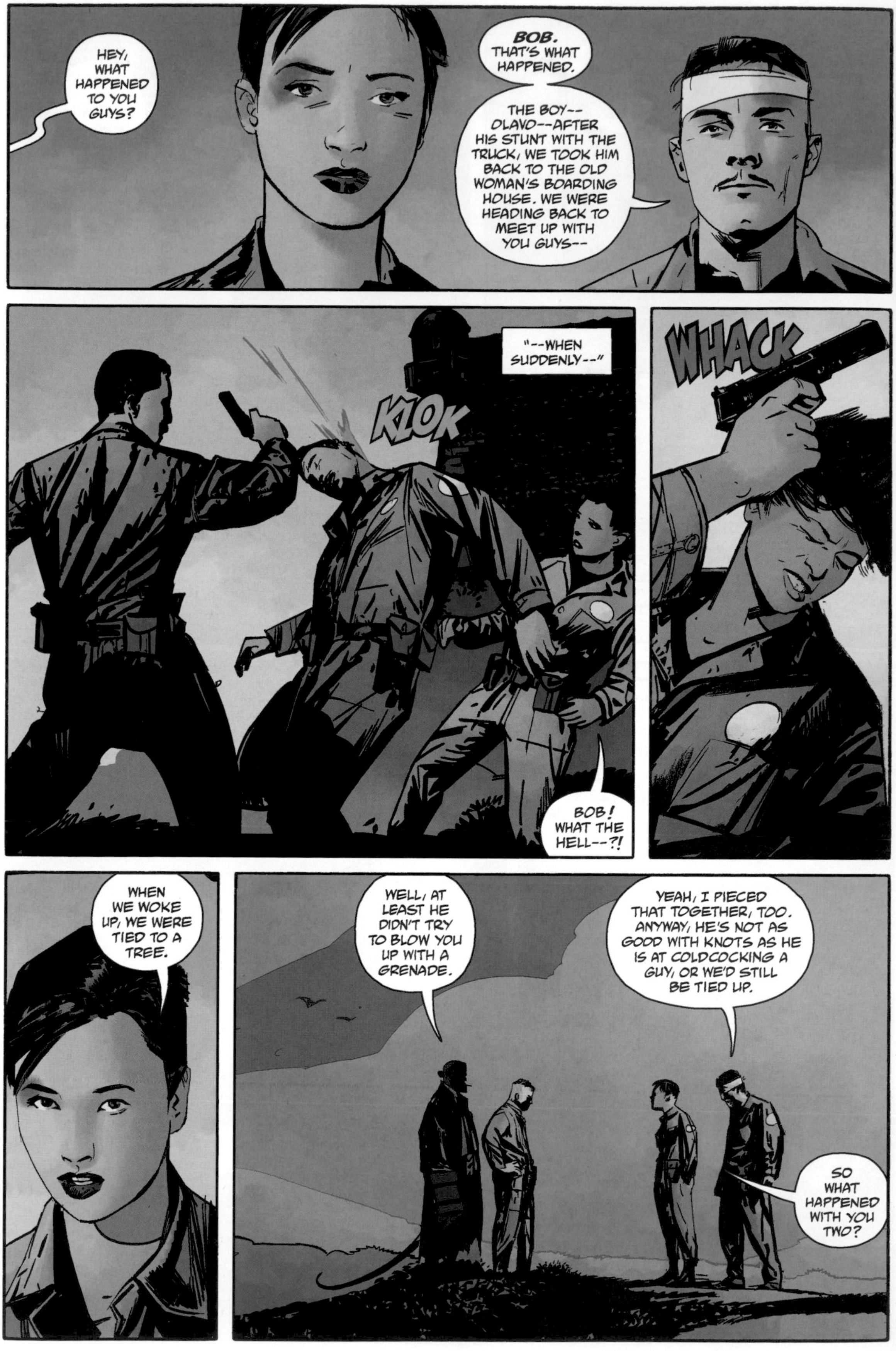
HEY, WHAT HAPPENED TO YOU GUYS?
BOB. THAT'S WHAT HAPPENED.
THE BOY--OLAVO--AFTER HIS STUNT WITH THE TRUCK, WE TOOK HIM BACK TO THE OLD WOMAN'S BOARDING HOUSE. WE WERE HEADING BACK TO MEET UP WITH YOU GUYS--
"--WHEN SUDDENLY--"
KLOK
BOB! WHAT THE HELL--?!
WHACK
WHEN WE WOKE UP, WE WERE TIED TO A TREE.
WELL, AT LEAST HE DIDN'T TRY TO BLOW YOU UP WITH A GRENADE.
YEAH, I PIECED THAT TOGETHER, TOO. ANYWAY, HE'S NOT AS GOOD WITH KNOTS AS HE IS AT COLDCOCKING A GUY, OR WE'D STILL BE TIED UP.
SO WHAT HAPPENED WITH YOU TWO?

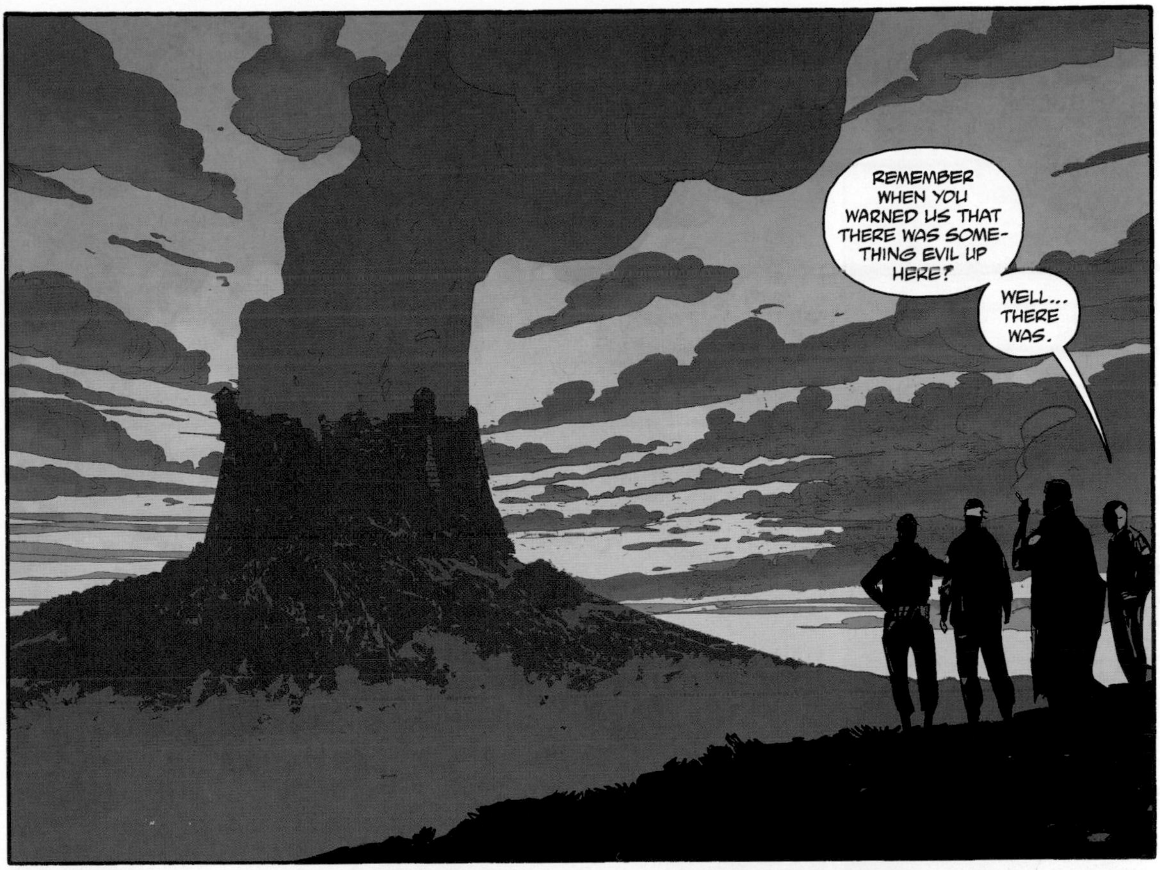
REMEMBER WHEN YOU WARNED US THAT THERE WAS SOME-THING EVIL UP HERE?
WELL... THERE WAS.

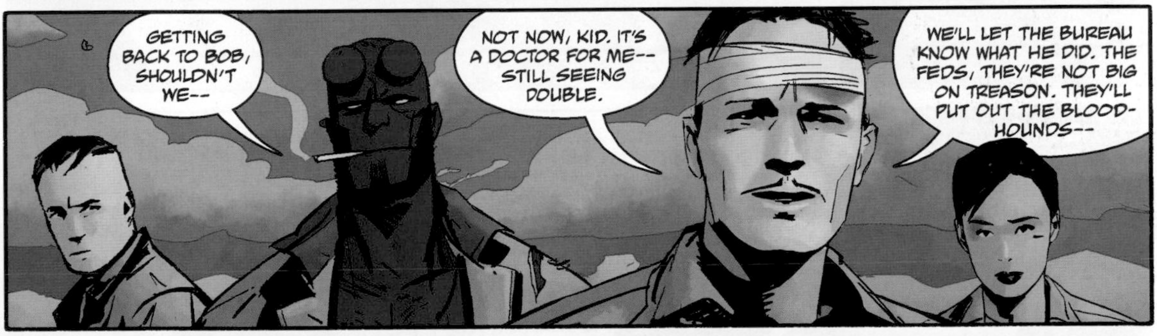
GETTING BACK TO BOB, SHOULDN'T WE--
NOT NOW, KID. IT'S A DOCTOR FOR ME--STILL SEEING DOUBLE.
WE'LL LET THE BUREAU KNOW WHAT HE DID. THE FEDS, THEY'RE NOT BIG ON TREASON. THEY'LL PUT OUT THE BLOOD-HOUNDS--

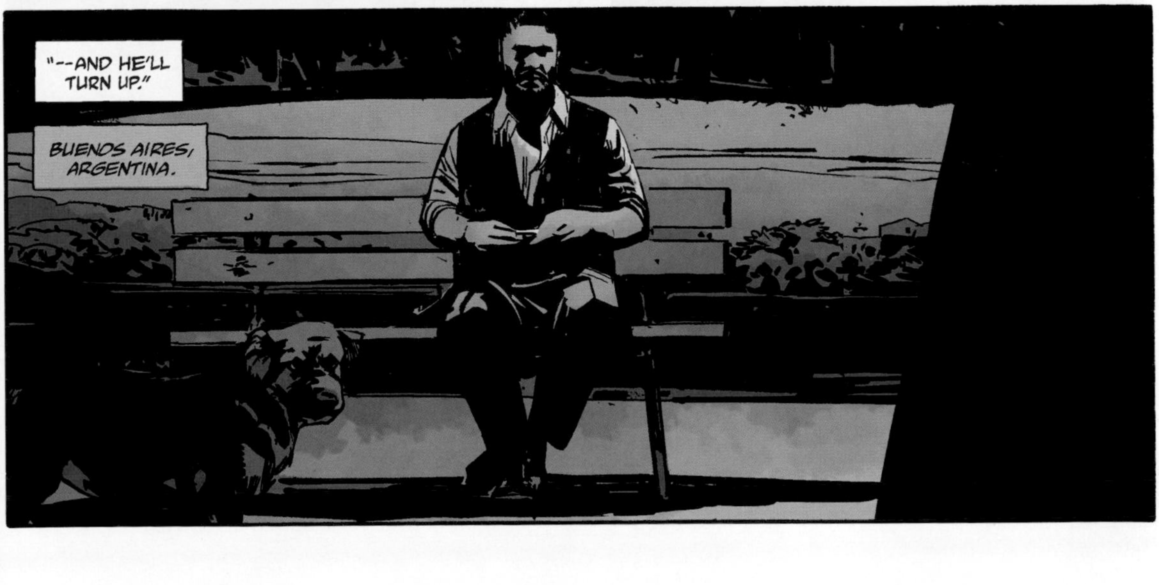
"--AND HE'LL TURN UP."
BUENOS AIRES, ARGENTINA.

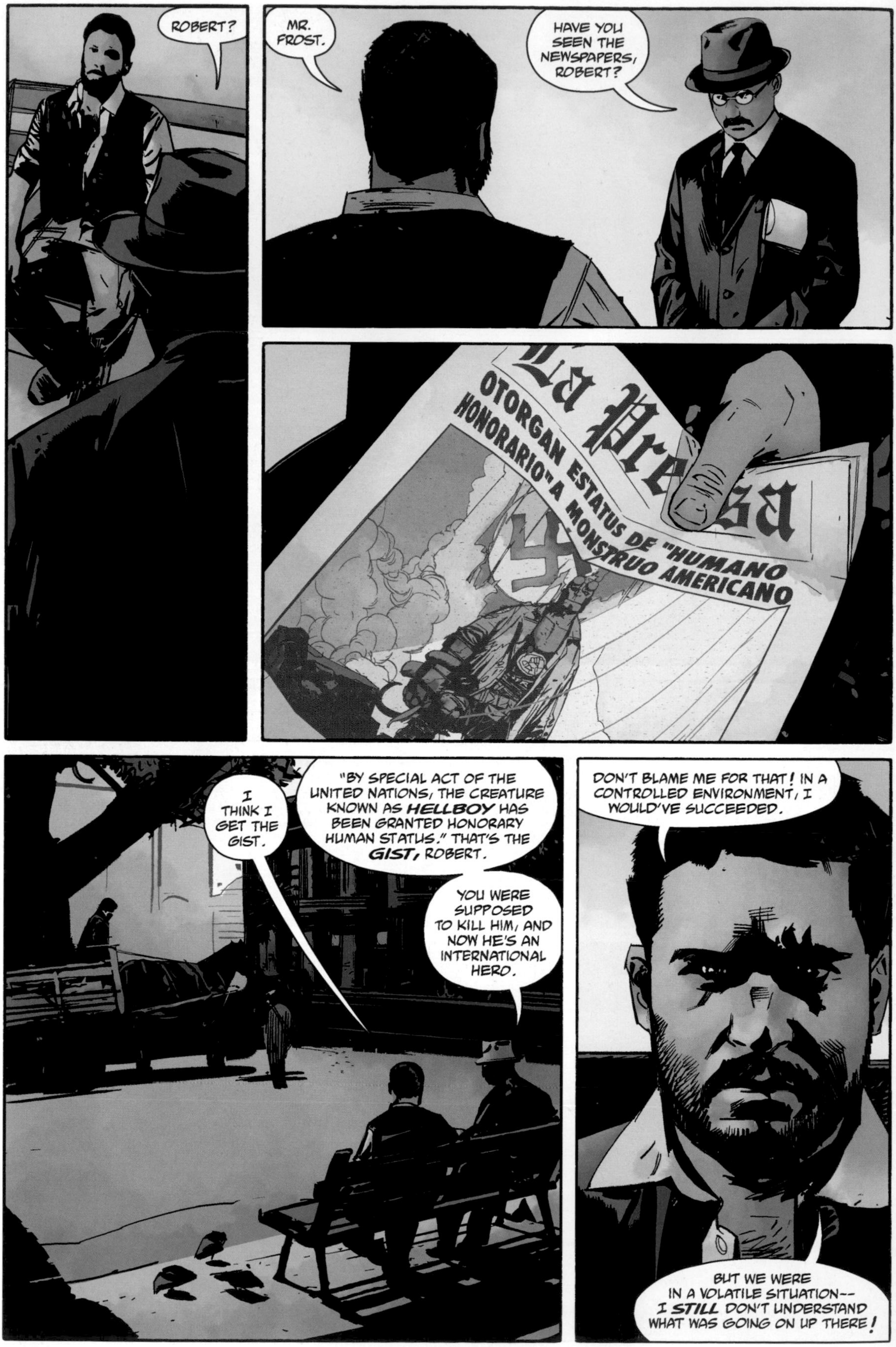
ROBERT?
MR. FROST.
HAVE YOU SEEN THE NEWSPAPERS, ROBERT?
La Prensa
OTORGAN ESTATUS DE "HUMANO HONORARIO" A MONSTRUO AMERICANO
I THINK I GET THE GIST.
"BY SPECIAL ACT OF THE UNITED NATIONS, THE CREATURE KNOWN AS HELLBOY HAS BEEN GRANTED HONORARY HUMAN STATUS." THAT'S THE GIST, ROBERT.
YOU WERE SUPPOSED TO KILL HIM, AND NOW HE'S AN INTERNATIONAL HERO.
DON'T BLAME ME FOR THAT! IN A CONTROLLED ENVIRONMENT, I WOULD'VE SUCCEEDED.
BUT WE WERE IN A VOLATILE SITUATION-- I STILL DON'T UNDERSTAND WHAT WAS GOING ON UP THERE!

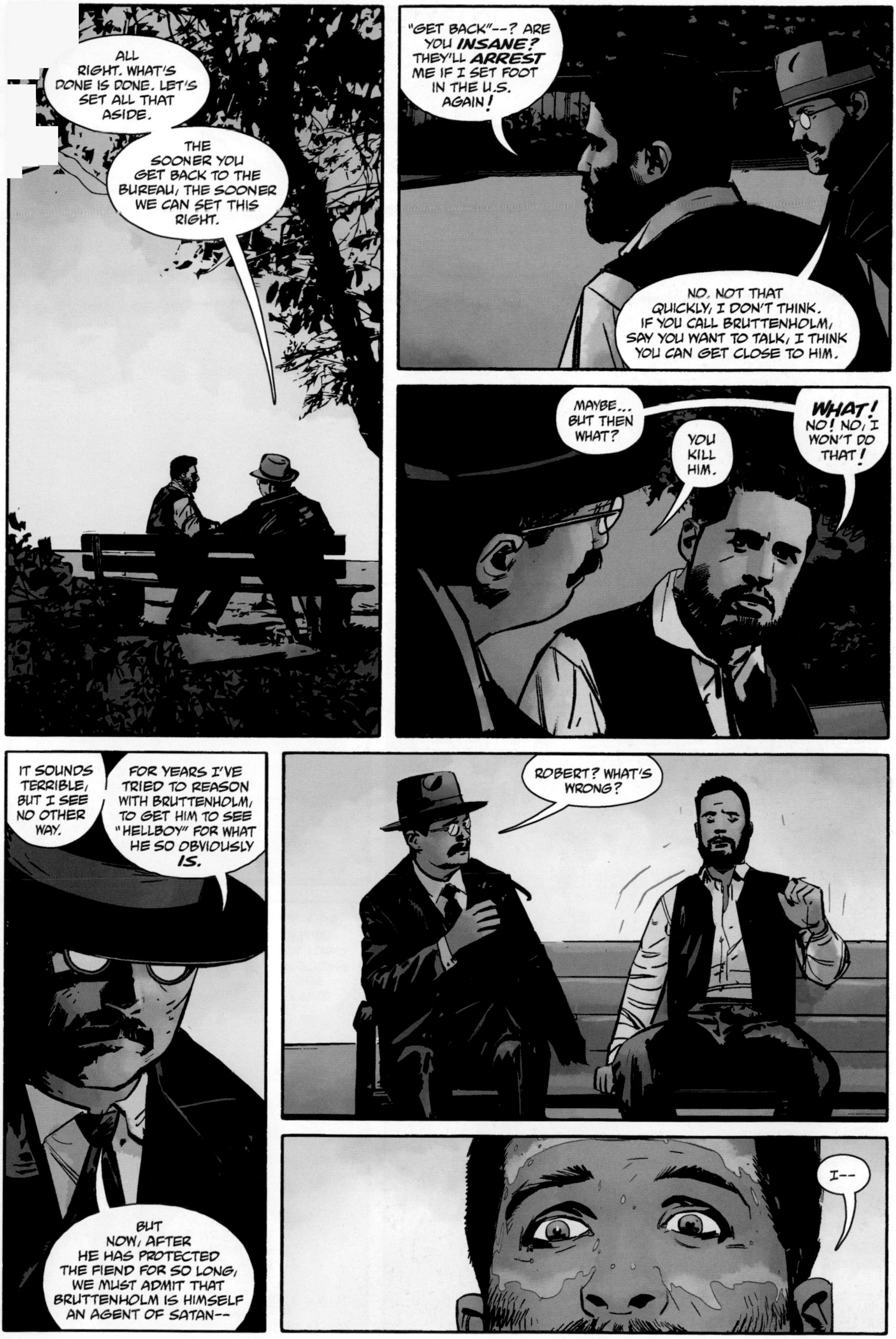
ALL RIGHT. WHAT'S DONE IS DONE. LET'S SET ALL THAT ASIDE.
THE SOONER YOU GET BACK TO THE BUREAU, THE SOONER WE CAN SET THIS RIGHT.
"GET BACK"--? ARE YOU **INSANE?** THEY'LL **ARREST** ME IF I SET FOOT IN THE U.S. AGAIN!
NO, NOT THAT QUICKLY, I DON'T THINK. IF YOU CALL BRUTTENHOLM, SAY YOU WANT TO TALK, I THINK YOU CAN GET CLOSE TO HIM.
MAYBE... BUT THEN WHAT?
YOU KILL HIM.
WHAT! NO! NO, I WON'T DO THAT!
IT SOUNDS TERRIBLE, BUT I SEE NO OTHER WAY.
FOR YEARS I'VE TRIED TO REASON WITH BRUTTENHOLM, TO GET HIM TO SEE "HELLBOY" FOR WHAT HE SO OBVIOUSLY **IS.**
BUT NOW, AFTER HE HAS PROTECTED THE FIEND FOR SO LONG, WE MUST ADMIT THAT BRUTTENHOLM IS HIMSELF AN AGENT OF SATAN--
ROBERT? WHAT'S WRONG?
I--

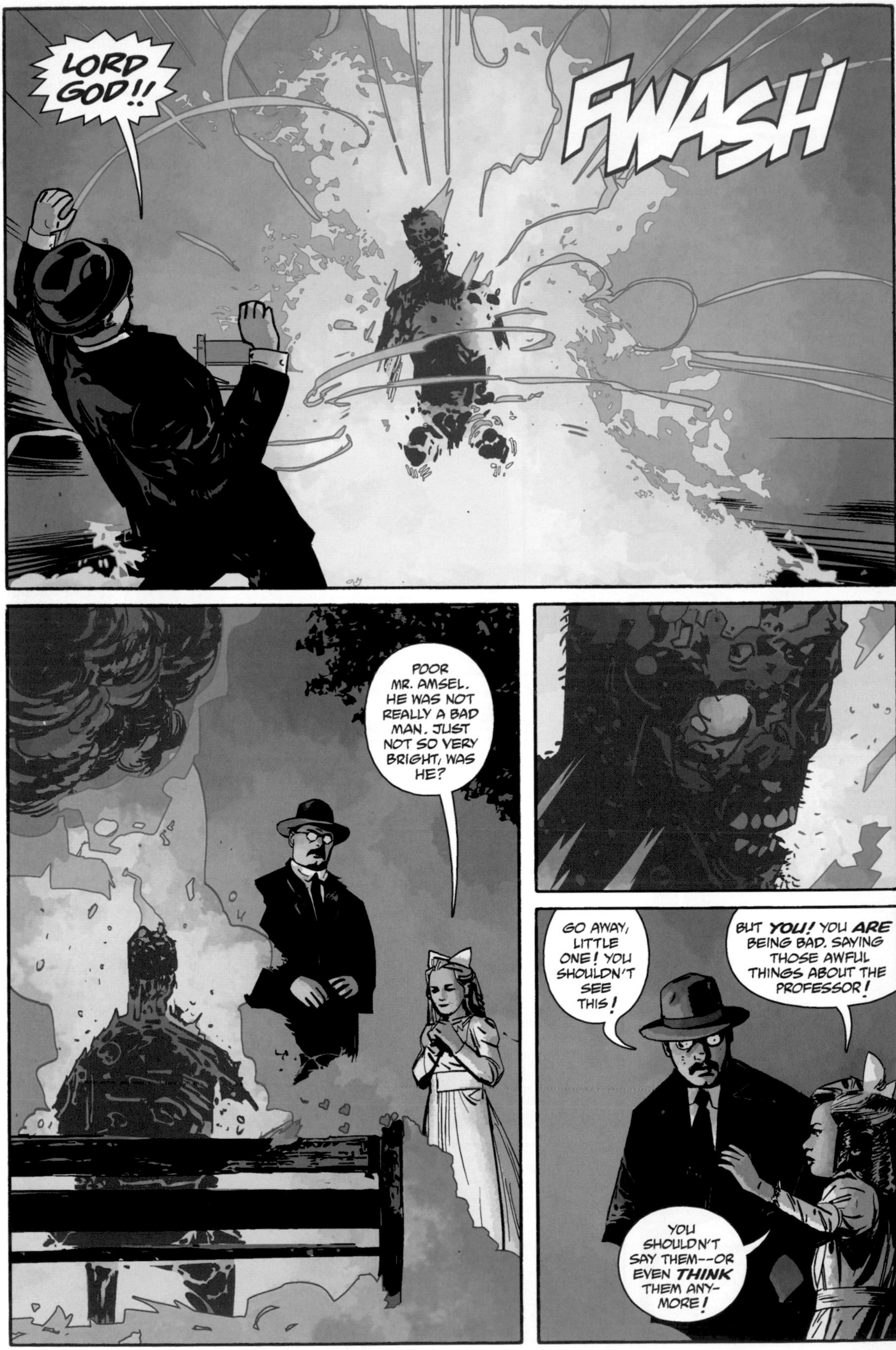
LORD GOD!!
FWASH
POOR MR. AMSEL. HE WAS NOT REALLY A BAD MAN. JUST NOT SO VERY BRIGHT, WAS HE?
GO AWAY, LITTLE ONE! YOU SHOULDN'T SEE THIS!
BUT YOU! YOU ARE BEING BAD. SAYING THOSE AWFUL THINGS ABOUT THE PROFESSOR!
YOU SHOULDN'T SAY THEM--OR EVEN THINK THEM ANY-MORE!

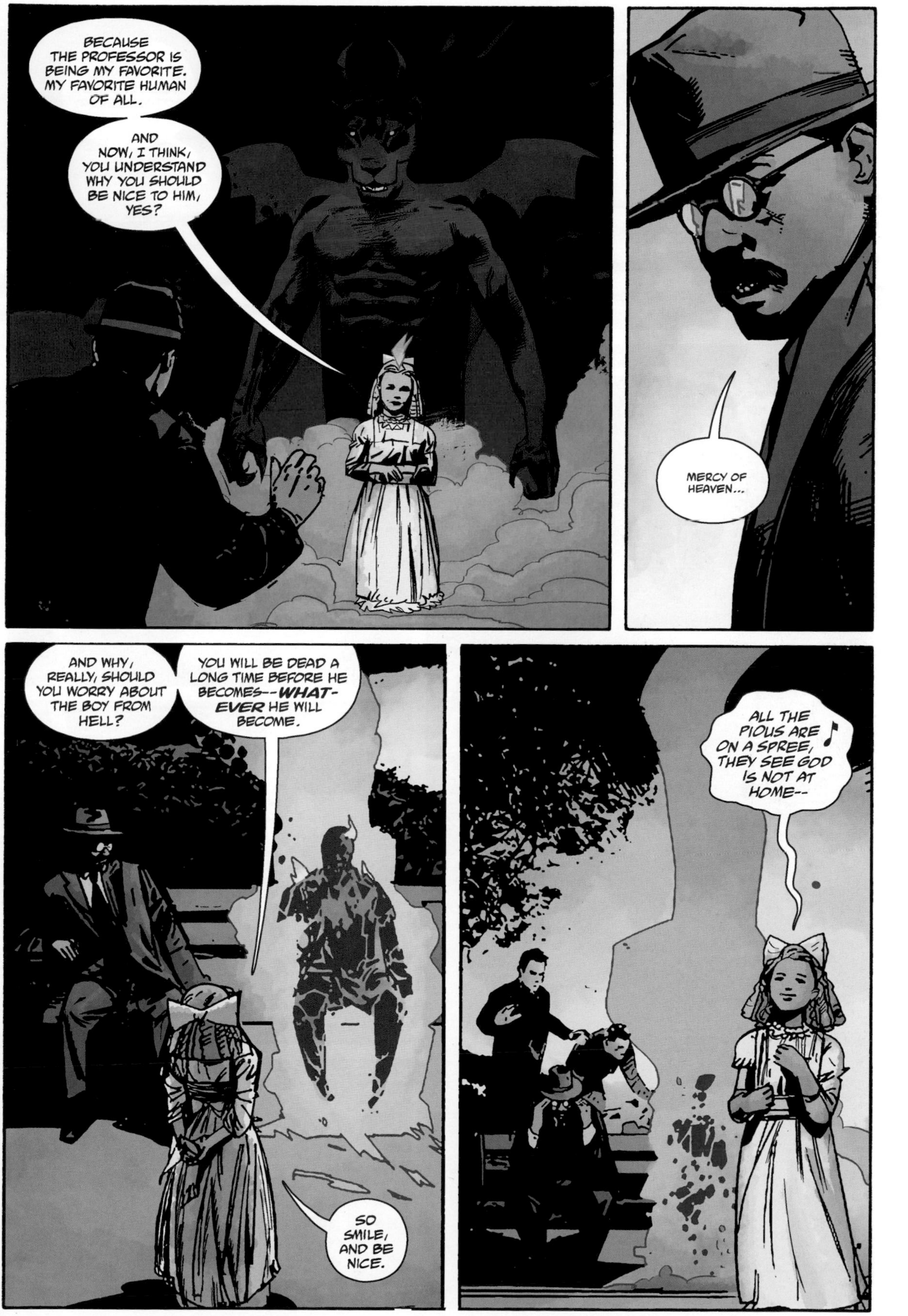
BECAUSE THE PROFESSOR IS BEING MY FAVORITE. MY FAVORITE HUMAN OF ALL.
AND NOW, I THINK, YOU UNDERSTAND WHY YOU SHOULD BE NICE TO HIM, YES?
MERCY OF HEAVEN...
AND WHY, REALLY, SHOULD YOU WORRY ABOUT THE BOY FROM HELL?
YOU WILL BE DEAD A LONG TIME BEFORE HE BECOMES--WHAT-EVER HE WILL BECOME.
SO SMILE, AND BE NICE.
ALL THE PIOUS ARE ON A SPREE, ♪ THEY SEE GOD IS NOT AT HOME--

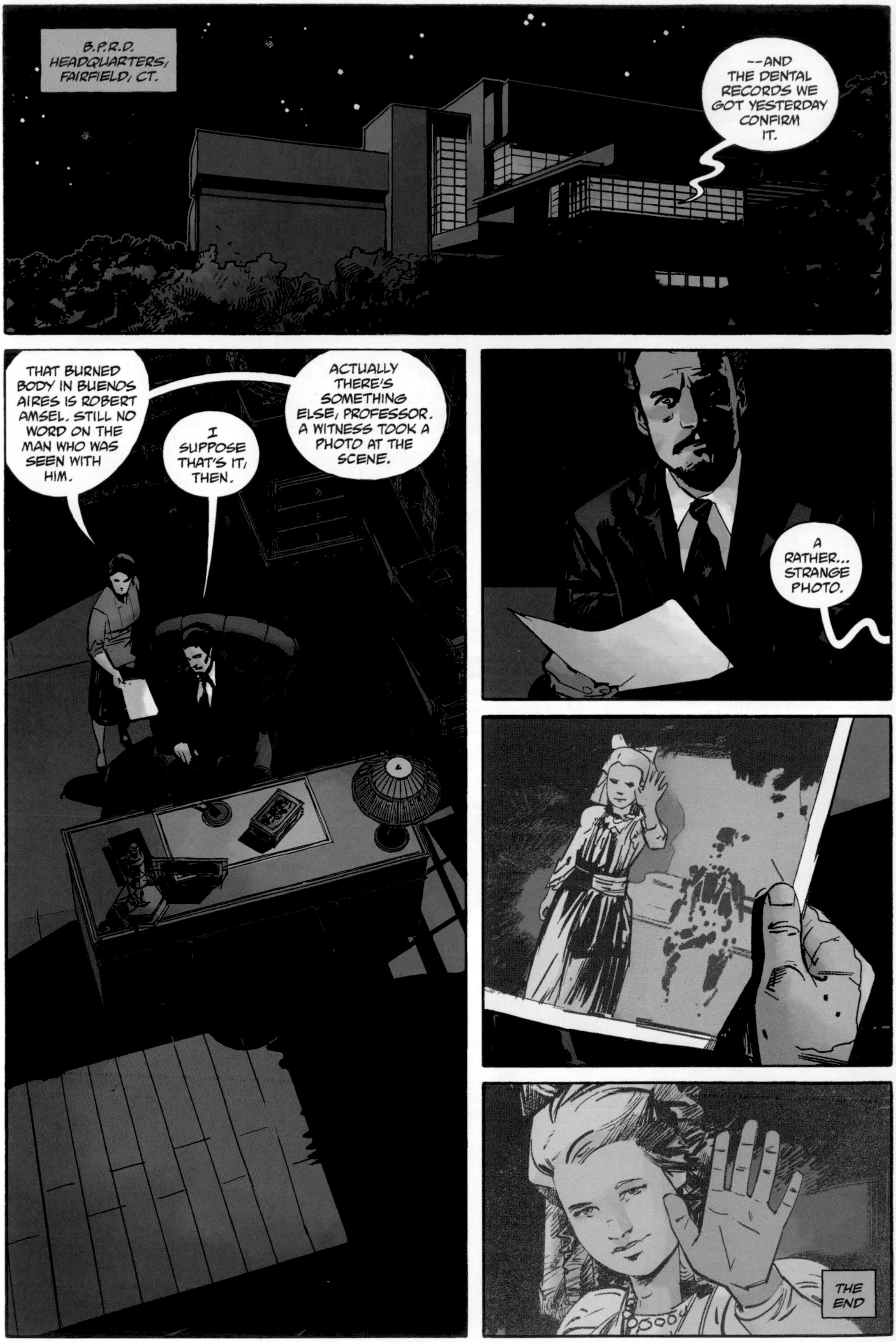
B.P.R.D. HEADQUARTERS, FAIRFIELD, CT.
--AND THE DENTAL RECORDS WE GOT YESTERDAY CONFIRM IT.
THAT BURNED BODY IN BUENOS AIRES IS ROBERT AMSEL. STILL NO WORD ON THE MAN WHO WAS SEEN WITH HIM.
I SUPPOSE THAT'S IT, THEN.
ACTUALLY THERE'S SOMETHING ELSE, PROFESSOR. A WITNESS TOOK A PHOTO AT THE SCENE.
A RATHER... STRANGE PHOTO.
THE END

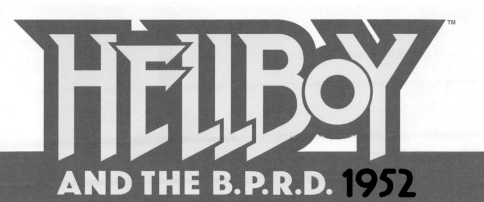

HELLBOY™ AND THE B.P.R.D. 1952

SKETCHBOOK

COOL!

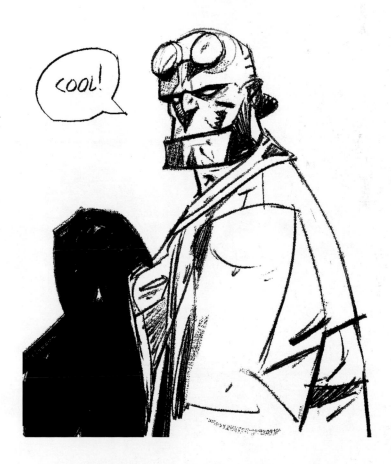

Hellboy by Alex Maleev.

Following pages: Cover sketches for Hellboy and the B.P.R.D. *#1 by Alex.*

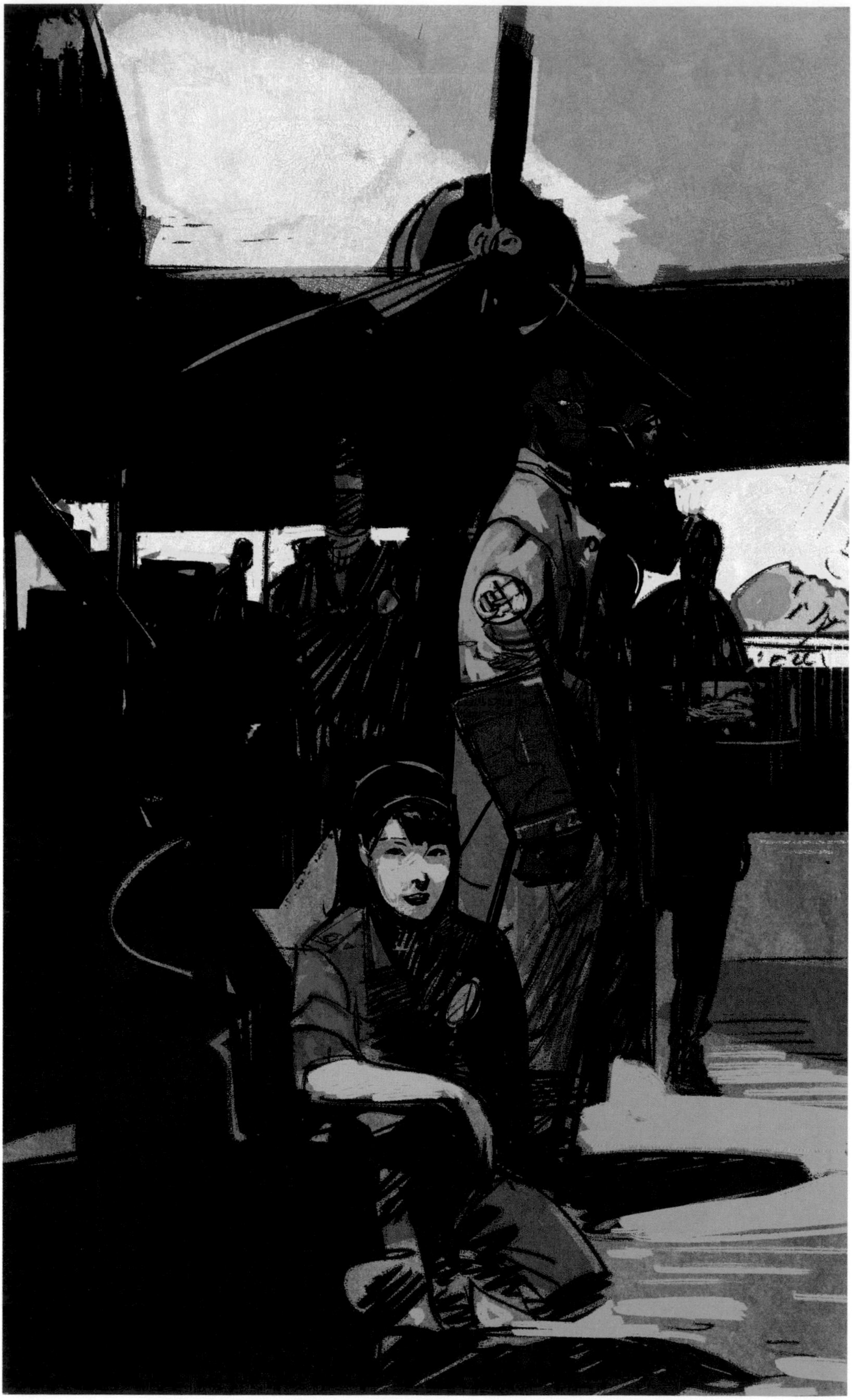

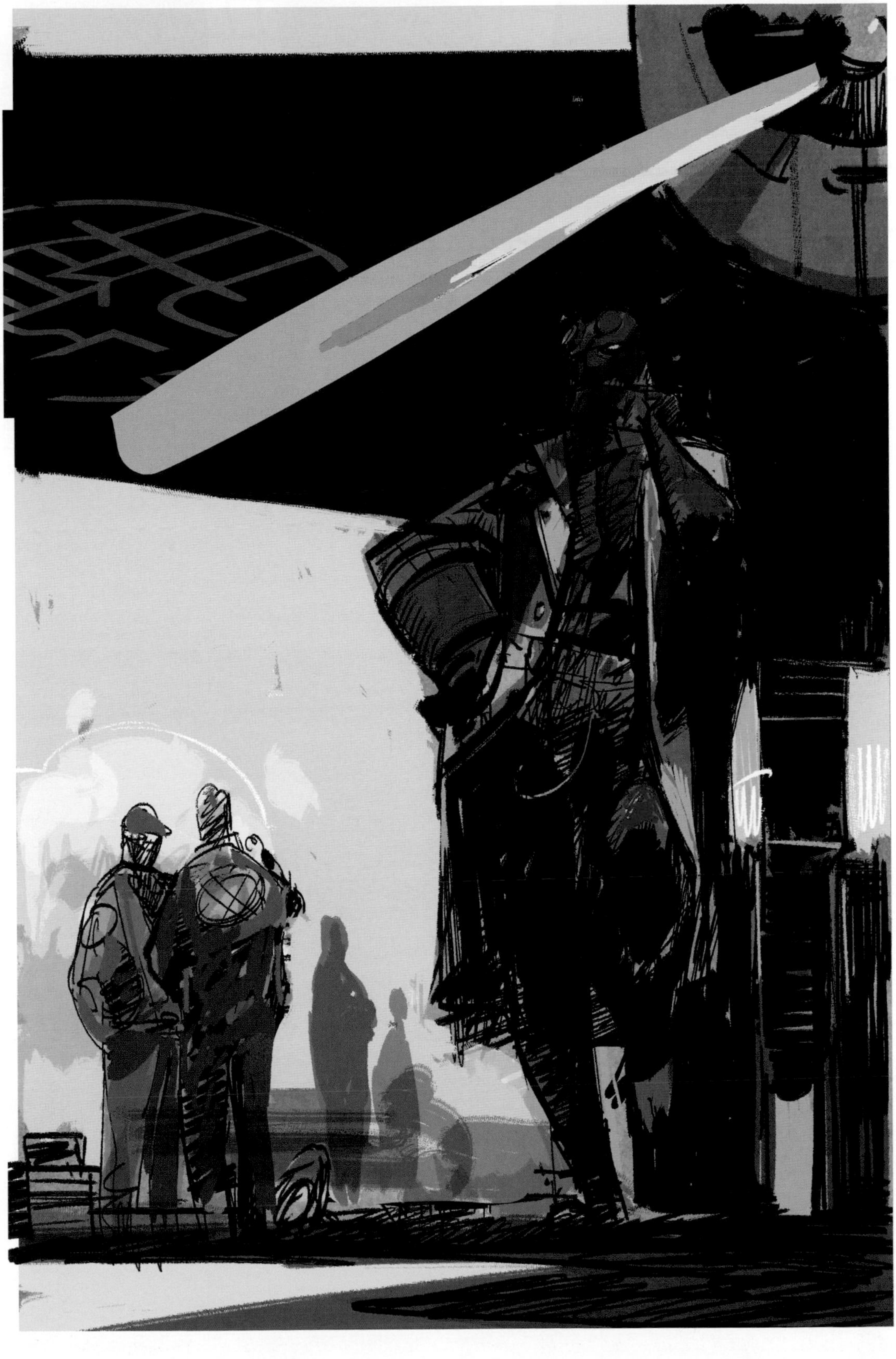

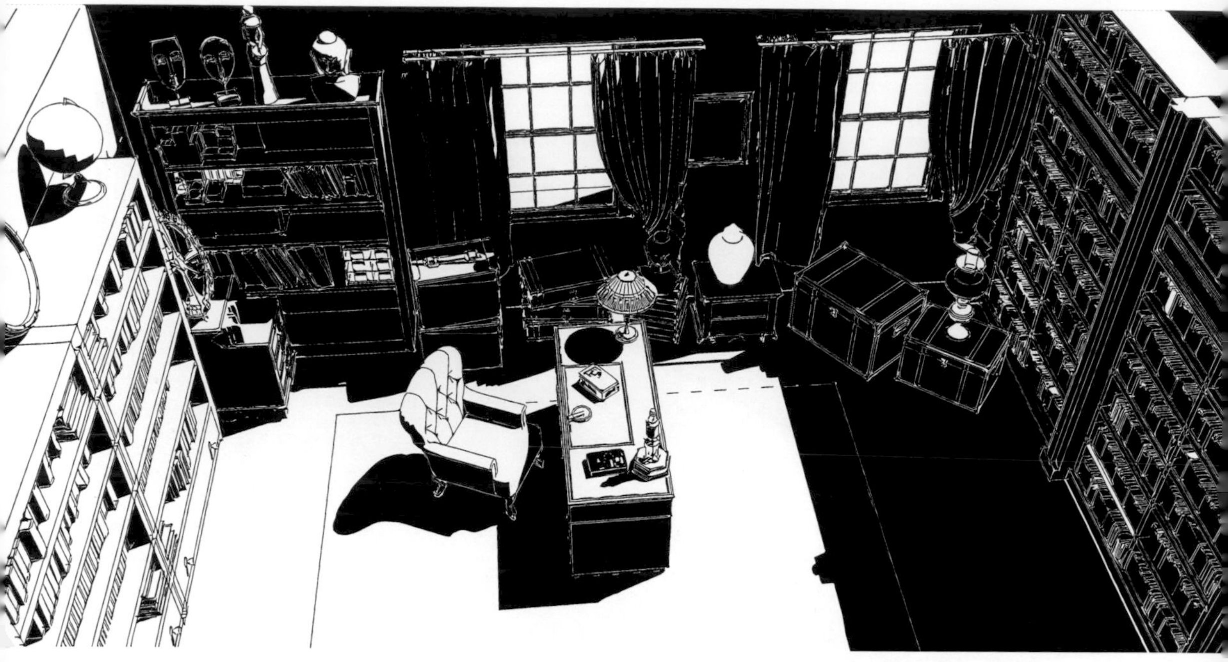

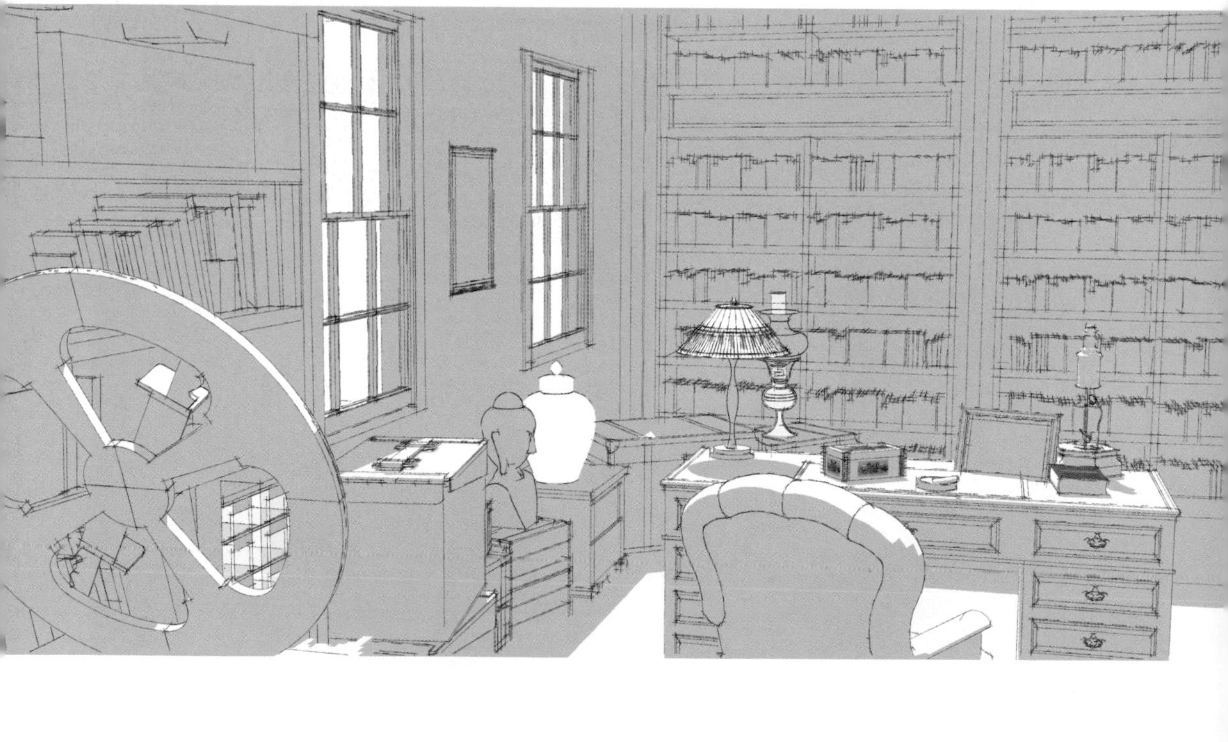

Studies for BPRD headquarters done by Alex in SketchUp.

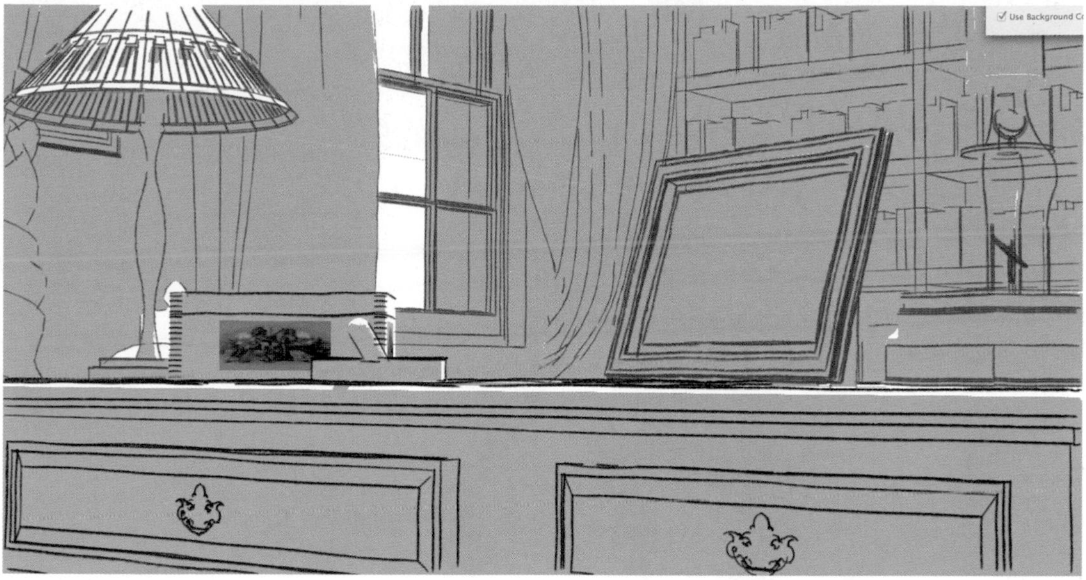

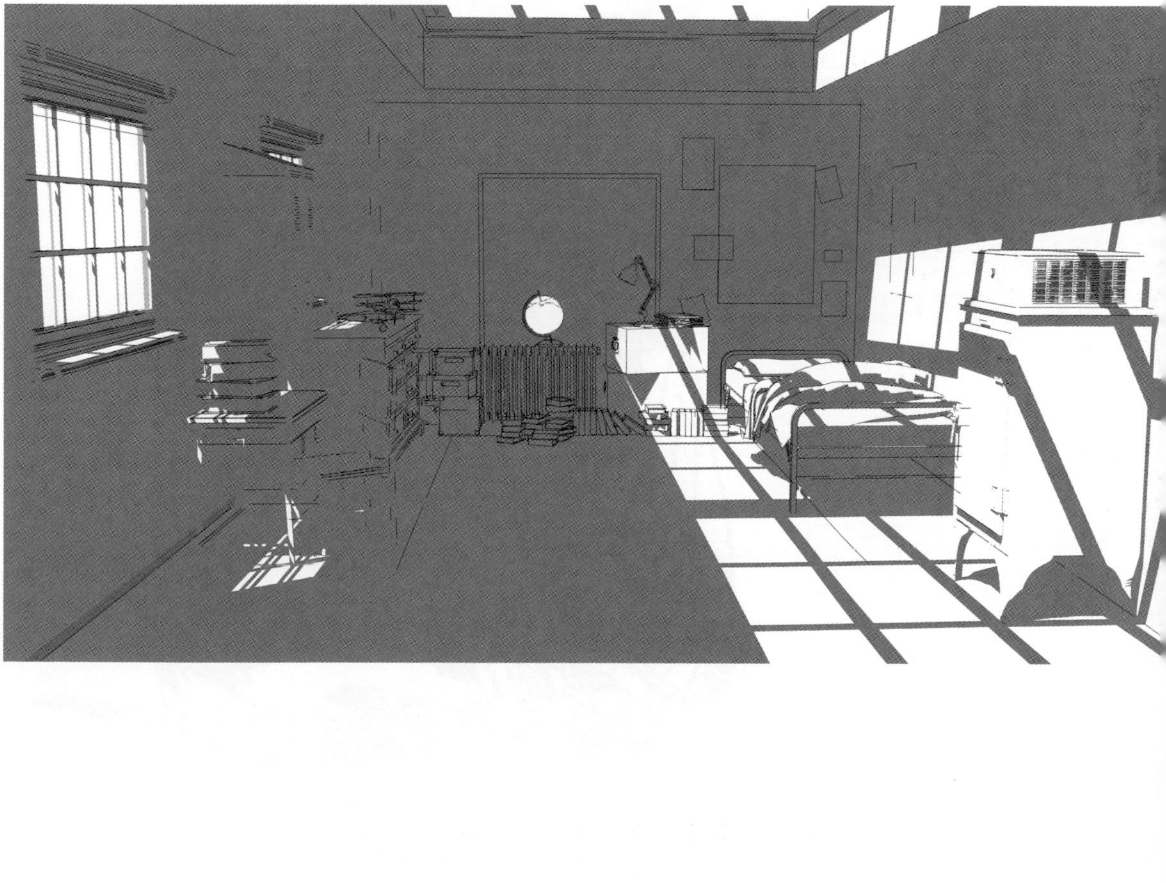

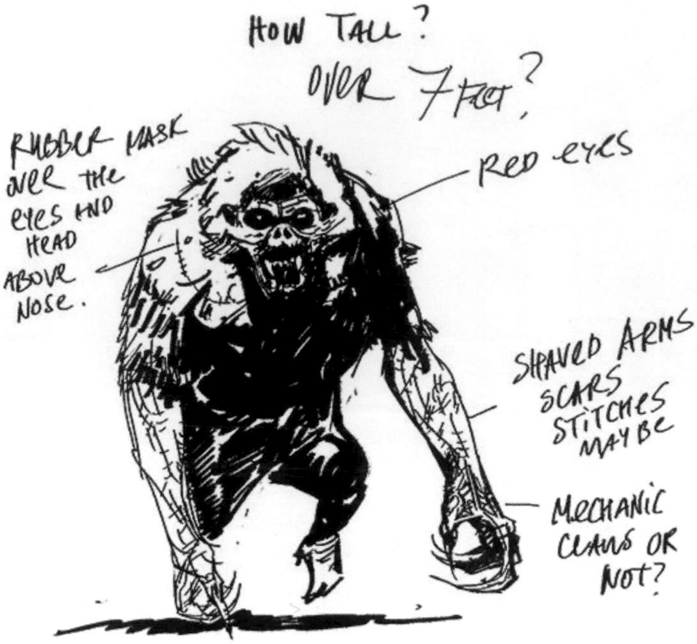
HOW TALL?
OVER 7 FEET?
RUBBER MASK OVER THE EYES AND HEAD ABOVE NOSE.
RED EYES
SHAVED ARMS SCARS STITCHES MAYBE
MECHANIC CLAWS OR NOT?

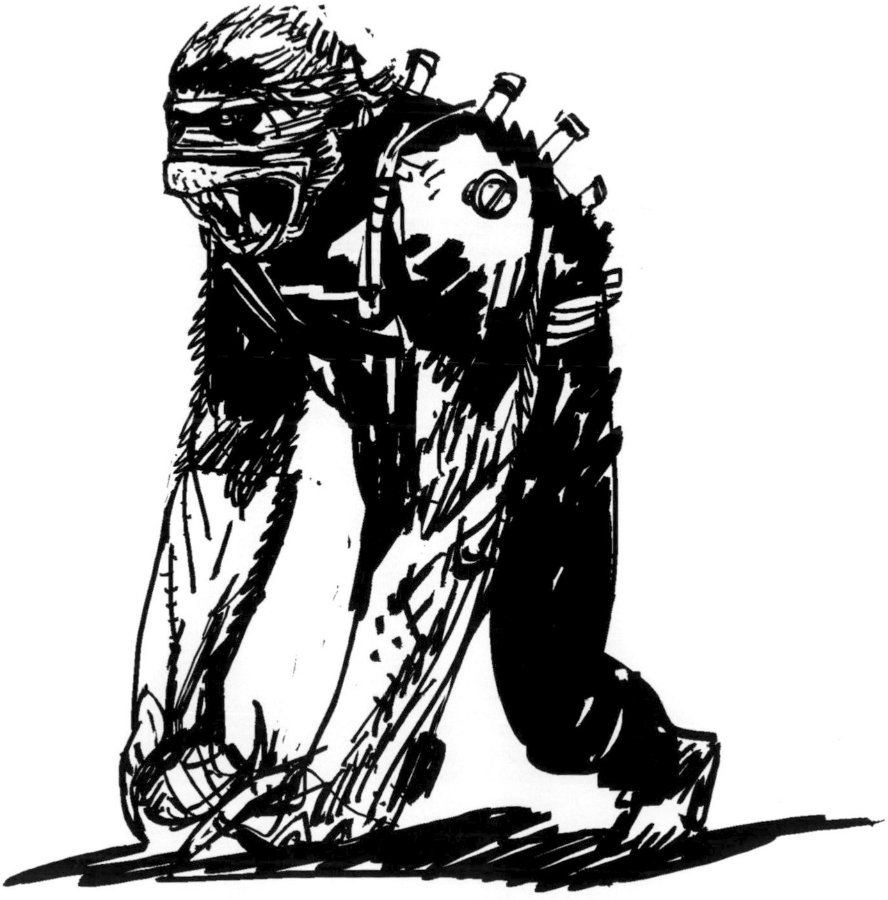

Alex's initial designs for the monster, based on the script. Mignola followed up with the designs on the facing page.

VAMPIRE CREATURE — HB · BPRD 1952

pointed ears - part of wig
↓

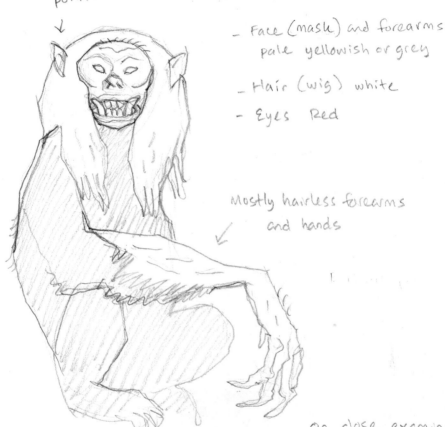

- Face (mask) and forearms
  pale yellowish or grey

- Hair (wig) white

- Eyes Red

Mostly hairless forearms
and hands
↓

On close examination
we will find that
his fingers have been
extended with metal
parts and claws.
But this is not clear
till after he's killed
in issue 3.

Mignola: I pretty much always knew what I wanted this guy to look like—something a little exotic, maybe even slightly Asian, and demonic, rather than obviously created in a laboratory. Plus, I just love the idea of somebody disguising an ape with a rubber mask and a wig.

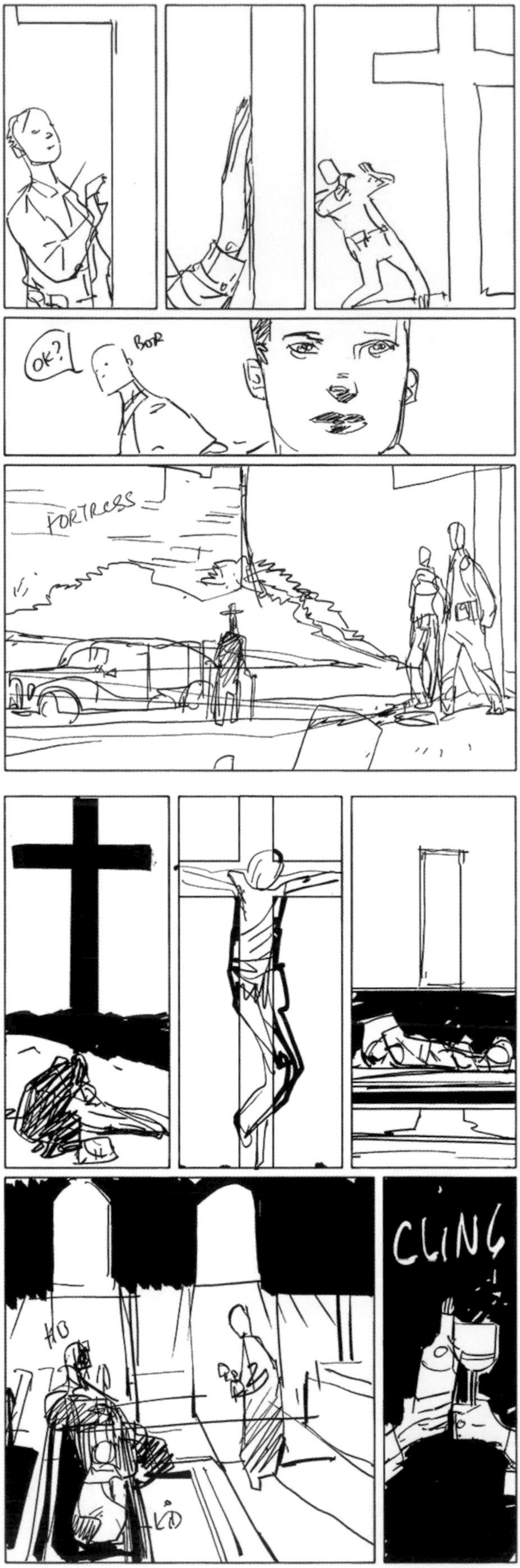
OK?
FORTRESS
CLING

Alex's layouts based on Mike's script for issue one.

Mignola (facing): A couple notes just to show Alex how to vary the pacing a little bit—and to show what a horrible control freak I can be.

TO ALEX & SCOTT

Page 12

Issue 2
TOP OF Page 8

- Last panel on page 7 - make sure to make sue look curious - like she senses something --

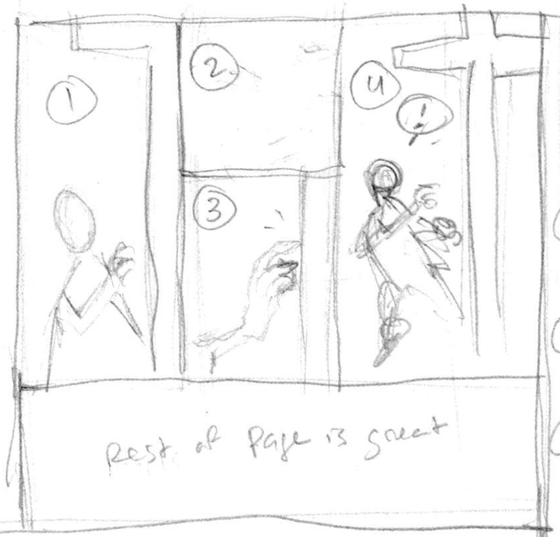
1
2
3
4
!
Rest of Page is great

Page 8

1. she reaches out toward cross hesitantly -- curious but just a little afraid.
2. close on her face -- So we see her concern - we see she is nervous
3. she just barely touches it with one finger --
4. And instantly recoils. As if she just touched a hot stove.

TOP OF Page 10

Just zoom in a bit closer on crucifix

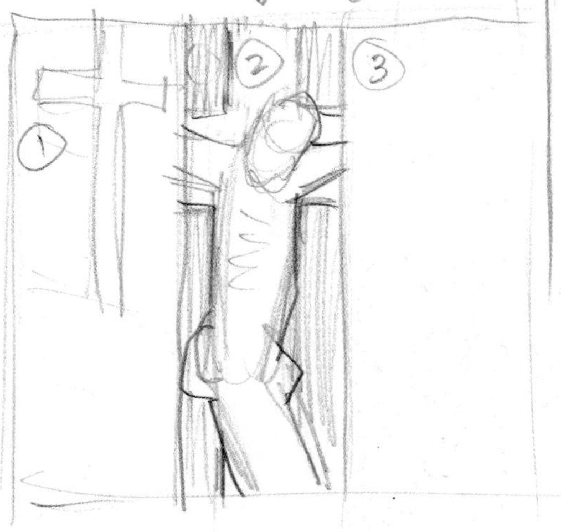
1
2
3

HB - BPRD
1952
Issue 2
Thumbnails for ALEX

PAGE 20

we see Bob and Sue through open window -- They are still inside the church.

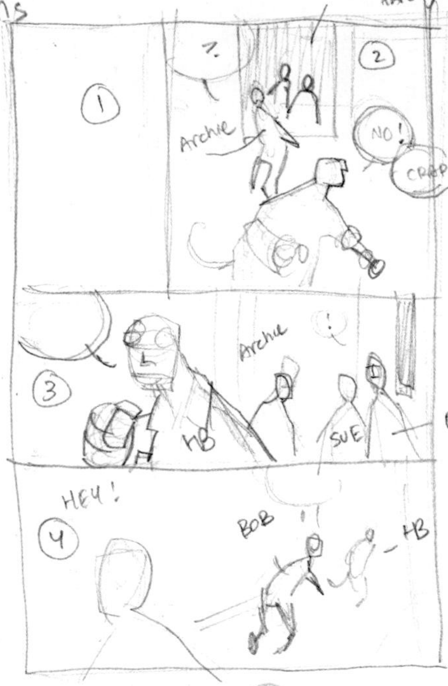
1
?
2
Archie
NO!
CRAP!
3
Archie
!
HB
SUE
BOB
HEY!
4
BOB
HB

1. As written in plot - Stegner and kid and screaming old woman
2. Archie dropping out of broken window, asking HB if he saw where the monster went. HB, frustrated, says No.
3. HB is looking towards us - moving towards us. Archie is looking down the street the other way - Away from HB, away from us.
   - Bob and Sue have come down between HB and Archie. Bob is looking towards HB. HB is already telling the guys to go the other way - He's going to go this way.
4. HB is running away from us and Bob is going after him. Archie is turning away from us to see HB taking off - says something like "HEY." Bob calls over his shoulder to Archie, telling him not to worry - He'll look after HB.

PAGE 21

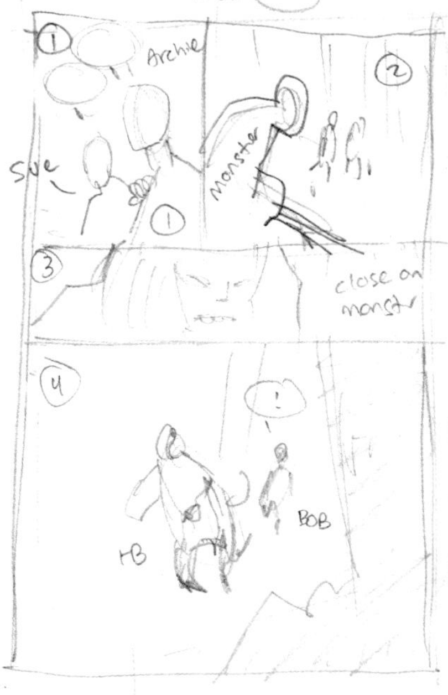
1
Archie
2
Sue
Monster
!
3
close on monster
4
!
HB
BOB

1. Archie and Sue. Archie is thinking of going after BOB and HB but Sue is telling him to come along - HB's right - best thing to do is split up.
2. We look down past monster at Archie and Sue running down the street.
3. I'm adding this - a close up of the monster looking down at the off panel Archie and Sue.
4. As in plot - HB and Bob running down the street - Bob yelling for HB to stop

*Facing: Mignola's thumbnails
for a scene in issue two.*

Mignola: Eventually I realized
it was just easier to do crude
thumbnails for certain scenes,
rather than try to describe the
layouts I had in mind.

*Right: Alex's loose pencils,
based on Mike's layouts.*

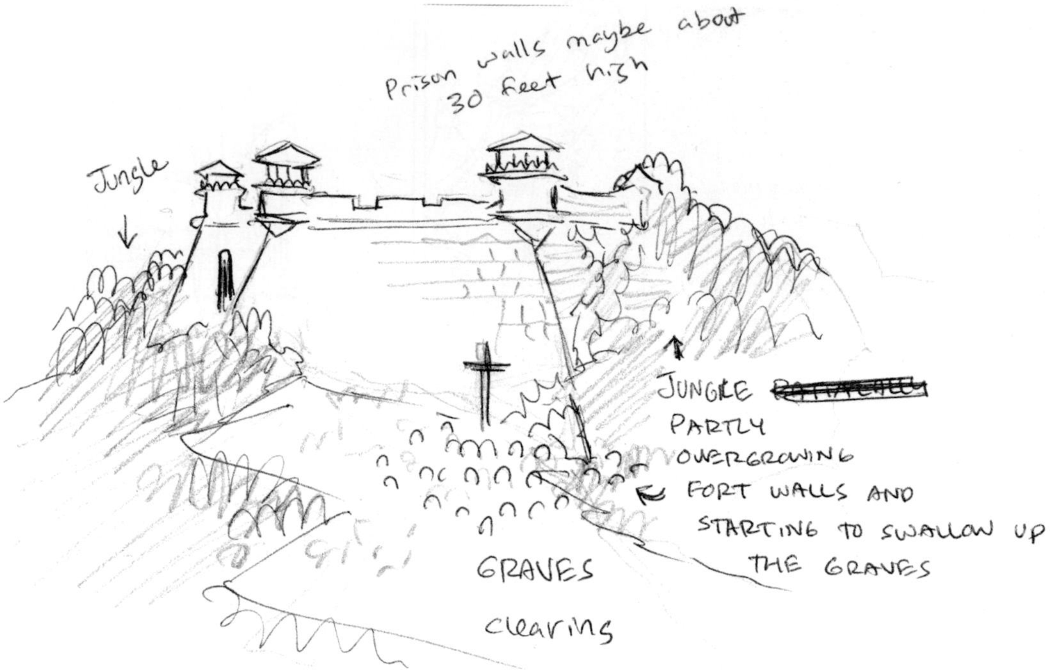
Prison walls maybe about 30 feet high
Jungle
JUNGLE
PARTLY OVERGROWING FORT WALLS AND STARTING TO SWALLOW UP THE GRAVES
GRAVES
clearing

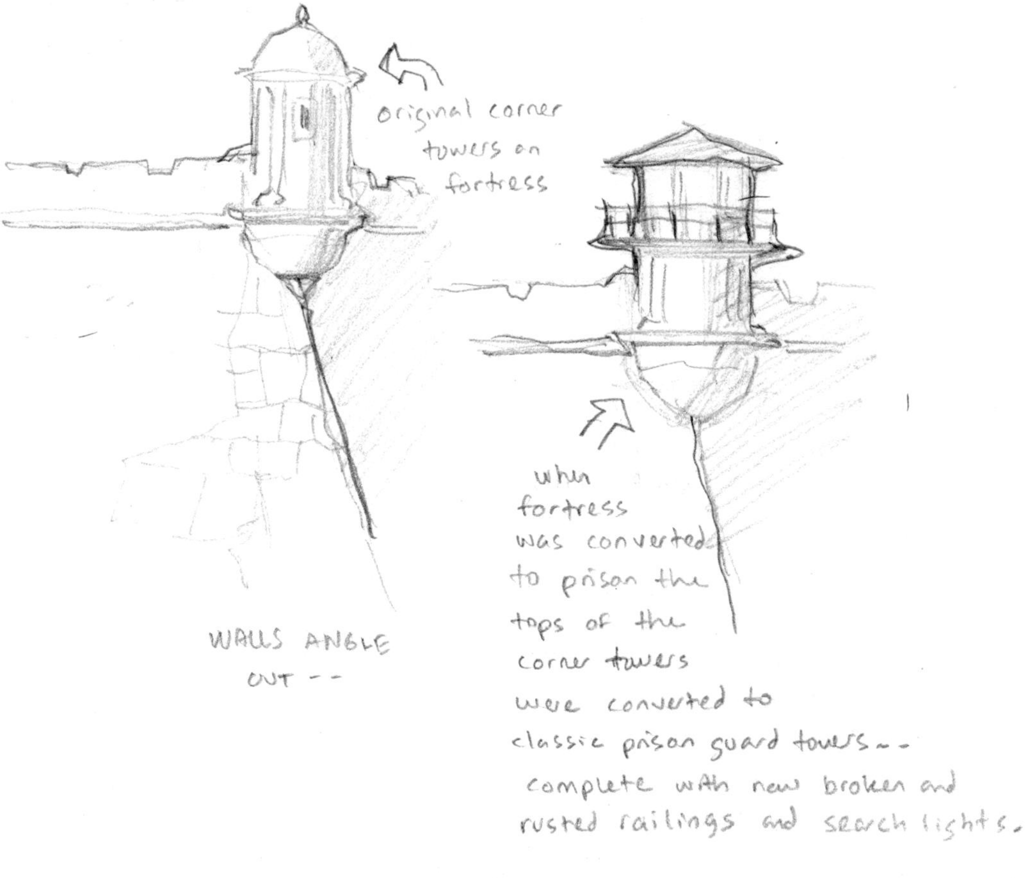
original corner towers on fortress
WALLS ANGLE OUT --
when fortress was converted to prison the tops of the corner towers were converted to classic prison guard towers -- complete with new broken and rusted railings and search lights.

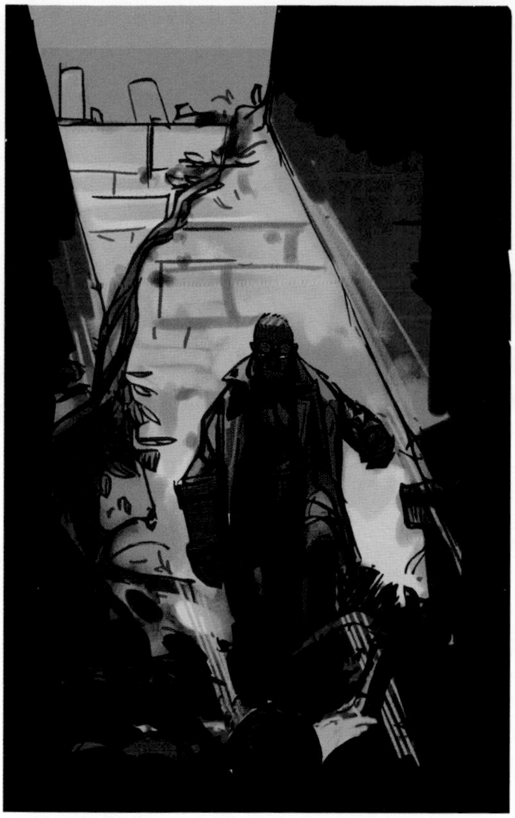

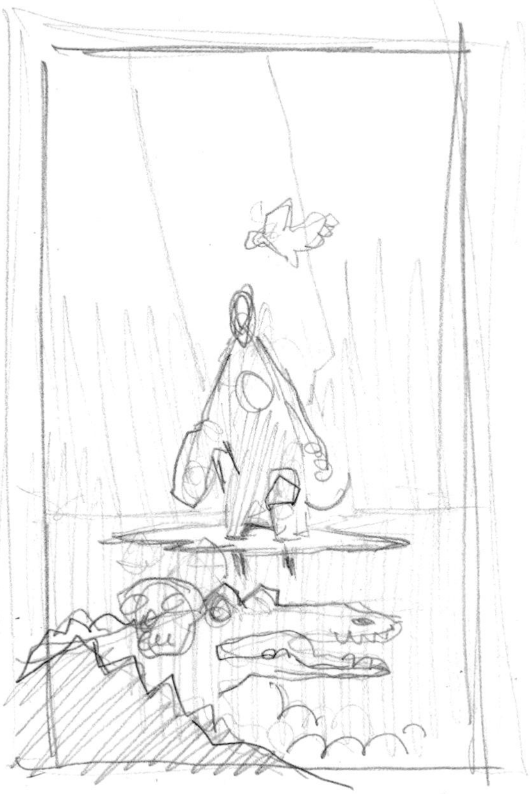

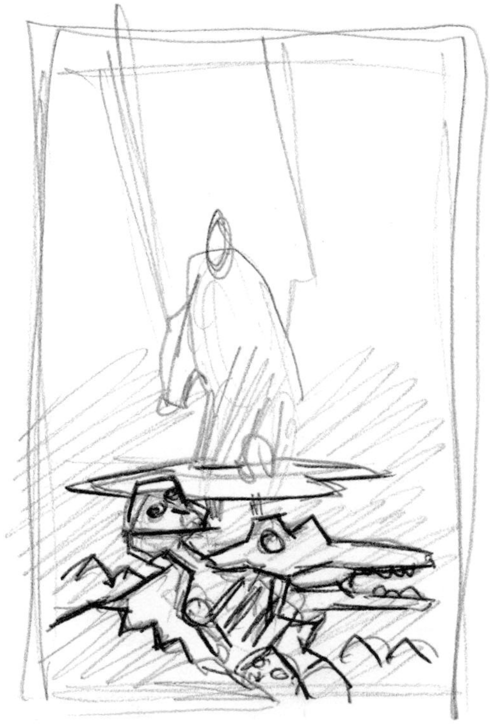

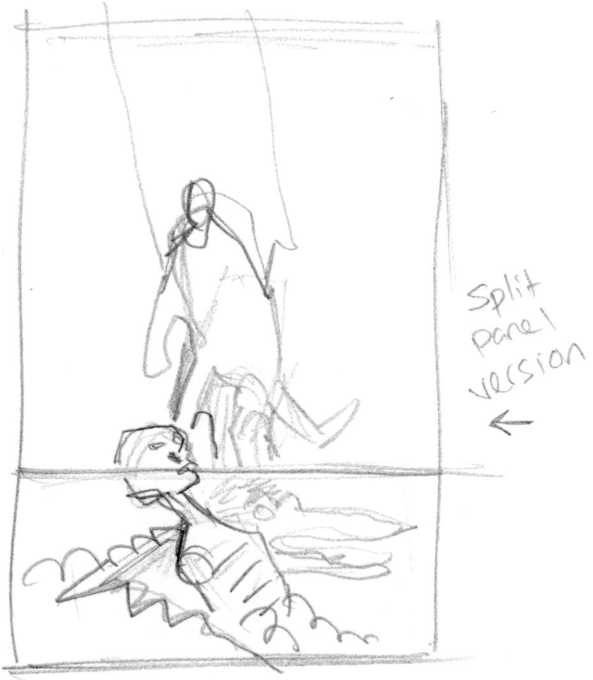
Split panel version

Mignola (facing): Rough idea for the fort turned prison, based on an actual Portuguese fort. Again, much easier to show what I had in mind, rather than try to describe it.

Inspired by Alex's sketch for the issue three cover (*upper left*), I came up with a couple ideas.

HELLBOY & BPRD 1952 #3
THUMBNAILS 1
TO ALEX & SCOTT
PAGE 7
PRIEST
DRIP
BLAM
BLAM
SUE - STARTLED OUT OF TRANCE BY GUNSHOTS
PAGE 15
BOB AND STEGNER
ARCHIE
INSIDE THE TUNNEL - BLOOD TRAILING OFF INTO THE DARK
RUBBLE FROM COLLAPSED TUNNEL ROOF AND HOUSE

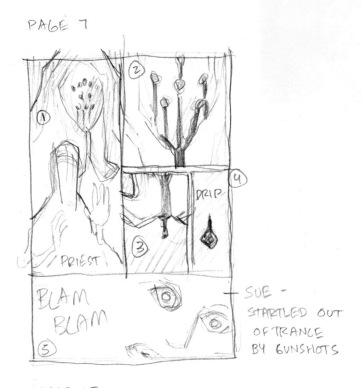

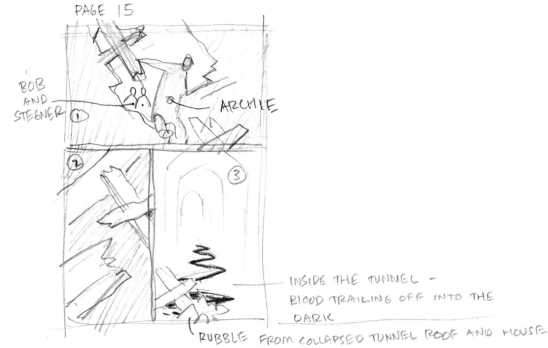

My thumbnails, now with the fancy addition of color to indicate blood and Lovecraftian goo.

HELLBOY & BPRD 1952 #3
THUMBNAILS ②

PAGE 16

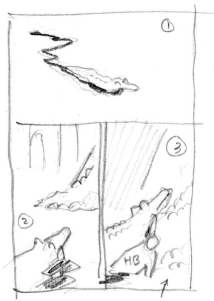

PAGE 17

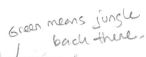

Green means jungle back there.

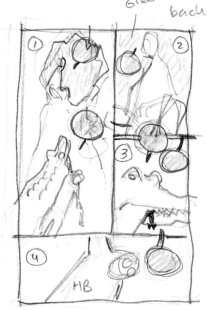

STARTING TO
CLIMB UP DIRT-
INTO THE LIGHT

PAGE 18

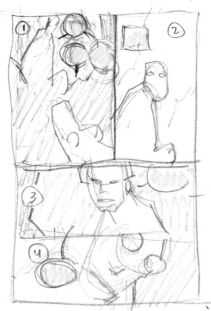

Green means
Jungle.

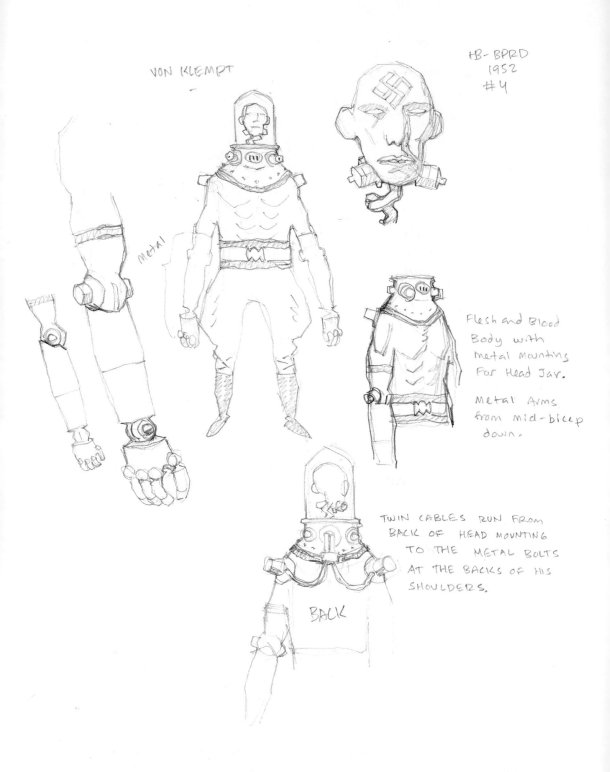

VON KLEMPT

Metal

Flesh and Blood
Body with
metal Mountings
For Head Jar.

Metal Arms
from mid-bicep
down.

TWIN CABLES RUN FROM
BACK OF HEAD MOUNTING
TO THE METAL BOLTS
AT THE BACKS OF HIS
SHOULDERS.

BACK

Von Klempt. This design was just too much fun. His robot arms are based (as are most robot things I draw) on the classic 11 ½-inch G.I. Joe, the greatest toy ever.

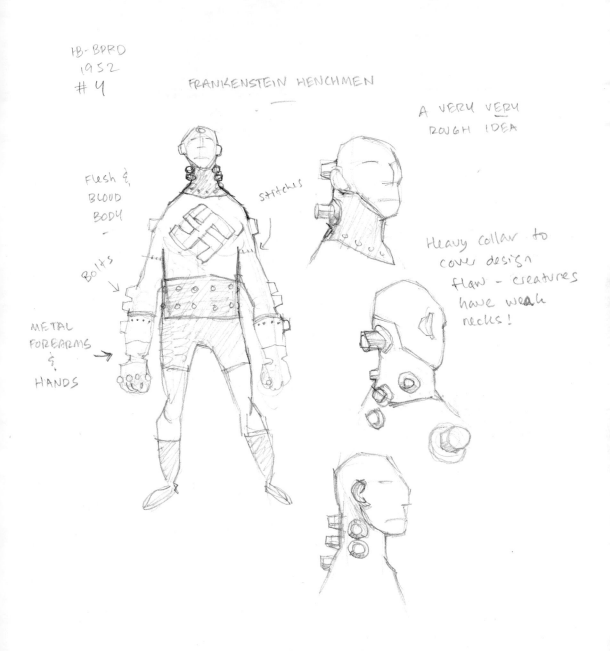

HB-BPRD
1952
#4

FRANKENSTEIN HENCHMEN

A VERY VERY
ROUGH IDEA

Flesh &
BLOOD
BODY

stitches

Bolts

METAL
FOREARMS
&
HANDS

Heavy collar to
cover design
flaw - creatures
have weak
necks!

I didn't have much of a design idea for the henchmen when I started. Then when I was plotting issue four I had to have Archie fight one of the Frankenstein guys, so I came up with the idea that they have weak necks—a pretty major design flaw for Nazi super-soldiers—which led to me giving the couple guys we see at the end these cool neck braces. I also didn't want to be too subtle with the Nazi message on these guys.

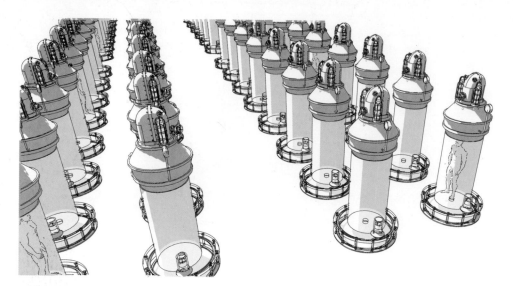

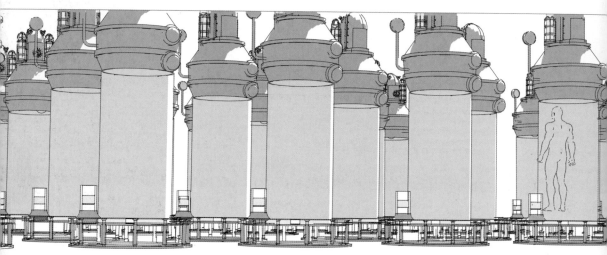

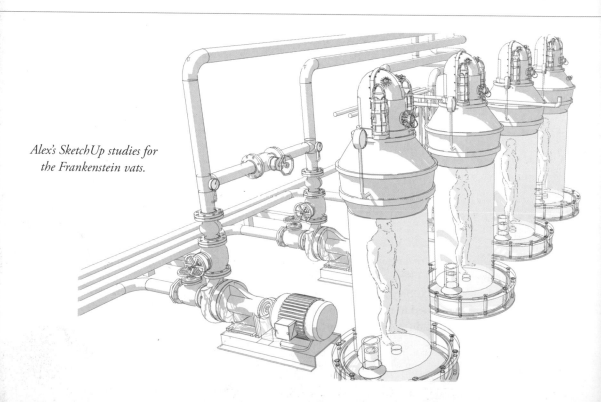

Alex's SketchUp studies for the Frankenstein vats.

HELLBOY

by MIKE MIGNOLA

HELLBOY LIBRARY EDITION VOLUME 1:
Seed of Destruction and Wake the Devil
ISBN 978-1-59307-910-9 | $49.99

HELLBOY LIBRARY EDITION VOLUME 2:
The Chained Coffin and The Right Hand of Doom
ISBN 978-1-59307-989-5 | $49.99

HELLBOY LIBRARY EDITION VOLUME 3:
Conqueror Worm and Strange Places
ISBN 978-1-59582-352-6 | $49.99

HELLBOY LIBRARY EDITION VOLUME 4:
The Crooked Man and The Troll Witch
with Richard Corben and others
ISBN 978-1-59582-658-9 | $49.99

HELLBOY LIBRARY EDITION VOLUME 5:
Darkness Calls and the Wild Hunt
with Duncan Fegredo
ISBN 978-1-59582-886-6 | $49.99

HELLBOY LIBRARY EDITION VOLUME 6:
The Storm and the Fury and The Bride of Hell
with Duncan Fegredo, Richard Corben, Kevin Nowlan, and Scott Hampton
ISBN 978-1-61655-133-9 | $49.99

SEED OF DESTRUCTION
with John Byrne
ISBN 978-1-59307-094-6 | $17.99

WAKE THE DEVIL
ISBN 978-1-59307-095-3 | $17.99

THE CHAINED COFFIN AND OTHERS
ISBN 978-1-59307-091-5 | $17.99

THE RIGHT HAND OF DOOM
ISBN 978-1-59307-093-9 | $17.99

THE TROLL WITCH AND OTHERS
with Richard Corben and others
ISBN 978-1-59307-860-7 | $17.99

DARKNESS CALLS
with Duncan Fegredo
ISBN 978-1-59307-896-6 | $19.99

THE WILD HUNT
with Duncan Fegredo
ISBN 978-1-59582-431-8 | $19.99

THE CROOKED MAN AND OTHERS
with Richard Corben
ISBN 978-1-59582-477-6 | $17.99

THE BRIDE OF HELL AND OTHERS
with Richard Corben, Kevin Nowlan, and Scott Hampton
ISBN 978-1-59582-740-1 | $19.99

THE STORM AND THE FURY
with Duncan Fegredo
ISBN 978-1-59582-827-9 | $19.99

HOUSE OF THE LIVING DEAD
with Richard Corben
ISBN 978-1-59582-757-9 | $14.99

THE MIDNIGHT CIRCUS
with Duncan Fegredo
ISBN 978-1-61655-238-1 | $14.99

HELLBOY IN HELL VOLUME 1: THE DESCENT
ISBN 978-1-61655-444-6 | $17.99

HELLBOY: THE FIRST 20 YEARS
ISBN 978-1-61655-353-1 | $19.99

THE ART OF HELLBOY
ISBN 978-1-59307-089-2 | $29.99

HELLBOY II: THE ART OF THE MOVIE
ISBN 978-1-59307-964-2 | $24.99

HELLBOY: THE COMPANION
ISBN 978-1-59307-655-9 | $14.99

HELLBOY: WEIRD TALES

HELLBOY AND THE B.P.R.D: 1952
with John Arcudi and Alex Maleev
ISBN 978-1-61655-660-0 | $19.99

NOVELS

HELLBOY: EMERALD HELL
By Tom Piccirilli
ISBN 978-1-59582-141-6 | $12.99

HELLBOY: THE ALL-SEEING EYE
By Mark Morris
ISBN 978-1-59582-142-3 | $12.99

HELLBOY: THE FIRE WOLVES
By Tim Lebbon
ISBN 978-1-59582-204-8 | $12.99

HELLBOY: THE ICE WOLVES
By Mark Chadbourn
ISBN 978-1-59582-205-5 | $12.99

SHORT STORIES
Illustrated by Mike Mignola

HELLBOY: ODDER JOBS
By Frank Darabont, Charles de Lint, Guillermo del Toro, and others
ISBN 978-1-59307-226-1 | $14.99

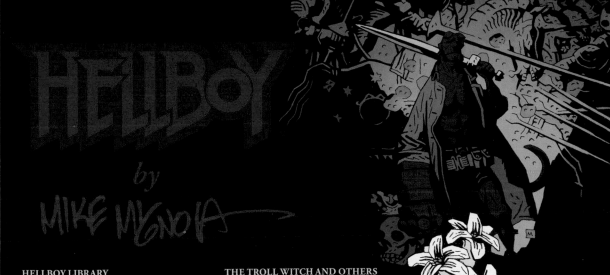

Also by
MIKE MIGNOLA

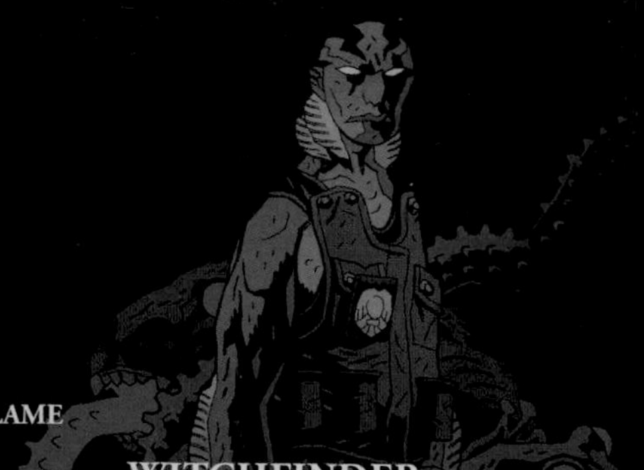

B.P.R.D.

PLAGUE OF FROGS
Volume 1
with Chris Golden, Guy Davis, and others
HC: ISBN 978-1-59582-609-1 | $34.99
TPB: ISBN 978-1-59582-675-6 | $19.99

Volume 2
with John Arcudi, Davis, and others
HC: ISBN 978-1-59582-672-5 | $34.99
TPB: ISBN 978-1-59582-676-3 | $24.99

Volume 3
with Arcudi and Davis
HC: ISBN 978-1-59582-860-6 | $34.99
TPB: ISBN 978-1-61655-622-8 | $24.99

Volume 4
with Arcudi and Davis
HC: ISBN 978-1-59582-974-0 | $34.99
TPB: ISBN 978-1-61655-641-9 | $24.99

1946–1948
with Joshua Dysart, Paul Azaceta, Fábio Moon,
Gabriel Bá, Max Fiumara, and Arcudi
ISBN 978-1-61655-646-4 | $34.99

BEING HUMAN
with Scott Allie, Arcudi, Davis, and others
ISBN 978-1-59582-756-2 | $17.99

VAMPIRE
with Moon and Bá
ISBN 978-1-61655-196-4 | $19.99

B.P.R.D. HELL ON EARTH

NEW WORLD
with Arcudi and Davis
ISBN 978-1-59582-707-4 | $19.99

GODS AND MONSTERS
with Arcudi, Davis, and Tyler Crook
ISBN 978-1-59582-822-4 | $19.99

RUSSIA
with Arcudi, Crook, and Duncan Fegredo
ISBN 978-1-59582-946-7 | $19.9

**THE DEVIL'S ENGINE
AND THE LONG DEATH**
with Arcudi, Crook, and James Harren
ISBN 978 1 59582 981-8 | $19.99

**THE PICKENS COUNTY
HORROR AND OTHERS**
with Allie, Jason Latour, Harren,
and Max Fiumara
ISBN 978-1-61655-140-7 | $19.99

THE RETURN OF THE MASTER
with Arcudi and Crook
ISBN 978-1-61655-193-3 | $19.99

A COLD DAY IN HELL
with Arcudi, Peter Snejbjerg, and
Laurence Campbell
ISBN 978-1-61655-199-5 | $19.99

THE REIGN OF THE BLACK FLAME
with Arcudi and Harren
ISBN 978-1-61655-471-2 | $19.99

THE DEVIL'S WINGS
with Arcudi, Campbell, Joe Querio, and Crook
ISBN 978-1-61655-617-4 | $19.99

LAKE OF FIRE
with Arcudi and Crook
ISBN 978-1-61655-402-6 | $19.99

ABE SAPIEN

THE DROWNING
with Jason Shawn Alexander
ISBN 978-1-59582-185-0 | $17.99

**THE DEVIL DOES NOT JEST AND
OTHER STORIES**
with Arcudi, Harren, and others
ISBN 978-1-59582-925-2 | $17.99

**DARK AND TERRIBLE
AND THE NEW RACE OF MAN**
with Allie, Arcudi, Sebastián
Fiumara, and Max Fiumara
ISBN 978-1-61655-284-8 | $19.99

THE SHAPE OF THINGS TO COME
with Allie, S. Fiumara, and M. Fiumara
ISBN 978-1-61655-443-9 | $19.99

SACRED PLACES
with Allie, S. Fiumara, and M. Fiumara
ISBN 978-1-61655-515-3 | $19.99

A DARKNESS SO GREAT
with Allie and M. Fiumara
ISBN 978-1-61655-656-3 | $19.99

LOBSTER JOHNSON

THE IRON PROMETHEUS
with Jason Armstrong
ISBN 978-1-59307-975-8 | $17.99

THE BURNING HAND
with Arcudi and Tonci Zonjic
ISBN 978-1-61655-031-8 | $17.99

SATAN SMELLS A RAT
with Arcudi, Fiumara, Querio,
Wilfredo Torres, and Kevin Nowlan
ISBN 978-1-61655-203-9 | $18.99

GET THE LOBSTER
with Arcudi and Zonjic
ISBN 978-1-61655-505-4 | $19.99

WITCHFINDER

IN THE SERVICE OF ANGELS
with Ben Stenbeck
ISBN 978-1-59582-483-7 | $17.99

LOST AND GONE FOREVER
with Arcudi and John Severin
ISBN 978-1-59582-794-4 | $17.99

THE MYSTERIES OF UNLAND
with Kim Newman, Maura McHugh,
and Crook
ISBN 978-1-61655-630-3 | $19.99

THE AMAZING
SCREW-ON HEAD
AND OTHER
CURIOUS OBJECTS
ISBN 978-1-59582-501-8 | $17.99

BALTIMORE

THE PLAGUE SHIPS
with Golden and Stenbeck
ISBN 978-1-59582-677-0 | $24.99

THE CURSE BELLS
with Golden and Stenbeck
ISBN 978-1-59582-674-9 | $24.99

**A PASSING STRANGER
AND OTHER STORIES**
with Golden and Stenbeck
ISBN 978-1-61655-182-7 | $24.99

CHAPEL OF BONES
with Golden and Stenbeck
ISBN 978-1-61655-328-9 | $24.99

**THE APOSTLE AND THE WITCH
OF HARJU**
with Golden, Stenbeck, and Peter Bergting
ISBN 978-1-61655-618-1 | $24.99

NOVELS

**LOBSTER JOHNSON:
THE SATAN FACTORY**
with Thomas E. Sniegoski
ISBN 978-1-59582-203-1 | $12.95

**JOE GOLEM AND THE
DROWNING CITY**
with Golden
ISBN 978-1-59582-971-9 | $99.99

AVAILABLE AT YOUR LOCAL COMICS SHOP OR BOOKSTORE! • To find a comics shop in your area, call 1-888-266-4226.
For more information or to order direct visit DarkHorse.com or call 1-800-862-0052 Mon.–Fri. 9 AM to 5 PM Pacific Time.
Prices and availability subject to change without notice.

Hellboy™ and B.P.R.D.™ © Mike Mignola. Abe Sapien™ © Mike Mignola. Lobster Johnson™ © Mike Mignola. Sir Edward Grey: Witchfinder™ © Mike Mignola. The Amazing Screw-On Head™ ©
Mike Mignola. Baltimore™ © Mike Mignola & Christopher Golden. Joe Golem and the Drowning City™ © Mike Mignola & Christopher Golden. Dark Horse Books® and the Dark Horse logo are registered
trademarks of Dark Horse Comics, Inc. All rights reserved. (BL 6061)